Imperial Venus

Pauline Bonaparte

by Robert Lefèvre

Imperial Venus

The story of
Pauline Bonaparte-Borghese

Len Ortzen

STEIN AND DAY / *Publishers* / New York

First published in the United States of America by
Stein and Day/*Publishers* in 1974
Copyright © 1974 by Len Ortzen
Library of Congress Catalog Card No. 73-92186
All rights reserved
Printed in the United States of America
Stein and Day/*Publishers*/Scarborough House, Briarcliff Manor, N.Y. 10510
ISBN 0-8128-1689-7

To Anne
with love

Contents

Illustrations

Acknowledgements

During my travels about France and Italy, in the footsteps of Pauline, I received help from a number of people, officials and private individuals, who kindly gave me local information or permission to visit property. I should like to thank in particular: Monsieur Gay, mayor of Gréoux-les-Bains, and his predecessor in office, Monsieur Gravier; Madame de Colbert, Château de Bouillidou; Monsieur le Marquis de Forbin; Signor Mario Palmieri, Portoferraio. My thanks are also due to the Chief Librarian, Bibliothèque Municipale, Aix-les-Bains, and to Mr W. Morris of the British Embassy, Paris.

Here in England I am greatly indebted to the Gloucestershire County Library for a constant supply of needed books and help with research, and I wish to express my appreciation to the County Librarian, Gloucester, and his staff, in particular to Mr R. A. Carroll (now with the British Council in Vienna), Mr T. T. Thewlis, Miss M. J. Maliphant and Mrs B. M. Swarbrick.

Books which have been of much assistance will be found in the Bibliography.

The photographs of portraits and paintings are reproduced by arrangement with the Mansell Collection, and the photographs of Elba by arrangement with the Ente per la Valorizzazione dell'Isola d'Elba.

Giovanni-Girolamo Ramolino (d. 1755)
m. Angela-Maria de Pietra-Santa,
m. (2) Joseph Fesch

Giuseppe (1762–1839)

Maria-Letizia (1749–1836)

Luciano Buonaparte
(the archdeacon)

Giuseppe Buonaparte
m. Maria Arrighi

Carlo-Maria (1746–85)

m.

- **Giuseppe (1768–1845)**
  (Joseph)
  **King of Naples, 1806
  and Spain, 1808–13**
  m. Julie Clary
  2 daughters

- **NAPOLEONE**
  (1769–1821)
  m. (1) Josephine
  de Beauharnais
  (2) Maria Luisa,
  Archduchess of
  Austria
  1 son

- Luciano
  (Lucien)
  (1775–1840)
  m. (1) Catherine Boyer
  2 daughters
  (2) Marie-Alexandrine
  de Bleschamps
  6 sons
  4 daughters

- Maria-Anna
  (Elisa)
  (1777–1820)
  m. Felice Bacciochi
  3 sons

- Luigi
  (Louis)
  (1778–1846)
  King of Holland
  1806–10
  m. Hortense de
  Beauharnais
  3 sons

- **MARIA-PAOLA**
  (PAULINE)
  (1780–1825)
  m. (1) Victor-Emmanuel
  LECLERC (d. 1802)
  Dermide (1798–1804)
  (2) Prince Camillo
  BORGHESE
  (1775–1832)
  no issue

- Maria-Annunziata
  (Caroline)
  (1782–1839)
  m. Joachim Murat
  2 sons
  2 daughters

- Girolamo (Jerome)
  (1784–1860)
  King of Westphalia, 1807
  m. (1) Elizabeth
  Patterson
  1 son
  (2) Catherine of
  Württemberg
  2 sons
  1 daughter

Imperial Venus

Corsican childhood

In the late eighteenth century Ajaccio was little more than a large village, nestling between wooded slopes and the bluish-green Gulf. Within its ramparts the flat-roofed houses with walls painted pink or blue, but faded and flaking, were huddled together protectively against summer heat and wintry blasts. Between them were just three long, unpaved streets sloping down to the sixteenth-century Genoese citadel overlooking the harbour. But a number of alleyways ran across the streets, and in one near the cathedral – the *strada Malerba,* the street of weeds, too narrow for a carriage to pass – stood the two-storeyed house with blue shutters and two front doors where the Buonapartes lived. There were steps up to the ground-floor living-rooms, which were over the stabling and storages spaces, set high as protection from sewage, the rains, and men pursuing a vendetta.

Here Letizia Buonaparte had given birth to thirteen children and brought up the eight who had survived infancy. The sixth of those eight had been christened Maria-Paola, but all the family called her Paoletta. When she was born in 1780 Corsica had been part of the French realm for only twelve years, and Italian – or rather the Corse dialect – was still the language of the people and was her mother tongue, as it was of all her brothers and sisters. Her father, Carlo, had spoken French in addition, but she had hardly known him, for he had died while travelling in France when she was only four years of age.

Paoletta's childhood would be the envy of many children today. Except for her weekly catechism class and a few elementary lessons from the local priest she had no schooling to take her from play. Her mother was unable to give her any education; Letizia, like nearly all Corsican women at that time, was almost illiterate. Paoletta had plenty of free time and spent it playing in the alleys or running wild, often barefoot, about the hillsides overlooking the blue Gulf, stirring up sleeping dogs and putting

peaceable ducks and hens to flight, and further enlivening these
excursions by raiding an orange orchard. Sometimes she went
down to the beach with other children and they all bathed in
the nude, as was the custom for those who had not reached the
age of puberty. Her pranks and impish tricks were numberless.
She would return home at the end of the day covered with dust,
her dress all torn and her shoes (when she wore any) scuffed and
scratched. Vigorous whippings by her mother had no effect.

By the time Paoletta was ten or eleven she was her mother's
chief help about the house, for her elder sister, Maria-Anna, was
at school in France, at the establishment for young ladies founded
by Madame de Maintenon at St Cyr, near Paris. This difference
in opportunity was due to their father, handsome, vain, extravagant Carlo, who by assiduous efforts and providing proof
of noble descent had obtained free places in French institutions
for his four eldest children, Giuseppe, Napoleone, Luciano and
Maria-Anna, and for his wife's half-brother, Giuseppe Fesch.
But then Carlo had died at the early age of thirty-nine, from a
scirrhus in the stomach, leaving his family perilously near to ruin
and the four youngest children without any provision.[1]

Paoletta's help about the house was of dubious worth, for her
impulsive movements were a constant threat to any object near
at hand. Darting here and there about the sparsely-furnished
house, she took frequent tumbles down the stone staircase, but
fortunately without breaking any bones. Once when Letizia
was hard put to make ends meet she sent Paoletta up to uncle
Luciano's room on the first floor, where the old archdeacon lay
bedridden with gout, to try while playing around to sneak a
gold louis or two from the hoard which the avaricious priest
kept under his mattress. It was an exciting game but not one in
which Paoletta had had much practice – and the whole bagful
fell out and burst open. The gold coins rolled about the bare
flagged floor, uncle Luciano almost leapt out of bed and gave
piercing cries of distress that brought Letizia hurrying upstairs.
She gathered up the coins and the old man counted them carefully,
swearing by all the saints that none of it belonged to him, that
he was holding it in trust for someone else.

At eleven years of age Paoletta was a mischievous child with

[1] See Notes at the end of the book on pp. 201-15.

dark, vivacious eyes, by turns a tousled-haired tomboy and a light, graceful girl already showing promise of beauty. Her elder brothers and sister had all been pursuing their studies in France since her babyhood, and she hardly knew them; except one – Napoleone. Since being commissioned second-lieutenant he had already shown his contempt for authority – such as it was at that time – and had contrived to spend long periods away from his regiment, on leave, amounting to more than four years out of his first six-and-a-half as an officer, and most of this time was spent at home in Corsica. Even allowing for the fact that, under the monarchy, French army officers were required to spend only six months of the year with their regiment, Napoleone had achieved something of a feat, especially as he had always managed to draw his pay.

Paoletta's first sight of her 'big brother' had been when she was six and he had arrived home after nearly eight years in France. All the family had gone down to the quayside to meet the ship – Letizia, Paoletta and the other children at home, the old grandmother and the three aunts who lived almost opposite the Buonaparte house; even the old archdeacon had struggled along. Then the whole clan had walked back to the house proudly showing off 'Nabulione' – as all the neighbours had known him – in his fine, new, blue uniform with scarlet epaulettes. How could little Paoletta not admire him? But Napoleone was shy; for all the outward signs of maturity, he was quite young. He had gone from home to the military academy at nine years of age, and now he was seventeen, a thin youngster with long lank hair and a piercing, ardent look, and an outsider, a stranger among his own family. He looked round for some response – and there was the little six-year-old girl with tousled hair and wide friendly eyes. To cover his embarrassment he bent down suddenly and picked her up, and she threw her arms round his neck with a child's willing abandon. All the adults exclaimed joyfully, the difficult moment was over, and Napoleone dandled her on his knee while telling the roomful of relatives about his adventures. He had found his favourite sister, and a bond was established between the two which was to endure for both their lifetimes.

Since that first meeting (Napoleone had stayed for a year,

applying himself to putting order into his father's confused estate, and dabbling in local politics), Paoletta had always looked forward to Napoleone's next leave; and each lasted long enough for her to build him up into a comforting father figure. His stay at home never failed to be a time of excitement . . .

In the late summer of 1791, just before her eleventh birthday, Napoleone was home on leave once more; he had been promoted lieutenant, but doubted whether he would ever reach the rank of major. Giuseppe was at home too, recently returned from Pisa University with a law degree; but he had no practice and little likelihood of starting one. He was Napoleone's senior by more than a year and therefore the titular head of the family. But it was Napoleone who made the decisions, and their mother already regarded him as the real head; he showed the necessary respect, nevertheless, to his plump and vain elder brother, who was turning out to be as much of a dilettante as his father had been. Luciano, the third son and the only one whose intelligence approached that of Napoleone, was still at the seminary at Aix-en-Provence.

In mid-October it became obvious that their great-uncle the archdeacon had only a short time left to live. Although a cleric, his real vocation would seem to have been in business. Throughout his long life he had made business deals in whatever appeared likely to show a profit, however small – wine, horses, corn or pigs – had lent money at high interest rates, bought and sold properties, and never hesitated to take people to court (five in one year, 1777, including his sister-in-law) whenever some advantage could be obtained. His acute business sense allied with peasant craftiness had enabled him to amass what was, for Corsica, a small fortune.

He was the patriarch of the family, and since the death of his nephew Carlo – his only male descendant – in 1785 he had been the guardian of the latter's eight children during their minority. On 16 October 1791 the six of them at home, Letizia and her aunts, crowded into the high-ceilinged room on the first floor where the old priest's monumental bed took up much of the space. The shutters were half closed; the bright light filtering in and making regular patches on the flagged floor was just enough for the dying man to see the faces of his kin when they came to receive his last blessing. It was a solemn scene, enough to repress young Paoletta as she stood in the background with her brothers Girolamo and Luigi and her nine-year-old sister Maria-Annunziata. Paoletta's birthday was in four days' time, and she must have been wondering whether there would now be any celebration. In any case, this death scene impressed itself on her young mind.

Letizia was weeping silently. She was losing a man she respected and who had counselled her during her widowhood, even though he had done little to help financially. But she had never really held that against him, for she had learnt the value of money the hard way herself, through always being short of it. Although she was just past forty, always a forlorn age for Mediterranean women, Letizia was still fine-looking with a dignified bearing; one could easily believe that she had been the loveliest girl in Corsica in her time. Now the stern lines to her features and a tinge of sadness in her eyes gave her a matriarchal air.

Suddenly the man in the bed raised himself on his pillows and pointed a quavering finger at Giuseppe. 'You're the eldest of the family, but Napoleone is the head of it. Remember that.' Then it was Napoleone's turn. '*Tu poï, Napoleone, serai un omone.*' ('As for you, Napoleon, you'll be a great man.')

These prophecies were almost his last words. Uncle Luciano died later that day. After the funeral his will[2] was read and it was learnt that he had appointed Letizia's five sons as his joint heirs, but none could sell any of the land or property without the agreement of the other four. Paoletta and her two sisters were each to have a 'reasonable' dowry on marrying but would then lose all claim to the family house in Ajaccio and a small farm called the Milleli some five or six miles away. These two properties were entailed; the archdeacon had struggled hard to hold on to the former – a lawsuit against some cousins who claimed ownership had gone on for years – and to acquire the latter, and he had no desire for either to pass out of the Buonaparte family after his death. In actual fact the whole house did not belong to the Buonapartes; all that the archdeacon could dispose of in his will were the ground and first floors. The top floor had been part of the dowry of a cousin who had married a Pozzo di Borgo, and this family still occupied it; which was the reason for the two front doors.

It did seem to Letizia that the difficult days were now over. The Buonapartes were not really poor; it was just that they rarely had any money. This was a common state of affairs in Corsica, where as much as possible people obtained the necessities of life by a system of barter. The Buonapartes were better placed than most: the family owned a mill and a large public oven (part of Letizia's dowry), and people paid for the use of the one and the other in flour and fish; their small vineyards and pieces of land kept the Buonapartes supplied with wine, olive-oil, milk and goat's cheese, and the butcher was paid with an agreed number of sheep and goats. The important thing was not to part with that rare commodity, hard cash, except for imported and indispensable goods and articles such as clothing, coffee and sugar.

Certainly Letizia had no intention of spending any of uncle Luciano's hoard of gold, but the thought of it being available if needed was sweet indeed. As for Paoletta, she had grand notions of some new clothes and of a servant being employed. But the two men of the family had different ideas. Napoleone in particular saw the archdeacon's money as 'the sinews of war' which he had always lacked. Not that there was a war imminent in Corsica; but there were elections brewing, and a Corsican election campaign was not unlike a state of war.

There were two parties struggling for supremacy on the island. The largest was led by the veteran patriot, Pasquale Paoli, who was still striving to break the French connection and to achieve the independence of Corsica. The other party wanted to maintain the union and it was chiefly made up of ardent supporters of the principles of the French Revolution. Napoleone, and to a lesser extent Giuseppe, were active adherents of this French party. Not that Napoleone was particularly in favour of the Revolution, but he was convinced that the best interests of Corsica – and his own too – were in the union with France.

The elections to the island's Assembly had already taken place, resulting in an overwhelming majority for Paoli's party. Giuseppe had been a candidate, urged by the absent Napoleone, but had failed to gain enough support. There remained the elections of the officers to command the battalions of the National Guard then being formed in Corsica. Napoleone saw this as an opportunity to obtain a leading role; and, unlike his elder brother, he would have the means to advance his cause by bribery and intrigue.

Paoletta was delighted – not about the elections, of which she knew little and cared less, but over Napoleone extending his leave and staying on at home. The poll was to be held in March, and his leave expired at the end of December; but that was just another minor hindrance, easily shrugged off – his personal ambitions came first. And Paoletta had all the excitement she could wish for. Now the house was always full of people; there was a constant coming and going of friends and relatives – the Buonaparte clan – arriving from villages in the mountains and often spending the night in the house. Then mattresses were put down in the living-room and on the landings, and Paoletta slept with her young brothers and sister in one small room. One morning she saw an armed group of Napoleone's supporters usher a bewildered man into the house. He was one of the three scrutineers for the elections, appointed by the French authorities on the island, and he had taken lodgings all unwittingly with an influential opponent of the Buonapartes named Peraldi. The armed group had burst into the Peraldi house and politely escorted the unfortunate scrutineer to Napoleone, who expressed regret at his lodging in a house where people would attempt to influence him.

'But here you are free to do as you wish,' Napoleone added, giving one of his piercing looks. 'No one will talk to you about your mission.'

As the man had no acquaintances in Ajaccio, he decided to stay with the Buonapartes, either through prudence or the influence of a few of uncle Luciano's gold louis.

By such high-handed tactics and by making considerable inroads into the money left by the archdeacon, the result of the election was never really in doubt. On polling day there was a minor disturbance over the appointment of polling officers, but otherwise everything went well for Napoleone and he easily headed the poll with 422 votes out of the 522 cast, or rather acknowledged. That evening the house in the *strada Malerba* was packed with people. Wine flowed freely, guns were let off, and, to the joy of Paoletta and the other children, the band of the National Guard came and played in the alley.

The two defeated candidates at the poll had been the choice of the elderly Paoli. He was furious at the success of this young contender and gave orders that Buonaparte's battalion was not to be allowed to mount guard at the citadel of Ajaccio. On Easter Day, while Paoletta was helping her mother prepare the meal, there came sounds of men marching down the main street, then shouting and shots being fired. It was Napoleone leading his men to take the citadel by force – against a garrison belonging to a French infantry regiment! He was forced to withdraw, with several men wounded.

A few weeks later news reached Ajaccio that France was at war with Austria. It was then May 1792, and Napoleone had been absent from his regiment since the first days of September. He was thoughtful for a day or two, then announced that it was advisable for him to return to France. After his departure the house seemed dull and empty to Paoletta.

Before the heat of the summer began to beat down on Ajaccio, Paoletta and other children of her age took their first Communion in the cathedral, followed by a celebration at their homes. Like Napoleone before her, she said it was the happiest day in her life until then – by which she meant, as he had, that the first communicant had new clothes and received presents from all the assembled relatives.

In her long white dress she was the centre of attraction at the family table laden with good food. A great day indeed for the eleven-year-old tomboy!

During the hot summer Letizia occasionally took the children to the Milelli for a day or two, walking the few miles out into the country. Giuseppe had had some repairs carried out to the cottage and had some of the rough land brought into cultivation. That summer Luciano arrived home unexpectedly from the seminary at Aix, due to lack of money and of vocation. In revolutionary France this tall, self-opinionated seventeen-year-old had become an ardent Jacobin, and at Ajaccio he spent much of his time making fiery speeches at the political club. Then in late September Napoleone turned up again, bringing his sister Maria-Anna.

The school at St Cyr had been closed as being a Royalist establishment, and Napoleone had seized the opportunity to apply for permission to escort his fifteen-year-old sister back through the troubled provinces to Corsica – and, never lacking in audacity, for travelling expenses for both of them. He had obtained the one and the other: 352 *livres*, equal to about three months of his pay as captain. For Napoleone had not only succeeded only in explaining away the adverse reports on his conduct and obtaining reinstatement, he had been promoted as well. This was due to the confused situation in the Ministries and to the fact that so many army officers had fled the country and joined the Royalists. The new French Republic was badly in need of trained officers, but Napoleone had more personal matters on his mind. He had no thought of returning once he had seen his sister safely home. He resumed command of his battalion of the National Guard and took up his intrigues where he had left off five months earlier.

For the first time ever, Letizia had all her eight children at home. Paoletta was overjoyed at seeing Napoleone again so soon, but Luciano and Maria-Anna got on her nerves, especially the strictly brought-up elder sister who kept criticising her free-and-easy behaviour and dress. Oddly enough, Luciano and Maria-Anna got on well together, although their youthful views on the world were so very different – he the rabid Jacobin, she an ardent Royalist. But the two were about the same age, were both pedantic and loved to air their knowledge of French and cultivated manners.

Just before Christimas a French fleet dropped anchor off Ajaccio. Paoletta badly wanted to go down to the quayside when she heard of this exciting event, but her mother sternly ordered all three girls to stay indoors. The ships were carrying troops for an attack on Sardinia – a lot of drunken riff-raff, said Letizia – and with them ashore the streets were not safe even for hardy men. However, Luciano brought the young rear-admiral, Truguet, to the house. He was soon followed by a number of officers and dignitaries, including the *ci-devant* Marquis de Sémonville, ambassador designate to the Grand Porte. The chief attraction was Maria-Anna; not that she was pretty – rather the opposite in fact – but with her knowledge of French and worldly ways she was unique in Ajaccio. Unfortunately for the young officers, her mother kept a stern eye on the flirtations, and her younger sister was always hanging around.

In Corsica, as in all Mediterranean countries, girls reach puberty at an early age. Letizia had been married at fourteen. Paoletta was in her thirteenth year, and her mind must have been on boys if not on young men. Her future seemed to be in marriage to some uncouth islander, probably a remote cousin avid for her small dowry. But now there were glittering young Frenchmen calling at the house, romantic visitors from a different world, all paying court to her simpering sister. It was an aspect of life she had not seen before, an aspect which made her conscious of her own femininity and her potential attractions. She may also have realised that from their French education Maria-Anna and Luciano had acquired something that she, brought up in the wilds, might never possess – poise. But it probably occurred to her, too, that she had been endowed with two great advantages which her sister lacked – vivacity and beauty.

The excitement did not last long. In mid-January the ships sailed for Bonifacio, which was to be the base for a two-pronged attack on the neighbouring island.[3] With them went Napoleone and his battalion of the National Guard; he was also in command of the expedition's artillery – two guns and one mortar. Luciano, too, left home again, as secretary to Sémonville. The ambassador had decided to return to France as British patrols were preventing him from sailing to Constantinople, and having been impressed by Luciano's attentions to him had offered the young man temporary employment.

A calm settled on the street of weeds – until mid-March when Napoleone arrived, fuming. The assault on Sardinia had been a dismal fiasco, he angrily told his mother and family. Paoli had done all he could to hinder the operation against what he considered to be the natural ally of Corsica, and was preparing to call on the aid of the British fleet in the Mediterranean to cast off the French yoke. Napoleone wrote to Luciano in Toulon and sent Giuseppe off to Bastia, the seat of French government of the island, to urge the Commissioners there to take vigorous action. These three Commissioners – one of whom, Saliceti, was a friend of the Buonapartes – had been sent by the Convention in Paris to supervise Paoli and report on conditions in the turbulent island.

Then came a bombshell. Napoleone received an exultant letter from Luciano: 'I've dealt our enemies a decisive blow . . . and our fortune is made!' The young hothead had addressed the Jacobin club in Toulon and denounced Paoli; a motion to this effect had been voted and sent to Paris. The Convention declared Paoli a traitor to the Republic and ordered his arrest.

The news spread like wildfire through Corsica. The effect was to draw the loyalties of the local patriots still closer to Paoli, and they began an active persecution and proscription of their opponents. Paoli, issuing furious orders from his mountain capital of Corte, declared a personal vendetta against all the sons of Carlo Buonaparte.

On 3 May Paoletta woke to find that Napoleone had vanished during the night. A messenger had come secretly to the house with a warning for Napoleone: a group headed by his old enemy Peraldi intended to seize him and take him to Paoli's headquarters at Corte. A word to his mother, and then Napoleone had crept out of the house to where the messenger had a horse tethered. By daybreak he was heading north along mule-tracks and through mountain gorges, making for Bastia, about one hundred miles away.

Letizia was left alone with the five youngest children in a town now openly hostile. A week passed and she was still without news of Napoleone. Even Paoletta was affected by the seriousness of the situation. As a precaution, Letizia took her two youngest children across to her mother's house, where her half-brother Giuseppe Fesch, then a priest, was living. If she had to flee, the two youngsters would be safe and she would have more freedom of movement.

A few days later a messenger arrived with the long-awaited news. Paoletta and the other two gathered round their anxious mother to hear the man's dramatic account. Napoleone was safe, he had reached Bastia, but on the way he had twice narrowly escaped capture by Paolists. In the village of Bocognano, high up in the mountains, a group of them had surrounded the inn

where he was having a meal; but some of his supporters had
helped him get away, over a wall at the bottom of the garden.
As he got into his saddle the Paolists had appeared at the bend
in the lane levelling their guns. *'A morte il traditore della patria!'*

The man was describing the scene with expansive gestures,
and Paoletta exclaimed indignantly with the others. Napoleone
had escaped unhurt. He galloped away, and for the next few days
had made his way towards the coast; one night he slept in a cave,
another night a cousin, Girolamo Levis, gave him shelter.
Finally he had reached Bastia by boat, and now he and Giuseppe
were urging Saliceti and the other Commissioners to mount a
seaborne attack on Ajaccio!

Letizia passed the word round to members of the Buonaparte
clan. The house seemed strangely quiet without the two youngsters and the vehement discussions of the elder brothers and their
supporters. More news reached Letizia on 20 May – Napoleone
had sailed from Bastia with a force of two hundred men in half-a-
dozen coasting vessels. While from another source she heard
that Paoli, well aware of this threat, was sending some fifteen
hundred armed men to repel any attempt by Napoleone to land
near Ajaccio.[4]

Late in the evening of 24 May there came a gentle but insistent
knocking at the Buonapartes' front door. Paoletta and the other
two had gone to bed, but Letizia's half-brother Giuseppe was
sitting with her. She peered down through the slatted shutters
and made out half-a-dozen armed men in the dim alley. She
recognised one of them as a trusty friend of the family – Costa,
from the mountain village of Bastelica – and went and unlocked
the door.

'You must leave at once, signora Letizia! Paoli's men will be
here any minute to take you off somewhere. Quick, there's not a
moment to lose!'

She hesitated; it was not in her nature to flee, to abandon the
family home. But Costa pointed out that her children would be
in danger too. That decided her; in a matter of minutes the three
were roused and had got dressed; Letizia packed some food and
clothing, and the whole party set off on foot through the night
for the Milelli cottage.

Even there they were not safe; while Letizia and the children were still sleeping after their night flight, Costa and his men standing guard saw a horseman galloping towards them. As he drew near they recognised him and lowered their guns. He was a priest named Coti, one of the Buonaparte clan, and he had come to warn Letizia. The Paolists had been furious at finding that the family had escaped; they had broken in and ransacked the house, and were now searching all the places where Letizia might have taken refuge. Soon they would extend their search to the Milelli.

Costa woke *la signora*. A hasty council was held. Costa and his men were prepared to fight, but against a more numerous enemy they would have little chance. So the party moved on again, and soon after leaving the Milelli met a couple of shepherds who were looking for Letizia. They had a message from Napoleone. He and his small force had landed at the northern tip of the Gulf of Ajaccio but had been beaten back and forced to re-embark; he was now aboard a three-masted vessel, sheltering from a rough sea in the small bay of Provenzale.

Letizia decided to try and reach the bay and join Napoleone; it seemed the only solution to her predicament. The party worked its way round to the north of Ajaccio, avoiding the beaten paths, floundering across streams and stumbling through the mauve, pungent *macchia*, a dense mass of aromatic shrubs, wild herbs, ferns and broom, six feet high in places. Maria-Anna was the first to complain; the curriculum at St Cyr had not included assault courses. Paoletta was made of sterner stuff and took the opportunity to decry her sister.

'Stop snivelling,' her mother said severely to Maria-Anna. 'I'm suffering too, but I don't complain.'

Then they came to a fast-running stream, the Capitello. The usual way of crossing it was to plunge in up to the waist and wade across. Letizia refused, saying that her children were too tired and risked being carried away by the current. Yet they had to get across; there was no way round. Costa suddenly remembered that a friend of his often kept a horse in a clearing a little way upstream. He hurried off, found the animal grazing peacefully, and led it back to the party of fugitives. One by one, they crossed the stream on the horse's back – Letizia, Luigi, Paoletta, Maria-Anna, and the two priests, Giuseppe Fesch and Coti.

Costa told his men to return home; they were to spread the story that they had accompanied Letizia and her children in a different direction to the one taken. Then on went the little party again, Costa going ahead and leading the horse, in case it should be needed again.

Suddenly they heard voices approaching, and hurried to hide in a small wood. It was a group of Paoli's men on their way back to Ajaccio. As they passed by the wood Letizia and the others heard them cursing the Buonapartes. It only needed the horse to stamp or to neigh, and all would be up! But the good animal stayed quiet, and the Paolists disappeared from view.

The party spent part of the night in a shepherd's hut, resting; they moved on at daybreak and an hour or two after sunrise came within sight of the sea. Paoletta's clothes were torn, her legs scratched, and she was hungry and weary; the others were in no better state. They sat down near the shore, and after a time saw a xebec, a three-masted coasting vessel, working along close to land as if searching for something. The Republican flag was flying from the stern. Letizia waved some clothing; the vessel hove to and lowered a boat. A few minutes later Napoleone was splashing through the surf to embrace his mother. Paoletta's eyes sparkled; never had she been so glad to see her big brother, who had now come miraculously to the rescue.

Costa declined to go aboard with the others. Letizia thanked him warmly there on the beach, and Napoleone added his own gratitude. (Nearly thirty years later, when making his will at St Helena, Napoleon included: 'To Costa of Bastelica in Corsica I leave one hundred thousand francs.')

The xebec sailed up the coast to Calvi, where the Buonapartes found temporary refuge at the house of yet another cousin. Letizia sent to Ajaccio for her two youngest children, and with their returning escort came news of the family's home having been pillaged and damaged. In her distress Letizia must have spared a thought for uncle Luciano – less than two years after his death the work and savings of a lifetime had almost vanished. The family was ruined, outlawed and homeless.

'*Questo paese non e per noi,*' Napoleone admitted sadly to his mother. 'This country isn't for us.' There was only one thing to do – for them all to go with him to France. After all, he was still an army captain, even if he had been absent from his regiment for nearly nine months. And revolutions were good opportunities for army officers with spirit and courage.

The family went across to Bastia and joined Giuseppe. A few days later, on 11 June, they sailed for Toulon in the fishing vessel *La Belette*. Napoleone had taken the precaution of obtaining from Saliceti a certificate confirming 'the necessity of Captain Buonaparte's presence in Corsica for the past six months'. They had been months of failure. But no one thought of blaming him, least of all Paoletta, straining her eyes against the dazzling blue of sea and sky for a first glimpse of France. Family solidarity, the clan spirit, was too strong to blame any member for the disastrous turn of events, not even the absent one, safe in Toulon.

Chapter 2

First love

In Toulon in June 1793 no one was safe. The anarchy and
bloodshed were more horrible than any battlefield. The crews
of two warships had mutinied and joined the released convicts
and the dockyard workers on strike. This mob was led by members
of the Jacobin club, extremists who flouted government orders.
At every front door hung a list of the house's occupants and
their means of livelihood. Prominent citizens were being arrested
and sent without trial to the guillotine. There was a food
shortage and even bread, so sacred to the French, was rationed.
Luciano was used to the situation, and when he hurried to the
town hall on hearing of the arrival of his family he was surprised
at their exclamations of horror and dismay.

The two eldest brothers quickly agreed that their mother and
the youngsters could not remain in Toulon. Lodgings were found
for them at La Valette, a village in the hills just outside the town.
On their passports, which they needed in order to leave Toulon,
Paoletta was described as 'dressmaker', like her mother and
sisters. Then Napoleone set off to rejoin his regiment, which was
stationed at Nice as part of the newly-formed Army of the Alps,
while Giuseppe went to Paris with other Corsican refugees to
seek financial aid from the Convention.

Letizia, Paoletta and her sisters and the two boys had cramped
quarters on the top floor of No. 23 in the Grande Rue of the
village. Food was easier to obtain there, the air was pure and the
countryside lovely, and the cost of living was cheaper – which
was just as well in the family's reduced circumstances. Letizia
began to look for work, and then a triumphant letter and some
money arrived from Napoleone. Once again, due to the massive
emigration of military officers, he had been reinstated and had
drawn all his back pay; and he was being sent to Avignon with
a troop of men and carts to collect ammunition. He soon found
himself in the midst of civil war.

The southern provinces, always strongly Royalist, had risen in revolt against the bloody excesses of the central government. Fifty thousand troops were marching to suppress the rebellious towns, bringing in their train the most evil and revengeful of the Commissioners of the Convention – Fouché and Collot d'Herbois, Barras and Fréron. Communications were cut, food was short; word spread south of massacres and atrocities, of churches being desecrated and plundered. People lived in fear and terror, never knowing what the next day would bring. From Lyons to Marseilles, the whole Rhône valley was up in arms, and in mid-July the insurrection spread to Toulon. The National Guard overthrew the hold of the Jacobins; the admiral commanding the fleet called on the aid of the British and Spanish ships blockading the port, and they landed troops to help in the defence of the town.

La Valette was in the danger zone. Letizia and her children gathered up their bundles again and moved on. For the remainder of that hot summer of 1793 they wandered about Provence, staying a fortnight in one village, three weeks in another, living from hand to mouth amidst the chaos and the sporadic fighting. Letizia knew no French and had to rely on her eldest daughter. In early September they reached Marseilles and found lodgings in a slum area down by the port – three small rooms on the fourth floor of a dilapidated house, No. 7 in the rue Pavillon.

There was no lack of accommodation in Marseilles at that time. It had fallen to the Republican troops a fortnight earlier, and the usual scenes of horror had followed; hundreds of suspects had been carted off to be shot or guillotined by order of the all-powerful Commissioners; and such grim sights were by no means over. Many fine houses were unoccupied, but to obtain possession of one Letizia needed money or influence, and she had neither.

The Convention had voted financial aid to Corsican families driven from the island as a result of loyalty to France – for this, Christophe Saliceti, who was himself a Corsican and who had returned to Paris, had been largely responsible – but the chaotic state of communications prevented the Corsican exiles from benefiting from this measure. Letizia was reduced to applying for the dole allowed to 'needy patriots'. Never had the family's fortunes been so low. But then, as often happens when it seems impossible for things to get worse, an unexpected sequence of events turned the tide of fortune for all the Buonapartes.

First, Giuseppe arrived from Paris in the company of Saliceti. Despite a difference of a generation in age, the two had become very friendly, and when the Commissioner was sent on mission to the army in the south he had invited Giuseppe to accompany him. Both were aghast at the situation in which they found Letizia and her children. Within a day or two Saliceti requisitioned for them the fine town house of a Monsieur de Cypières who had emigrated. A job as clerk in the army stores out at St Maximin was found for Luciano; while Giuseppe was given an appointment in the army contracting service which carried a high salary and many fringe benefits. But this was not all the good fortune. Napoleone, dissatisfied with his obscure duties of trundling ammunition along the dusty lanes of Provence, sought out Saliceti to obtain a transfer to more promising employment. He found him in the village of Beausset, outside Toulon, which was being invested by the army which had taken Marseilles. It so happened that one of the divisional artillery commanders had been severely wounded; Captain Buonaparte was appointed in his place.

Toulon was a much harder nut to crack than Marseilles had been. The besieged allied force held out for three months; then a strategic fort overlooking the harbour was captured by Republican troops, it was in Napoleone's sector and he at once installed his batteries on the heights. In a matter of hours, the British and Spanish ships sailed away with their troops, the French defenders surrendered, and the besiegers swarmed into the town to pillage, slaughter and burn.

Napoleone had distinguished himself in several ways; in addition to his successful action he had been the most active of officers throughout the siege, and he had been wounded in the leg by a bayonet-thrust during an attack on a fort. Moreover, while besieging Toulon he had not omitted to besiege the representatives of the Convention on mission in the area, notably Saliceti, Paul Barras and Robespierre the Younger, whose wide powers included the nomination of senior officers. On 22 December, three days after the end of the siege, Napoleone was

promoted acting brigadier-general. The decree that Barras and
Saliceti sent to the War Ministry for confirmation (which it
received two months later) was countersigned by the GOC,
Dugommier, who added the ironic yet prophetic comment:
'If this officer is not promoted, he will promote himself.'

Napoleone, never satisfied, also obtained the post of Inspector-
General of the coastal defences between Marseilles and Cannes.
His pay was 15,000 livres a year (equivalent to more than £3,000
today) with many extra allowances and rations. The headquarters
of his Inspectorate was at Marseilles, and there he went early in
January 1794. One of his first calls was at the Cypières town house
to see his mother and family.

For Paoletta, after the privations and horrors of that terrible
summer, life was suddenly wonderful. There was money and
comfort such as she had never known. Everything was strange,
exciting, new – including the dame school which she attended,
not very willingly, with her younger sister and Girolamo. But
these lessons came to an end in the spring, when Napoleone
invited his mother and sisters to join him at Antibes. The young
brigadier-general had moved his headquarters there when the
Army of the Alps, commanded by Masséna, began making
limited attacks on the Austrian forces in Piedmont.

Paoletta clapped her hands in delight when she saw the fine
country house and grounds that her brother had requisitioned.
The Château Sallé, as it was called, stood a little way inland from
the seaside town. Its white frontage sparkled under the Provençal
sun; it had gaily painted shutters and almost tropical gardens in
which grew orange-trees, palms, mimosas and eucalyptus. It was
a far cry from the poor lodgings of the previous summer.
Napoleone had given his mother a good allowance but, thrifty
as ever, she engaged only one servant and did the family washing
herself in the stream at the bottom of the garden – she knew
it would be done properly that way. Paoletta, as free as air,
roamed over the countryside and tasted to the full the joys of
this happy release – and, as at Ajaccio, climbed the neighbours'
walls to taste their ripe figs and young artichokes. On one
occasion she only just escaped the wrath of a Monsieur Baliste
whose garden she had invaded and who chased her with a stick.

Thus she spent the last carefree summer of her girlhood in this quiet retreat in a far corner of France, while the Reign of Terror reached its peak in Paris and other cities. Her mother often spoke of their home in Ajaccio and wondered when she would see her beloved Corsica again; but Paoletta, like anyone of her age, lived for the present and looked forward to life, not backwards. In later years, however, she said that the weeks at the Château Sallé were among the happiest of her life; and fourteen years afterwards, when at the height of her amazing career and while staying in the region, she made a sudden sally to revisit the house and revive those happy memories.

Only one thing marred that delightful summer – Paoletta saw very little of Napoleone. When the probings and skirmishes beyond the Alps were called off, due to inadequate resources, Napoleone was sent on a secret mission to Genoa. But two brothers gave Letizia and her daughters plenty to talk about. Early in May Luciano wrote from St Maximin to announce that he had got married – without having given the family any warning or asked his mother's permission. As his bride, Catherine Boyer, was the illiterate daughter of the village innkeeper, Luciano's deliberate omission was understandable. Letizia was indignant at this flaunting of Corsican custom and Napoleone, when the news reached him, was furious at not having been consulted, especially as it was a marriage of which he strongly disapproved. A couple of months later Giuseppe wrote to say that he wished to marry; and this time Paoletta heard nothing but exclamations of delight from her mother and sisters. The fiancée was Julie Clary, daughter of a wealthy Marseilles merchant whose family was connected with some of the local nobility. Letizia had already met the Clarys in Marseilles; Giuseppe, through his relations with Saliceti, had obtained the release of one of the sons who had been arrested by the revolutionary tribunal. Julie had a sister, Désirée, who was as pretty as she was plain; but Giuseppe knew goodness and virtue when he saw them, and perhaps as compensation for her looks Julie's father agreed to give her a handsome dowry of 150,000 francs. The wedding took place on 1 August, and a few days later the couple arrived at the Château Sallé for a short visit.

Paoletta and Maria-Anna must have regarded their first sister-in-law – at least, the first they had seen – with mixed feelings. Maria-Anna, turned seventeen, was a few months older than the bride but was still unmarried. Paoletta could greet Julie with genuine warmth; in the company of such a plain face her own beauty was bound to be enhanced.

However, the quiet pleasures of this family party in idyllic surroundings were suddenly disrupted. Napoleone had been arrested! The news of 9 Thermidor had taken more than a week to reach the headquarters of the Army of the Alps at Nice: both the Robespierres had been guillotined, the Reign of Terror was over, France could breathe again. But those people who owed their power to the old order were now at risk. Napoleone's recent mission to Genoa and his cultivation of Robespierre the Younger made him an obvious suspect – or scapegoat. On 9 August he was arrested by order of the Commissioners with the Army of the Alps and two days later was incarcerated in the fort at Antibes.

This news was brought to the Château Sallé by Napoleone's aide-de-camp, Lieutenant Junot, a dashing cavalryman. He had been a frequent visitor, attracted by Paoletta, and now took the opportunity to console her during the general consternation that his message produced. Paoletta was upset more than anyone. There was apparently a possibility of Napoleone being sent to Paris under escort – she saw a vision of the guillotine over him. He must escape from the fort . . . everyone agreed . . . Junot was sent to consult with him . . . The young brigadier-general did not agree; to escape would compromise himself still further, and besides he was innocent, so he said. In any case, ten days later he was released, largely through the intervention of Saliceti, who probably feared being involved if Napoleone were brought to trial. But the brigadier-general lost his command and had to look elsewhere for employment; his family left the Château Sallé and returned to Marseilles, too thankful at Napoleone's release to feel much regret. Besides, winter was approaching and life would be much gayer in a large town – a thought that was uppermost in the minds of the three girls.

The Buonapartes' circle of acquaintances in Marseilles had greatly widened since becoming allied to the Clary family; and Giuseppe's new wealth enabled them to hold receptions and give balls. Napoleone obtained a command in the expedition being mounted painfully at Toulon to drive the British out of Corsica, and he frequently visited his mother and family. His staff officers too – Junot, Leclerc, Marmont – called at the house whenever they passed through Marseilles.

Paoletta – or rather Paulette, as she was now called – was undoubtedly the great attraction. Like most Corsican girls, she had matured early, and her slim, graceful figure was already suggesting the physical charms which the coming years were to bring to perfection. Her face was a pure oval, with a long straight nose, small mouth and pronounced little chin. She had a clear olive complexion, dark lustrous eyes and teeth with the regularity of a string of carefully selected pearls. She was very beautiful and she knew it.

Amorous by nature, flirtatious by temperament, she lived for frivolity; but it was balanced by a gaiety and good nature which charmed everyone who knew her. Beauty was indeed her sole asset, matrimonial or otherwise. She had no education in the accepted sense, nor had she revealed any artistic or other talent. Her experiences in her early teens had not been of a kind to inculcate high ideals nor create refinements of mind or manners; and the loose morals of the time – a permissive age if ever there was one – were an incentive to her instincts. Fortunately, Letizia was there to keep a stern eye on all her daughters; and the Corsican tradition of virtue in girls was innate.

Paulette could bring no dowry to anyone offering marriage, but several suitors presented themselves. In the spring of 1795 a Monsieur Billon, a soap manufacturer in Marseilles, made approaches to Letizia. He was forty and bald, but, so he told her, wealthy. But Napoleone vetoed the match. 'A certain citizen Billon, whom I am assured you know,' he wrote to Giuseppe, 'has asked for Paulette's hand. This citizen has no money. I have written to Mama that it cannot be considered.'

Soon afterwards, young Junot opened his heart to Napoleone. The two were in Paris, the brigadier-general having been summoned to another post. Junot was in despair at being so far from Paulette, with whom he had become infatuated, and begged Napoleone's support in pressing his suit. Instead the general advised him to forget about it.

'You say you will have an income of twelve hundred francs when your father dies,' Napoleone summed up realistically. 'But he is in excellent health and will probably live a long time. Meanwhile you have only your lieutenant's pay. Paulette hasn't even that. In short, you have nothing, she has nothing – total, nothing.'[1]

Already Napoleone was taking a hand in Paulette's affairs of the heart. But it is doubtful that she ever knew of these two proposals of marriage. The third, however, was a very different matter, and she fought with all her energy to have it accepted.

This suitor was Louis Stanislas Fréron, a libertine and political adventurer whose hands were steeped in blood from the massacres at Toulon and Marseilles. He came of a Royalist family; King Stanislas of Poland had stood godfather to him. At college in Paris, where one of his schoolfellows was the elder Robespierre, he had become imbued with the principles of the Revolution. In 1789 he founded and edited a violent, left-wing newspaper, *L'Orateur du Peuple*. Elected to the Convention, he voted for the death of Louis XVI, became one of the most powerful of the representatives and was sent to the south during the Terror. He was completely without scruples and was implicated in most of the disreputable schemes of the time. A man of intelligence and good taste in some respects, he dressed in an elegant but foppish manner, in tight-fitting rose-coloured breeches and a coat with a huge collar over which his powdered hair fell in long locks. To the gilded youth of the day, who dressed even more extravagantly, he was known as 'the king of the dandies'. He was not handsome but he had presence and style; like most of his kind, he was an inveterate pursuer of women, and at the time he met Paulette he had been openly living with a Paris actress named Masson for five years, and she was expecting her third child by him.

He became a visitor to the Buonaparte house while on mission in Marseilles, and was dazzled by Paulette's beauty and freshness. As for the emotionally precocious Paulette, she could scarcely fail to be flattered by the attentions of a man so obviously superior by birth, talents, and position. The undisguised admiration of a man twice her age – Fréron was in fact turned forty – gave her a thrill of pride, an exhilaration that she had never before exper-

ienced. She knew she was beautiful – but what a joy it was to be
told so, and for the first time! She did not know his past history
nor how expert he was at a game at which she was as yet a
novice. He read to her the most romantic passages of Petrarch's
Sonnets; he gave her locks of his hair and asked for some of hers
in exchange. There can be no doubt that he aroused the passionate
nature in her. They became secretly affianced lovers, awaiting
only the consent of Paulette's family to their union. But Letizia's
stern eye was on them, taking a caustic look at this plausible but
distasteful suitor. She learnt something of his past and refused
Paulette's pleadings to be allowed to marry him, then forbade
further meetings between the two. Letizia may have been playing
for time until Napoleone could be consulted; he was still in
Paris, on half-pay as a result of refusing the uninteresting posts
he had been directed to fill. This brought out the obstinate
streak in Paulette; the determination to have her own way
manifested itself for the first time, and she began sending passionate letters to her Stanislas.

Fréron returned to Paris as the Assembly was voting a new
Constitution to set up the Directory. Paulette's letters, fervent
and tender, followed after him. 'I swear to love but you alone;
my heart cannot be divided, it is given wholly to you. Who could
oppose the union of two souls who seek happiness and find it in
their love for each other? We will write to each other and that
will be some consolation for not seeing you . . .' At the end she
turned from French to her native tongue, as though that were
the only true means of expressing her feelings. '*Addio, anima mia,
ti amo sempre, mia vita.*'

In Paris, after the rage and cannon-shots of rainy 13 Vendémiaire, a grateful Assembly prepared to reward the army officers
who had saved it from the insurrection. The name of Buonaparte
had not been mentioned until Fréron seized a change of gaining
the support of Paulette's brother whose word was law in family
affairs at least. Fréron rose in his seat and with his usual eloquence
reminded the Assembly of the good work performed by Buonaparte during that memorable night and day, and proposed
recognition of his services. The representatives applauded these
fine sentiments, though most of them had never heard the
name before. Then Paul Barras, the leading light of the Assembly

and recently appointed commander of the Army of the Interior, seconded Fréron's proposition and asked that Buonaparte become second-in-command to himself; this was approved, and the appointment was published the following day.[2] A fortnight later Barras became one of the five members of the Directory and resigned his army command; he used his influence to have Buonaparte appointed in his stead, believing that in this way he was ensuring the general's future loyalty.

On 3 October 1795, Napoleone had been on half-pay, a slovenly-dressed, thin, pale, unemployed officer with few prospects. On 4 October he was reinstated brigadier-general, on the 10th he became second-in-command of the Army of the Interior, on the 16th major-general and on the 26th GOC of that Army, in other words military commander of Paris, one of the most powerful positions in the country. Again he owed his rapid advancement to civil strife, but this time also to his favourite sister's love affair.

How thrilled Paulette would have been if she had known! But it is most unlikely that word of the part Fréron had played ever reached her. Fréron might have reminded Napoleone of it, but to have boasted of it to others would have been a bad move. His intervention in favour of Napoleone was forgotten in the turmoil and swiftly-moving events of the time; and the beneficiary glossed over it in later years.

Fréron returned to Marseilles armed with friendly letters of introduction from Napoleone, who did not oppose the marriage to Paulette but did not give his consent to it either; he was still feeling his feet in his new position, and Fréron was an associate of the all-powerful Barras.[3] In Marseilles, however, Fréron found Paulette's mother still adamant. Letizia must have told Paulette some home-truths about him, but they made no difference to the lovesick girl. She continued to write to Fréron:

> On my return from the country I found your charming letter, which made me very happy . . . You came very near losing your Paulette, for I fell into the water while trying to step into a boat. Fortunately I was helped out quickly . . . I am not going to say anything more about your mistress. All that you tell me is reassuring. I know the uprightness of your heart

and approve of the arrangements you are making with regard to her. The water I swallowed has not chilled my heart towards you . . .

And another time:

My dear one, you must be anxious at not receiving my letters, but I suffer just as much as you do . . . we are being thwarted and made miserably unhappy . . . Lucien showed me your letter; I see that your situation is the same as ever. Ah, how I kissed that letter! I pressed it to my breast, holding it close to my heart. How I wish I were with you to comfort you in the midst of the wrongs being done you.

The postscript was more passionate than ever:

Ti amo sempre e passionatissimamenta, per sempre ti amo, ti amo, sbell' idolo mio, sei cuore mio, tenero amico, ti amo, amo, si amatissimo amante.

The wrongs being done to Fréron, to which Paulette had alluded, were in fact the evils of his past catching up with him. He had failed to be elected to the new Chamber; old political enemies had demanded his removal as Commissioner. He hastened to Paris to defend himself, but in vain. He was in a decline, while Napoleone was in the ascendancy, which caused the latter to harden his attitude.

Nevertheless, the affair struggled on. Paulette remained Fréron's one hope of recovering himself. Her brother was a rising star – Barras had just given him command of the Army of Italy – and there was at least a chance that Napoleone would give way to his sister's urgent pleas. If he did, Fréron felt confident of restoring his fortunes through the Buonaparte connection. Paulette was as much in love with him as ever and she remained blindly loyal; his political disgrace left her unmoved.

'Everyone is against us,' she wrote to him in the spring of 1796. 'I see by your letters that all your friends have failed you, including Napoleone's wife, on whose support you counted. In fact she told her husband that I should demean myself by marrying you, and that she hoped to prevent our marriage! What harm have we done to her? Everyone is against us, we are in a miserable situation. Do write to Napoleone. I would like to write to him myself. What do you think? I shall love you all my life. . . .'

There has always been some mystery about Paulette's letters to Fréron. They were first published in Paris in 1834, in the *Revue Rétrospective,* and have been reproduced in several biographies. Some writers have doubted their authenticity, and certainly Paulette did not escape the attention of fabricators of Buonaparte letters. A number of fake letters by her were the work of a Royalist refugee in London named Peltier, who was the earliest propagator of the myth of Paulette the shameless. They were repeated by anti-Napoleonic pamphleteers, who originated the stories of her having been Fréron's mistress and contracting syphilis from him – an obnoxious libel still being repeated by certain modern French writers obliged to rely on the sensational. But the authenticity of the remaining letters, including those quoted here, can be questioned only because of one factor – at their date Paulette was barely able to read or write elementary French. Two years later, when she attended a finishing school in Paris, she still had much progress to make. But there is a simple explanation: Luciano wrote them for her, or dictated them to her. He was still smarting from the family's refusal to accept his wife (though Letizia had relented when Catherine presented her with a first grandchild, a girl), and so he supported Paulette against all the others in her efforts to marry the man of her choice. Moreover, he had attached himself to Fréron early on, as a means of advancing his own political ambitions without help from Napoleone. When Fréron fell into disfavour, Lucien (he had gallicised his name) was even more concerned to help him back by having him become brother-in-law to the GOC of the Army of Italy, a protégé of the all-powerful Barras. The Italian postscripts to the letters were, however, Paulette's own work. It was Lucien who wrote to Fréron to ask for the return of Paulette's letters when the affair came to an end; presumably Fréron never did return them.

It came to an end when Fréron gave up, defeated by Letizia's opposition and Napoleone's temporising. He saw Napoleone briefly when the latter stopped at Marseilles on his way to take up his command at Nice, and apparently left Fréron still with a little hope, for a few days later he wrote to Napoleone:

> Before we parted, my dear Buonaparte, you promised me a letter to your wife. We arranged that you would inform her of my marriage so that in the event of my presenting Paulette to her, she should not be taken by surprise . . . Your mother is standing in the way of my haste just a little. I still hope that the wedding may take place at Marseilles within four or five days . . . I implore you to write to your mother directly to waive all objections. Tell her to give me a free hand in deciding what date to fix for the happy moment . . . My dear Buonaparte, help me to overcome this new obstacle. I rely on you.

Napoleone was having his own difficulties with his mother because he, too, had married without her consent or knowledge. This probably made Letizia even more determined to exercise her control over her daughters. Eventually Napoleone made up his mind; he was much more decisive in military matters than in emotional affairs, and besides he had been hoping that Paulette would grow tired of Fréron or fall in love with someone else. From the midst of his early victories in Piedmont and Lombardy he wrote in May 1796 to Josephine: 'Please tell Fréron that it is not the intention of my family to allow him to marry my sister, and that I have decided to do whatever may be required to prevent it.' He followed this up with a note to Giuseppe the next day: 'Pray arrange Paulette's affairs. I do not intend Fréron to marry her. Tell her so, and let him know it too.'

Paulette accepted his ruling with dignity and courage. She may have received some help from Lucien in composing the letter she wrote in return, but it is unlikely; he was away in Paris at about this time, and in any case she could write in Italian to Napoleone, the words coming from her heart:

> I have received your letter. It has caused me the deepest pain. I did not expect such a change on your part. You agreed to my union with Fréron . . . I send you his last letter; from it you will see that all the accusations against him are untrue.
>
> As for me, I prefer unhappiness to marrying without your

consent and drawing your curse upon me. If you, for whom I have always had the tenderest affection, could see the tears your letter caused me to shed you would be touched by them, I am sure. You, from whom I expected happiness, you compel me to renounce the only man I can ever love. Young as I am, I have a steadfast character. I feel it is impossible for me to give up Fréron after all the promises I have made to love him alone. No one can prevent me from keeping my heart for him, receiving his letters, answering them, and repeating that I will love only him. I know my duties too well to turn aside from them. I'm not one to change according to circumstances.

I had to say this to you. Be happy, and in the midst of your victories think sometimes of my life full of bitterness and the tears that I shed every day.

Paulette had been saved from a disastrous marriage, but she still loved Fréron – or thought she did. The long opposition she had met with and the final sacrifice imposed upon her – as she saw it – inevitably left enduring effects upon her mind and character.

Napoleone thought he knew Paulette better than she did herself, and he was sure that she would soon forget Fréron; but to help her to do so he invited her to join him at his headquarters in Milan when the approach of winter brought a halt to campaigning. She was the first of the family to be thus invited. Escorted by her uncle, Giuseppe Fesch, to whom Napoleone had promised a situation as an army contractor and who already saw his fortune made, Paulette sailed from Marseilles for Genoa in December 1796.

Chapter 3

A marriage has been arranged

It was a new and changed brother that Paulette found awaiting her in Milan. He had quickly won the esteem of senior officers by a series of lightning victories which had humbled Austria, based on a sound knowledge of the terrain acquired two years before; he had transformed a shambling collection of ill-provided units into a cohesive, well-equipped army by demanding and obtaining from the Directory all that it lacked and by promising the troops the loot of a lifetime. His conquests of rich Italian towns and duchies had filled the empty coffers of the French Republic and turned the Louvre into a depository of plundered art treasures. His dispatches to Paris were of this kind: 'The more men you send me, the easier it will be to feed them. There are twenty old masters, from Correggio to Michelangelo, on the way to you . . . I trust things are going well, as I'm able to send twelve millions to you; that will help out for the Army of the Rhine. Send me four thousand unmounted cavalrymen, I'll find horses for them here. I should also like two or three more generals with fire in their belly . . .' He was not only the head of a conquering army; he had been given power to negotiate treaties too, and had begun to sign himself 'Bonaparte', after the manner of kings. He was the sole arbiter of peoples' destinies, the dispenser of all fortune. He was twenty-seven years of age, and some of his generals were even younger.

He held 'court', with Josephine, giving receptions and balls attended by the delegates of princes and kings, by famous artists, scholars and men of letters, leaders of high society, Italian contessas in gay dresses and army officers in splendid uniforms. There were intrigues and shady deals, flirting and love-making, in a nervous, feverish, exuberant atmosphere such as prevails between one victorious battle and the next.

Into this setting Paulette slipped with astonishing ease. Her brother gave her a comfortable apartment in the Serbelloni palace in Milan which he had taken over for his personal use. A daily round of pleasures now filled her life – dinners and balls, amateur theatricals, excursions and picnics to Lake Como or Lake Maggiore, escorted by one or two of her brother's dashing young aides-de-camp. As he had predicted, this entire change of scene was the best remedy for Paulette; she forgot about Fréron, became again the gay, larking girl, a little older and perhaps a little wiser in the ways of the world. There were tales of her dashing into the offices of the general staff where a group of handsome young men was always to be found; of listening at keyholes, and spying on Josephine in the hope of surprising her in a compromising situation. Paulette still nursed a bitter feeling against her sister-in-law for saying that her marriage to Fréron would be a disgrace; and she was at one with her mother and family in their antagonism to Josephine, that loose widow, whom they regarded as an intruder who would reap the major benefits from Napoleone's position.

A vivid sketch of Paulette was given by the poet and playwright Antoine Arnault, who was placed next to her at dinner one night:

> She remembered meeting me in Marseilles and treated me as an old friend. What a curious mixture she was of physical perfection and the most bizarre moral attributes! Although the loveliest creature one had ever seen, she was also the most frivolous. She acted like a schoolgirl, chattering continuously, laughing at everything and nothing, mimicking the most dignified personages, sticking out her tongue at her sister-in-law when the latter was not looking, and prodding me with her knee when I did not pay enough attention to her antics. Every now and then her brother gave her one of those terrible glances with which he recalled to order the most refractory of his men, but even this did not daunt her for long. She was soon at it again . . . Yet she was a good sort, by nature rather than purpose, for she had no principles, and was capable of kind actions if only in a fickle sort of way.

Such was the impression she gave to a sensitive observer.

In the spring, Napoleon (he and his brothers had gallicised

their names as well as dropping the 'u' from their surname, now that France held out great promise) moved his headquarters to Mombello, a square-built, rococo country seat on a hill a few miles outside Milan. It stood in a large park with many shady walks, grottoes and fountains, and a long, tree-lined avenue led up to a double flight of steps and a wide terrace, from which there were views of the tower of Milan cathedral, the distant misty Alps, and the fertile greenness of the Lombardy plain. Inside the mansion the vast, stone-flagged rooms were too chilly in winter, despite the huge fireplaces, but remained delightfully cool in the heat of the summer; and next to them were pleasant little rooms appropriate for intimate conversation. There at Mombello, Josephine reigned over the 'court' with grace and charm; in the evenings a military band played on the terrace, and sometimes Napoleon strolled among the 'courtiers' after his hasty dinner, bestowing a kind word on deserving people. And there, under the magnificent wide blue sky of the Milanais, Paulette became engaged in April and, two months later, was married.

Napoleon, among his many preoccupations, had thought that his sister would not only forget Fréron but would find someone she wanted to marry from among the glittering throng of handsome, brave young men. To his mind, marriage would wipe out the memory of Fréron and do something towards settling the volatile spirits of Paulette. But she showed no signs of wishing to marry anyone; so her brother, perforce, arranged matters for her. His first choice was one of his staff officers, Louis de Marmont, whom he had known at Toulon. But this clever and well-educated officer was looking for some amenable, dutiful, sweet little woman to take as his wife, and did not think Paulette would come up to his expectations. He politely refused the offer; and when he came to write his memoirs he declared that he was still more pleased than sorry at his decision. However, as he betrayed Napoleon in 1814 he might have been prejudiced.

Napoleon then turned to another old comrade from his Toulon days, Victor Leclerc. He had been a frequent visitor to the Bonaparte house in Marseilles and was one of the many to hover around Paulette. Since her arrival at Milan, two years older than when he had last seen her, he had often been in her company, and he only needed this hint of approval from his army chief to press his courtship. Paulette obviously felt no great passion for Leclerc, but she liked him well enough; and she realised that in order to rival Josephine she needed married status and an establishment of her own. Moreover, Napoleon desired her to marry Leclerc. So she accepted the proposal.[1]

Leclerc was twenty-five and had been in the army for six years. He came of good family; his father was a wealthy miller at Pontoise and his mother's dowry had included the château of Montgobert, near Soissons; and, unlike poor Junot, he had money of his own. But he was neither handsome nor dashing, just a small, neat young man, grave and polite, though pleasant enough, with fair hair and well-shaped features, yet lacking in determination and with little personality. Paulette referred to him as *mon petit Leclerc*. He idolised her and was devoted to Napoleon, who had complete confidence in him, even to the extent of putting him in charge of the political correspondence. A fortnight before the wedding Napoleon had him promoted to brigadier-general.

Before the wedding took place, Letizia arrived at Mombello accompanied by her two daughters and – a surprise for Napoleon and Paulette – a new son-in-law. He was a thirty-five-year-old Corsican, a captain in the French army, named Felice Bacciochi, and a month earlier he had married Elisa – as Maria-Anna now called herself on the advice of Lucien, a specialist in such matters (the youngest sister now went by the name of Caroline). Letizia fully approved of the marriage – after all, Elisa was turned twenty – but without Napoleon's approval the husband would remain a captain and Elisa be without a dowry. Napoleon took a dim view of this unexpected brother-in-law; any army man who was still a captain at thirty-five, when by seizing one's opportunity one could be a full general long before that age, must be a poor specimen. But Napoleon had never felt much regard for his eldest sister; if she was satisfied with her pudding-faced Bacciochi, so be it. He found time between various state negotiations to deal with family affairs, and at the same time as providing Paulette with a dowry of forty thousand francs he did as much for Elisa. The conqueror of Italy had money to spare!

Letizia was more pleased to hear of Paulette's betrothal than

Napoleon had been to learn of Elisa's wedding. Two daughters
off her hands in one summer! She knew of Leclerc's loyalty to
Napoleon, and she was happy at the prospect of seeing Paulette
'settled', but there was one point about the wedding that did not
satisfy her: no religious ceremony had been arranged. Napoleon,
who had managed without this formality for his own wedding,
did not think it necessary. The civil marriage banns had been
duly published. Signed by Berthier, Napoleon's Chief of General
Staff, the notice certified that 'the above declaration has been
affixed, in conformity with the law, to the door of the General
Staff office for the period decreed by the law, and that up to this
day, 20 Prairial, there has been no protest against it'. But this
meant nothing to Paulette's mother. Napoleon obtained a special
licence, or rather a dispensation from having the banns read in
church, from the Archbishop of Milan. And on 14 June 1797,
with many of her family present, Paulette was married to her
'petit Leclerc' in the chapel at Mombello by the local priest, the
civil ceremony having taken place earlier in the day.

A few weeks after the wedding, Arnault called on the young
couple: 'I found Leclerc intoxicated with happiness . . . His
wife seemed to me very happy too, not only because she was
married to him but also just because she was married. Her new
position had not made her more serious, as was the case with her
husband . . . She was just as much of a madcap as ever.'
   Leclerc's military duties kept him in Milan. Though hard-
working he was not very clever, and he had no sense of humour.
As he bore some resemblance to Napoleon in figure and general
appearance, he began to make this likeness more striking by
walking like Napoleon, his hands behind his back, talking like
him in brief, jerky sentences, and dressing in a similar grey
overcoat and cocked hat worn sideways. One can imagine how
this absurd affectation struck Pauline, as she had decided to be
called in her new status. It certainly did not increase her respect
for her husband. But she had affection for him, and she loved
being adored by him. On the other hand, her swiftly changing
moods disconcerted his slower mind; her fantastic actions shocked
his gravity; and her coquetry hurt his love and pride. Any man
married to this wild young Corsican beauty would have found her

difficult; but a stranger mate for her than Leclerc could hardly be imagined.

Arnault would seem to have hit the nail on the head – it was the married state that pleased her rather than the man who had led her into it. Her sexual appetite had been roused, and Leclerc kept her satisfied. Just before her seventeenth birthday she knew she was pregnant.

By then she was the only Bonaparte still in Milan, and she must have felt very lonely; at such an important period in her life she was without her mother or either of her sisters for the first time. The family was more scattered than it had ever been. Letizia was back in her beloved Ajaccio, restoring the old home; with her had gone Elisa and husband, the latter promoted lieutenant-colonel and given command of the citadel at Ajaccio. Napoleon was in Austria, putting finishing touches to the peace treaty; with him was Louis (Luigi), being groomed for an army career. Joseph (Giuseppe) was French Ambassador to the Holy See. Lucien had been elected to the Five Hundred, the lower Chamber, and was looking after Bonaparte interests in Paris. Caroline was there too, at Madame Campan's fashionable school for young ladies, with Leclerc's sister and Josephine's daughter. Jerome (Girolamo) was at sea, Napoleon having destined him for a navy career.

Pauline had a difficult confinement, and the effects were to trouble her for many years. She gave birth to a boy on 20 April 1798. There were post-natal complications, and it is highly probable that the doctors told her she would never be able to have another child. Although there is no evidence for this, she never did give birth again, nor was she ever pregnant – and it was certainly not for lack of opportunity. If it was indeed true that she knew she had given birth to her first and last child, it is unlikely that she grieved very much. Pauline was not cast for the role of a mother of a family. If anything, she felt relief that her figure would be inviolate, apart from the advantages of freedom from crude and unreliable contraceptives.

The child was baptised in Milan on 29 May and was given the names Dermide Louis Napoleon. From Toulon, and the organising of the expedition to Egypt, Napoleon had sent instructions on the naming of his first nephew (Lucien's and Joseph's wives had produced only girls, and he himself was still childless; Pauline's accomplishment raised her in his favour). Dermide was the peculiar name of a character in the poems of Ossian, a legendary Scottish bard whose works had been recently published in translation and been greatly admired by Napoleon.

Pauline had been pressing her husband to obtain a transfer to Paris, which she was longing to see and be seen in; and he himself was not happy in Milan, among the constant friction between the civil and military authorities. A month after the christening of their child, Leclerc was posted to the army in the north of France, which was waiting for an opportunity to invade England. He and Pauline and the baby arrived in Paris in July, and while on leave he rented a house for her in the rue de la Ville-l'Evêque, near the Madeleine; and as he was alarmed at her lack of education he arranged for her to attend Madame Campan's school.[2] Then he went to take up his appointment as chief of staff at headquarters in Rennes and, with much regret and not a little trepidation, left his wife to embark upon the social life of the capital she had heard so much about over the years. The reports of her brother's victories in the shadow of the Pyramids, whose forty centuries had never seen the like of him and his soldiers, and the fresh prestige his name acquired, made Pauline's head turn dizzy. All doors were open to her; she was the first lady in the capital, after Josephine.

Parisian society at this time was at a low ebb; it consisted chiefly of corrupt politicians, money-grabbing financiers, thieving army contractors and women of loose virtue. The elegant manners and sparkling conversation of the salons under the monarchy had been replaced by vulgar display, gluttony and gambling, and wife-swapping or, more often, mistress-swapping. Money was the dominating object; cynicism was prevalent. It was a time of instability and bewilderment for the mass of people. Their armies in Europe were being defeated everywhere, driven out of Italy, forced back to the Rhine.

There were, however, a few exceptions to the degenerate salons of the capital, and fortunately for Pauline her introduction to society in the winter of 1798 was by way of one of them. A girlhood friend of Letizia's had married a young Frenchman who had become receiver of taxes at Montpellier; it was at the house of this couple, the Permons, that Letizia's husband had died. When the Permons had moved to Paris they had befriended lonely young Napoleone while he was a cadet at the military school. Later, after 13 Vendémiaire, he had spoken to Madame Permon, by then a widow, about marrying her instead of Josephine, while one of his younger brothers would marry her daughter Laure. Madame Permon had laughed him out of it. But the two families had remained in touch. Madame Permon was very rich, her late husband having made a fortune as an army contractor and her son having succeeded him; but they were people of culture and had nothing in common with the wealthy racketeers newly emerged from the muck of the Revolution. Madame Permon received only the better elements of the Paris scene and old friends of Royalist antecedents.

Pauline went often to the Permon house, which was in the same district as her own, and became friendly with the daughter, Laure, who was about her own age.[3] There she met some of the Faubourg Saint Germain set, who still retained the old aristocratic traditions and atmosphere and who were gradually opening their salons again, to which Pauline was invited. Lucien and Joseph, back in Paris again, both had fine houses; and the latter's wife, Julie, did much entertaining. The fashionable hour for dinner was five o'clock or even a little earlier if the company were going to the theatre, as performances started at six. After the theatre there would be supper and dancing until the early hours. Everyone in this society rose late, if only because the houses were very cold in winter; until a good log fire had heated the rooms it was permissible to receive visitors in dressing-gown and nightcap or even in bed, as did Pauline and other ladies, or while at their *toilette*.

By the end of the winter Pauline had gained recognition as the most beautiful woman in Paris, and she was increasingly conscious of her powers. The adulation she received also led her to want her own way in whatever came into her wilful young head. In congenial company her manners were expansive and easy-going; her year in Italy had been an education to her and had developed her innate good taste. But when vexed or thwarted she could and did use sharp claws. Serious conversation, on the arts for instance, made her impatient; she knew nothing as yet of such subjects. But she often came out with some odd remark, not always relevant but very droll and made more so by the little air of seriousness and conviction with which it was uttered.

Pauline's sway as the leading beauty was not uncontested, and that winter she suffered one of the few defeats in her life. It happened at a ball given by Madame Permon, to which were invited her own set and the Bonapartes then in Paris, some of the more elegant officers who were good dancers, and the élite of the Faubourg St Germain. Among the last was Madame de Contades, daughter of the Marquis de Bouillé who had helped Louis XVI make his unsuccessful flight from Paris. This lady had a goddess-like head with luxuriant dark hair, flashing eyes, and a commanding presence. She disliked Napoleon intensely and would allow him no credit for his military victories, and with the same perversity she refused to admit the exceptional beauty of 'citizeness Leclerc'.

The ball was to be one of the highlights of the 'season', and Pauline prepared for it like Napoleon planning a battle – thoroughly and in secret. The best hairdresser and the most fashionable dressmaker in Paris were enrolled on her side. She asked Madame Permon's permission to dress at her house on the night of the ball, so that she could make her entrance quite unruffled. She made a sensation when she appeared and advanced slowly across the ballroom to the seat Madame Permon had kept for her. A short-sleeved white Greek tunic with a deep bordering of gold and held at the shoulders by cameos displayed her lovely figure to great advantage. Beneath her breasts, which seemed about to take flight from her corsage like plump birds out of a nest, she wore a golden girdle with a fine antique stone as a clasp. On her round white arms glistened bracelets of gold and cameos, and her piled-up hair was crowned with little bunches of golden grapes.

The room hummed with tributes of admiration, but soon feminine envy found something to attack. Madame de Contades moved regally across the room on the arm of her partner to the long sofa on which Pauline was reclining in what had become her favourite pose. She paid her compliments to her young rival, then gave a start and said to her escort in a loud whisper for all to hear: 'What a pity such a lovely creature should be so deformed! If I had such ugly ears I really think I would cut them off.'

All eyes turned on Pauline's ears. It was not surprising that no one had noticed them before; they were little, shapeless pieces of cartilage without any curl to them. Pauline was too inexperienced to meet such malicious remarks with the sweet venom they warranted. She retired, weeping, to Madame Permon's boudoir. And ever afterwards she kept her ears concealed by her hair or a bandeau.

She was spending so much money on clothes and jewellery – or rather, running up bills, for as Napoleon's sister her credit was good – that Leclerc was aghast when he came home on leave. Her mother, who returned to Paris in the spring of 1799 and went to live with Joseph and his family, also spoke sharply to her about her extravagances. One day, Pauline and her mother were driving out to Mortefontaine, a property about twenty miles north of Paris that Joseph had recently bought. The two were travelling in one of Joseph's magnificent carriages; Letizia was wearing a cheap cotton dress, and Pauline teased her about it. 'Be quiet, spendthrift that you are!' said her mother. 'I have to save for your brothers. They're not all in good positions yet. It is natural at your age to think of pleasure, but I have more serious matters to consider.' But neither the remonstrances of her mother nor of her husband had any effect on Pauline.

Napoleon, however, soon gave all the family a further increase in position, power and fortune. He returned unexpectedly from Egypt, reached Paris in the early hours of 16 October 1799, and less than a month later had overthrown the Directory and established himself as the head of State, the chief of three Consuls – preparatory to being proclaimed First Consul and moving into the Tuileries palace with absolute power over the country. France had found the man to lift her up from her knees, as had happened before and has happened since in her long history. But this *coup d'état* had its anxious moments, and its success was due in large part to the promptitude of Murat and his soldiers and, especially, to the coolheadedness of Lucien, then president of the lower Chamber.

On the evening of November 9th Letizia and Pauline, who

knew something of what was afoot, went to the Feydeau theatre with Madame Permon and her daughter. In their box they tried to present a calm and composed face to the public – but assuredly Pauline and her mother were thinking of other times when they had waited for news of Napoleon's scheming! This time there was much more at stake.

The curtain rose, the play began; halfway through the first act, the stage-manager rushed on to the boards and stopped the play. 'Citizens!' he cried. 'General Bonaparte has just escaped being assassinated by traitors to the country!'

Pauline screamed loudly and fell back fainting in her chair. Her mother went 'as white as a statue' but remained in command of herself. The audience was on its feet, struggling amid tumult to reach the exit to find out what was happening in the capital. Letizia grasped Pauline's hands and shook her. 'Your brother is all right, didn't you hear? Come along – we must go back.'

The four women hurried from the theatre and were driven to Napoleon's house in the rue de la Victoire, which they found crammed with people acclaiming the new Consul. Napoleon had been roughly handled by political opponents at a crucial moment, but the story of an attempted assassination was just another of Lucien's tricks; he had stage-managed the drama out at St Cloud, where the two Chambers were in session, but had neglected to keep his mother and sisters fully informed.

While Napoleon led the French armies to fresh victories in Europe, reconquering the lost ground, and then initiated his vast programme of national reconstruction, bringing order out of chaos, Pauline entered more into society and tried in her vain but sincere way to serve his interests. The salons slowly regained some of their social and cultural influence; life in general became gayer, and the Parisians were again treated to military displays and firework shows to celebrate victories. As the First Consul's power strengthened he restored the old, popular holidays such as Mardi Gras and New Year's Day, abolished the Décadi (tenth day of rest) and brought back Sundays. The Bonapartes were naturally at the centre of things and much of the social life of the capital revolved around them. Lucien had been appointed Minister of the Interior – at twenty-five – by Napoleon; Joseph had been made a member of the Legislature and given the rank of ambassador; while Louis was promoted colonel, 'a rise in rank as rapid as that of a prince of the blood in the time of the monarchy'. The whole family had been gathered together for the wedding in Paris of Caroline to General Joachim Murat in January 1800, and then for the celebrations at Mortefontaine. Later in the year Lucien lost his wife and soon took a mistress; and Pauline probably had her first lover.

If reports of memoir-writers be true, he was an actor who called himself Pierre Lafon (he had changed his name, understandably enough, from Rapenouille). He came from Périgord, and made his début at the Comédie Française in May 1800. He played romantic heroes, being tall, slender and handsome, and was very much a ladies' man; he was said to be adept at making love, which would have endeared him to Pauline. She undoubtedly knew him well, and first met him at Lucien's country house at Plessis-Chamant where he stage-managed the amateur theatricals in which Lucien, Elisa and Pauline took part with their retinues.

Napoleon expressed his annoyance over the realism of some of these performances. 'The ardour of the declarations, the expressiveness of the gestures, the too nude nature of the costumes, made a bad impression. Lucien was rebuked by the First Consul', reported one memoir-writer.[4]

Napoleon was becoming increasingly authoritarian, and his family did not escape his strictures. He was already developing his 'system' whereby his brothers and sisters would become part of his scheme of things, and he expected them to set an example to society in all matters, including morals. In this respect at least they failed him. All had mistresses or lovers; but the First Consul and Josephine were not exactly above reproach. Napoleon's love affairs, however, could easily be classed, in modern parlance, as having sex; on the rare occasions when he took a woman to bed it was almost as rapid a business as passing a warming-pan between the sheets. He was as under-sexed as Pauline was over-sexed.

If Lafon ever did become Pauline's lover, she was remarkably discreet about it, much more so than in her later love affairs – but by then her circumstances were very different. The first hint of his being her lover came when news spread in October 1801 that she was to accompany her husband on the expedition to San Domingo. An acress at the Comédie Française exclaimed: 'This will break Lafon's heart! It's enough to kill him!'

Napoleon's choice of Leclerc to command the expedition was an instance of his distrust of all men except those he believed, sometimes mistakenly, to be closely bound to him by ties of relationship or old-comradeship. Her insistence that Pauline should go with her husband was in keeping with his 'code' that the place of a woman of his family was at the side of her husband. But spiteful tongues, of which there were quite a few where Pauline was concerned, suggested that the First Consul was alarmed by her conduct and was sending her off to the West Indies as a means of putting a stop to her infidelities. Leclerc would have liked to refuse the command but dared not.[5] He was intelligent enough to know his limitations and doubted his ability to succeed in the task allotted him, which was to suppress the Negro revolt and re-establish complete French sovereignty over San Domingo (present-day Haiti). It was one of the richest French colonies and was inhabited by half-a-million slaves who, led by Toussaint L'Ouverture and inspired by the principles of the French Revolution, had wiped out the white planters and proclaimed their independence. Its submission was part of Napoleon's vast project to restore the lost French colonial empire.

Pauline's first reaction, too, was one of distress; but not at leaving her reputed lover. She felt despair, quite naturally, at the thought of leaving Paris and its pleasures to go to a distant island that she imagined peopled by cannibals. 'How can my brother be so hard-hearted as to send me into exile among savages and snakes,' she sobbed to her friend Laure, who had called to see her. 'Besides, I am ill. I shall die before I get there.'

She certainly acknowledged Napoleon's authority, but she was the only one of his brothers and sisters ever to fight it repeatedly, with her own particular weapons, when it did not suit her; and Napoleon was never able to hold out against her for long. But on this occasion she soon changed her mind, in her impulsive way. She saw herself as queen of the colony, the first lady in the land, instead of ever having to take second place to that hateful Josephine. Her friend Laure, then married to Junot, had something to do with her change of mind, too.

I told her she would look very pretty in the Creole costume (Laure wrote in her *Memoirs*). As I advanced in my arguments, Madame Leclerc's sobs became less hysterical. 'You really think, Laurette,' said she, 'that I shall look pretty, prettier than usual, in a Creole turban, a short waist, and petticoat of striped muslin?' She rang for her maid. 'Bring me all the bandannas in the house!' she ordered. She had some very fine ones that my mother had given her from a bale of Indian silks and muslins. We chose the prettiest, and as my mother had always worn silk handkerchiefs for night-caps, I was accustomed to the arrangement of the corners in the most becoming manner. Madame Leclerc, looking at herself in the mirror, was enraptured with my skill. 'Laurette,' she said, replacing herself on the sofa, 'you must come to San Domingo – you will be next to myself in rank. I will talk to Napoleon about it, and as he is partial to Junot, he will let you go. Junot shall be the commander of the capital. What is its name? I will tell Leclerc I expect him to give a fête every day.' As she said this, she pinched my nose and pulled my ears, for she liked to ape her brother, and thought such sort of easy manners had an air of royalty. The next time I saw her, she had forgotten everything but the bandanna.

This is Pauline to the life. Enthusiastic for the West Indies now, even to the point of taking her three-year-old son, she joined her husband at Brest, where the troops and ships comprising the expedition were assembling. She took with her countless dresses and hats and other indispensable articles that formed her wardrobe. Leclerc had problems enough and refused to give up valuable cargo space for all this impedimenta. Pauline peremptorily pointed out that, by her brother's express orders, she was a part – an important part – of the expedition; and her baggage was as necessary to her as arms and ammunition to him. Leclerc gave way. The admiral, Villaret-Joyeuse, arranged for a ball to be held in her honour, and her good humour was restored.

The expedition appeared to have every chance of success.

Leclerc had been given a good staff by Napoleon, also officers with experience of guerrilla warfare against the Royalists in the Vendée. There were thirty-two warships in the naval force, which was carrying the twenty thousand troops under Leclerc's command and a number of civilian officials. Among the latter was Stanislas Fréron. He had fallen on hard times, and Lucien in his eminence had kindly given him an appointment as Sous-Préfet in San Domingo.

On 14 December 1801 Pauline went aboard the flagship, *L'Océan*, and the fleet set sail.

Chapter 4

Death and desolation

A cabin had been specially fitted out with every possible comfort for Pauline, but when warm waters were reached she spent the days reclining in state on a chaise-longue on the quarter-deck, surrounded by an admiring court of military and naval officers. On 28 January, forty-five days out from Brest, the northern coast of Haiti was sighted; and next day the flagship and most of the fleet were tacking off the entrance to the wide harbour of Cap François, the capital of the French half of the island.

The sight of this large naval force convinced the Negro leaders – Toussaint L'Ouverture and his chief lieutenants, Henry Christophe and Dessalines, a mulatto – that the French had come to enslave the Negroes again. Christophe, who was in command of the native troops at Cap François, refused to allow the French ships to enter harbour. Leclerc's second-in-command, Rochambeau, landed a force on the coast east of the capital, while another division captured Port-de-Paix to the west; and the men-of-war bombarded the forts protecting the harbour of Cap François. Threatened by this pincer movement, Christophe withdrew to the mountains – but first set fire to the capital.

When the French entered what had been a fine new town with wide straight streets, several large squares and many handsome buildings, they found only one house in ten untouched by flames. The main powder magazine had exploded and most of the town had been reduced to smouldering embers. Leclerc sent columns of troops into the interior, captured most of the towns, and by the end of February had brought the colony under control.

Pauline had come ashore and was living in an undamaged house on the sea-front at Cap François. All around was a scene of desolation, and all she heard of this blood-drenched island was unnerving. The Negro slaves had been treated abominably by the white planters and after rising in revolt had returned like

for like; one of their favourite methods of disposing of a
prisoner, whatever his colour, was to bind him between two
planks and then saw them in half. They practised the hideous
rites of voodoo, whose spirits had the power of bringing the dead
to life in the form of 'zombies'; this obscene religion had become
a secret society linking the slaves on all the plantations, and it
was still flourishing. Pauline became fascinated by stories of
voodoo rites and mythology – perhaps it was the pagan in her
peeping out – and wanted to meet Baron Samedi, who haunted
cemeteries dressed in top-hat and tail-coat, and smoking a big
cigar. But there was no question of her or any of the French wives
being allowed to leave the comparative security of the capital.
Guerrilla warfare was continuing in the wooded hills and
mountain ravines of the interior, and atrocities were being
committed by both sides.

However, in late April Christophe and Dessalines submitted to
Leclerc and were allowed to keep their miltary commands for
the time being. Toussaint opened negotiations and dined with
Leclerc and his staff (though he ate only a small piece of cheese
and emptied a glass of water, for fear of being poisoned) at the
partially restored Government House. Pauline had moved there
and was staving off boredom by furnishing her rooms with the
contents of some of the crates brought out in the *Océan*. She had
her boudoir hung in blue satin with silver fringes, and her
bedroom decorated in white and gold. At her request, Leclerc
gave instructions for troops in the interior to send back rare
birds and wild animals for her to form a small menagerie. Trees
were uprooted and hauled into one of the courtyards of Government House, replanted and roofed over with sails, making a
vast cage in which parrots and monkeys could disport themselves
for Pauline's entertainment. She gradually had them shipped off
to the Paris zoo.

Each ship returning to France also carried reports from
Leclerc. He had lost more than two thousand men killed and
wounded, and he urgently needed reinforcements and supplies;
he complained that the hospital equipment had been badly
stowed and ruined, that inventories had been falsified and he
was short of eleven thousand pairs of boots and had not a
single water-bottle. He began to get flustered and, fearing that

Toussaint was untrustworthy, had him arrested by stealth, put him aboard a frigate and sent him as a prisoner to France (where, in the fortress of Jouy, he died from consumption and pneumonia less than a year later).

For the moment the colony was comparatively quiet. Pauline did her part by arranging receptions and concerts and generally presiding over the social life, military and civilian, of the little capital. The music was provided by a military band which wore a uniform of her own fantastic creation – a gold-laced coat, crimson trousers tucked up in Mameluke style, and a helmet of white horsehair. But this peaceful interlude came to an end when Leclerc nominated a reactionary council of twenty-two members who advocated the return of slavery; and, especially, when news arrived from France that a law had been passed re-introducing the slave trade.

Headed by Henry Christophe, revolt broke out afresh. So did yellow fever; this dread pestilence swept through the expeditionary force, killing off and laying low many more men than succumbed to the Negroes' attacks. The weather had changed abruptly too; the humid heat on the coastal plain became oppressive, prostrating. Pauline was aghast as she saw her features lose their bloom and become lined and yellowed; and she was fearful that her son, Dermide, would contract some unknown disease.

One of the first to die from yellow fever was Stanislas Fréron. He had kept away from Pauline ever since Brest, when he had had the decency, or tact, to sail on a different ship. He had married his mistress, but had not been able to obtain passage for her. Leclerc, who must have known Fréron's past association with his wife, wrote to Admiral Decrès, the Minister of Marine: 'Fréron is dead. He dies poor. I recommend his wife and children to you. He was a good sort and a pleasant fellow, and he went out of his way to assist me when power was his . . .'

Leclerc had his finest hour as he strove to roll back the tide of misfortune. He withdrew his headquarters – his wife and child too – to the offshore island of Tortuga, the original home of the French buccaneers, where the climate was healthier and the position safer. But the privations and danger brought out the hard core in Pauline; very conscious of her position and duty as the GOC's wife, she returned to the mainland and by action and manner tried to calm the fears of the ladies of the colony and to lessen the social misery. She visited the soldiers in field hospitals, as she thought Napoleon would require her to do, making a slow progress down the long rows of truckle-beds with their dying fever patients, giving what comfort she could – her presence and her smile. She opened her drawing-room at Government House to all who cared to come, and in the evenings the remnants of the military band in their bizarre costume played for any who cared to listen. In short she behaved as though disaster were not just around the corner.

Leclerc was doing his utmost to keep it at bay, but Christophe's forces were closing in and threatening to overwhelm the French base. By the end of September fifteen hundred officers, eleven thousand soldiers and marines, and hundreds of civilians had died, chiefly from the virulent disease. Reinforcements and supplies failed to arrive. The hospitals were overflowing with sick and dying men; army doctors were too few and medical supplies were hopelessly inadequate. When twelve thousand Negro troops made a determined attack on Cap François, Leclerc could muster barely three thousand fighting men to repel them. His advanced positions fell, the enemy broke into the town, and Leclerc became greatly alarmed for Pauline's safety.

She and other officers' wives had gathered at Government House, and the ladies were beseeching her to take refuge on one of the ships in the harbour, so that they could go with her. 'You may go if you wish,' she cried, 'but I am the sister of Bonaparte and I'm not afraid!' Then an aide-de-camp came hurrying back with orders from Leclerc that she and her son were to be put on board ship at once, by force if necessary. She refused to leave her chair; four grenadiers lifted her, chair and all, and made for the harbour. Another grenadier carried young Dermide on his shoulders. Some of the women followed, accompanied by servants, and the aide-de-camp and Leclerc's secretary walked alongside Pauline on her chair, the secretary holding a parasol over her head. She surveyed the procession and gave a ripple of laughter. 'We're like a masquerade at the opera house!' she exclaimed. They arrived at the waterfront and as Pauline, still on her chair, was being put into a boat, another aide came running with the news that the enemy had been repulsed and General Leclerc had ordered a return to Government House. 'There, you see,' remarked Pauline with a pout of her pretty lips. 'I knew very well I should not go aboard ship.'

Somehow there was always an element of farce where Pauline was concerned, even in the most tragic or dangerous moments of her life.

The attack had been repulsed, but it was only a short respite. The capital had been devastated again, the countryside had been ravaged, and food was in short supply. The French were confined to several small bridgeheads which Leclerc tried despairingly to hold, hoping against hope for reinforcements. Then, on 22 October, two days after Pauline's birthday, he too went down with fever. For a week, nursed by Pauline, he fought against the progress of the disease, but becoming weaker and delirious. As she watched her husband dying, she must have remembered her first forebodings on learning that they were being sent to this rebellious tropical island. Her worst expectations had been more than fulfilled, except that it was her husband who was dying, not herself – even though she was debilitated and had broken out in sores.

On 29 October Leclerc came out of his delirium for a short time. He summoned his staff and dictated orders for the evacuation of all non-combatants, including his wife and son, then handed over command to Rochambeau. Three days later, in the early hours of 2 November 1802, he died. He had not expected glory if the expedition had been successful; the credit, he knew, would have gone to Napoleon. As it was, faced with defeat, the responsibility for all the miscalculations and failure would fall on his shoulders and he would have returned to France to meet Napoleon's displeasure. He had known from the start that he had everything to lose and nothing to gain, and he died an embittered and disappointed man.

His body was embalmed and placed in a lead coffin. Pauline, remembering an ancient Corsican custom, cut off some of her hair and had it tucked under the cap where the bandaging of the body ended, and asked for a few locks of his in exchange. Leclerc's heart was enclosed in a lead vase, and this was put in a golden urn which bore the inscription: 'Pauline Bonaparte, married to General Leclerc on 14 June 1797, has enclosed in this urn her love together with the heart of her husband, whose perils and glory she shared . . .' Coffin and urn were put in a mortuary chapel on board the *Swiftsure,* a 74-gun captured British vessel whose name had been retained, and on 10 November Pauline and her son embarked.

She sailed from this island of desolation a sick and despondent woman, a grieving widow – for she had felt sincere affection for her 'petit Leclerc' – dreading the long sea journey yet wanting only to see France and her family again. She scarcely left her cabin, as she suffered from seasickness and other ills, and in any case there was little to induce her; there was no circle of gold-laced admirers, no young men full of enthusiasm for adventure and glory, aboard the *Swiftsure*; the decks were crammed with a doleful assemblage of army widows, wounded soldiers, prisoners and civilians without office.

The *Swiftsure* entered Toulon harbour on New Year's Day 1803. The last time Pauline had seen the quays and hills beyond swing into view was from the deck of a small fishing-vessel. Then she had been a homeless refugee. Now, nearly ten years later, she was arriving in very different but nevertheless dismal circumstances. Her first act, while still on board for the fifteen-day quarantine period, was to send a letter by courier to Napoleon in Paris. 'I have reached Toulon after a frightful voyage and in miserable health, which is, however, the least of my troubles. I have brought with me the remains of my poor Leclerc. Pity your Paulette, who is most unhappy . . .'

Napoleon, on receipt of her news, sent an aide-de-camp to escort Pauline to Paris, ordered State mourning for ten days, and with his now customary attention to detail issued instructions for the military honours to be accorded to Leclerc's coffin during its progress through France and for the imposing funeral ceremony to be held in Paris.[1] Pauline reached the capital at the end of January and went to stay with Joseph and Julie at their town house in the rue du Faubourg St Honoré. She was in a poor state of health. The torrid climate of Haiti and the distress of her husband's illness and death had taken a heavy toll; an ulcer which had formed on one of her hands had resisted all medical treatment.

Victor-Emmanuel Leclerc

by François Kinson

Pauline Bonaparte in 1806
by Jeanne Maudhuit

Moreover, her hair was beginning to fall out and her beautiful complexion had been ravaged by the tropical summer sun, which was quite disastrous for her morale. She was indeed a pitiful figure, and for a couple of months after her return saw no one and hardly ever went out.

She was now a widow of twenty-two with a five-year-old son, a mature woman who had experienced many vicissitudes. There can be little doubt that the violence and the disasters of the months spent in Haiti were a turning point in her life. She was not made for the horrible or the tragic. But those months had shown that she possessed some solid qualities beneath the frivolous and capricious exterior.

Throughout her life Pauline was a favourite subject of gossip in Paris drawing-rooms and elsewhere; spiteful tongues exaggerated and embellished every encounter between Pauline and her undoubtedly numerous admirers. This salacious gossip was all repeated later by various memoir-writers, and from 1802 onwards Royalist agents and anti-Napoleonic propagandists filled out their reports and pamphlets with inventive details of Pauline's escapades and love affairs.[2]

In point of fact, Elisa (Maria-Anna, the *demoiselle* of St Cyr) had more lovers in her life than ever Pauline did; but no one has ever troubled to count them. Elisa was not the attractive subject for gossip and memoir-writers that her sister proved to be.

Instances of the mingling of distorted fact and absolute fiction concerning Pauline abound. The placing of a few locks of her hair in her husband's coffin, and the loss of hair she was suffering on her return to Paris, gave rise to the story that at Cap François she had paraded her grief by cutting off all her hair as a sign of mourning.[3] She was said to have returned from Haiti with much loot and plunder extorted by her husband, valued at seven million francs according to one notorious pamphleteer, Lewis Goldsmith; other anti-Napoleonic writers put the value of the plunder even higher. Actually, she would have been in somewhat straitened circumstances if Napoleon had not made her an allowance until Leclerc's estate was settled, when she found herself in possession of property and monies amounting to half-a-million francs – by no means a large source of income for someone of her position and expensive tastes.

Such stories were accepted as truth and repeated by people who ought to have known better. Lady Bessborough, one of the many of London society who spent the winter of 1802–3 in Paris, wrote to her brother in England: 'Madame Leclerc . . . is very pretty, had many lovers, and at length an actor [a reference to Lafon], in consequence of which her brother ordered her to San Domingo . . . Leclerc, they say, behaved very ill there, oppressing the blacks by every kind of extortion. She has returned with his body and his riches . . .'

'They say . . .' At that time tongues were also wagging maliciously about a love affair between Pauline and General Jean Humbert during the Haiti expedition; memoir-writers later repeated the tale, and some modern French biographers still include it in their efforts to portray Pauline as *une garce,* a first-class bitch, or as a nitwit of the first order – sometimes as both, for the one does not preclude the other. Humbert was thirty-five when appointed to Leclerc's staff, a handsome giant of a man, as brave as any, but with diminutive brains – which was supposed to explain Pauline's attraction for him. The story was given further credence by the facts of his being known as a libertine and having been relieved of his appointment by Leclerc after the expeditionary force reached Haiti. According to the gossips, Humbert was Pauline's lover during the outward passage and continued to be during their return on the *Swiftsure*. But a secret liaison on board the crowded flagship, with Pauline and her husband sharing a cabin, is hardly credible. Opportunities on the *Swiftsure* might have occurred, but for one important fact – Humbert was not a passenger. He had been sent back to France before Leclerc died and was already in that country when Pauline reached Toulon. The name of the *Swiftsure*'s captain was Huber, and the close approximation of names (pronounced in French, the two are very similar) very likely set tongues wagging and enabled pamphleteers to weave their anecdote.

Humbert was deprived of his rank by the First Consul and retired without pay three weeks after arriving back in Paris, which substantiates that his dismissal by Leclerc was on military grounds and not, as Pauline's detractors have claimed, an act of revenge by a cuckolded husband. Not until 1809 was Humbert again given employment with the army, as brigadier-general, and less than a year later he was discharged without a pension.

Even a writer not usually favourable to the Bonapartes, Comte Remacle, reported that 'the love affairs with which Pauline Bonaparte is credited at Haiti are very improbable. She found the climate very trying, and at this date was in ill-health . . .'

There can be no doubt, however, that Pauline had a succession of lovers from 1805 onwards. Men were very necessary to her; and all the more so after her second marriage, even because of it.

Chapter 5

From one husband to the next

Pauline was feeling bored, terribly bored. By April she had recovered her health and strength, it was springtime in Paris, but both Joseph and Napoleon insisted on her observing all the conventions and restrictions of her official period of mourning for Leclerc; and this, as for any widow in public life or high society, had to last for a year and six weeks from the death of the husband. Although black became her well, it was a colour she detested. But worst of all were the long and tedious hours empty of excitement and pleasurable sensation. Reading wearied her, singing or playing the piano were as yet beyond her, and embroidery she regarded with utter disdain.

'I can't stand this any longer, Laurette,' she wailed to one of the few people she was permitted to receive and visit. 'If my brother continues to keep me cloistered like a nun, I shall do away with myself.'

However, she was now her old self and, not for the first or last time, jibbed at Napoleon's authoritarian ways. Moreover, he was often away from Paris, inspecting the army camps and preparations at Boulogne and other Channel ports for a possible invasion of England. Pauline had the bright idea, as a means of obtaining greater freedom, of acquiring a town house of her own. Both her sisters had establishments of their own, and for Pauline to follow suit was but a woman's natural desire; though of course hers had to be more sumptuous.

She soon found what she was looking for, not far from Joseph's town house. At the eastern end of the rue du Faubourg St Honoré a splendid mansion, known as the Hôtel de Charost, was for sale. It had been built in 1720 for the Duc de Charost, tutor to the young Louis XV, and had come unscathed through the Revolution because the last Duke had remained in Paris and been in sympathy with the political principles of the Republic. His widow wanted four hundred thousand francs for it. Pauline was charmed by the mansion, which had shady lawns and flower gardens extending to the Champs Elysées. She borrowed one hundred thousand francs from Joseph and obtained a mortgage for the remaining amount. Then she enjoyed herself by converting and furnishing it to her taste, spending large sums of money or signing bills for tables and consoles, candelabra, rugs and tapestries, and especially many of the bibelots and trinkets which she loved to have about her. It was as good a way as any of relieving her boredom, and it was all the more agreeable as there was no one to reproach her for her extravagances, as 'le petit Leclerc' had dared to do.

There was the fresh decoration of the rooms, too. On the ground floor of the mansion Pauline was going to have a yellow drawing-room, a reception room in crimson velvet, a state bedroom in light-blue satin, and a dining-room. The last was something of an innovation, for the usual practice was to have servants set up a table wherever the company happened to be when a mealtime arrived; this was the procedure even at the Tuileries when Napoleon was in residence, though as he gobbled his food and never spent much more than ten minutes at table, it suited him very well. But Pauline was far more conscious of the social occasion. On the first floor were more drawing-rooms and her own bedroom, sumptuously appointed, though the bed itself was small and low, with pink-embroidered muslin curtains round it; and adjoining was her bathroom, which became renowned; about five gallons of milk were delivered daily for her beauty bath. Pauline's town house soon became a veritable nest of seductive luxury; indeed, it got the name of *le nid de Pauline*.[1]

Soon after going to live there, Pauline met Prince Camillo Borghese at Lucien's house in the rue St Dominique. He was nearly twenty-eight and a bachelor, a handsome Roman with dark curly hair, shining dark eyes and an elegant bearing, though of medium height and tending to stoutness. He was also a man of incredible wealth, owning many villas and vast estates in Italy, and had an imposing roll of titles, being a Grandee of Spain, Prince of Sulmona, Prince of Rossano, Duke of Ceri . . . The family jewels were said to be the finest in the world and his art treasures formed one of the best private collections. The Borghese titles and wealth dated from the election of an earlier Camillo to the Papal throne, as Paul V, in 1605. Since then the family had become allied by marriage with many illustrious Italian and Spanish families, accumulating wealth and position over the generations.

Prince Borghese had arrived in Paris at the end of March and had rented a town house, the Hôtel d'Oigny, in the rue Grange-Batelière. He was presented to the First Consul by the Papal Legate, Cardinal Caprara, at a diplomatic reception and attracted immediate attention, partly through being the first man to wear court costume at a Consular audience. His dress-coat was dove-coloured, he wore a short sword crosswise and carried a black, plumed hat under his arm. Paris society took him up enthusiastically; the salons had regained something of their social and cultural influence, and dignity and decorum were gradually returning under the leadership of Madame Récamier, the elderly Marquise de Montesson and others. Borghese proved to be a good dancer and amiable in his ways. But it soon got around that 'he had nothing to say, though a lively manner of saying it', and 'no one was more capable than he of driving a four-in-hand but no one was less capable of carrying on a conversation'.

He became acquainted with the Bonapartes through Angiolini di Serravera, the Tuscan envoy, who was a close friend of Joseph. And before long the two diplomats were discussing between themselves the possibility of a marriage between Pauline and Prince Borghese. Joseph certainly thought it advisable for Pauline to marry again, and a connection with the influential Borghese family would be an advantage in pursuing Napoleon's policy towards Italy and the Papacy; in the nervous state of European politics, a safe channel of communication for the giving and receiving of secret information in times of stress would be invaluable to both sides. Angiolini consulted the Papal Legate, who gave his support. Joseph had a word with the First Consul, who gave his approval. And instructions were sent to Cardinal Fesch in Rome (Letizia's half-brother had obtained faster preferment, thanks to Napoleon, than the latter had been given promotion) to sound out opinion there on the proposed union. Only the two people most intimately concerned were not consulted at this stage. Arrangements were made, however, for them to be brought into contact.

The meeting at Lucien's house was followed by a family party at Joseph's country seat at Mortefontaine to which Borghese and the Papal Legate were invited. Pauline must have realised that something was in the wind, but Borghese seems to have been completely taken aback when, a few days later, Angiolini informed him of the happy future being prepared for him by his spiritual and temporal agents. However, Angiolini learnt that the lady in question pleased him, and on 21 June was able to write to Joseph: 'The thing is done. Prince Borghese will consider himself the happiest of men if the First Consul will graciously accord him the honour of marrying your very charming sister.' The Prince had still to obtain the consent of his mother, the Dowager (his father had died three years earlier), and he sent his secretary to Rome with letters for his family. And, of course, there was still Pauline to be considered before 'the thing was done'.

Her situation was very different from when she had become engaged to Leclerc, quite apart from her age. Now she had money and an establishment of her own. Although still officially in mourning, the time was approaching when she could fully enter the gay social round. In the meantime she gave intimate little supper parties and – what meant so much to her – had admirers at her feet. The image of Leclerc was fast fading from her mind, as was the memory of those horrible months in Haiti. She was never a woman to cling to the past, and was more than ready to give her impulses and frivolous nature free play. Thoughts of marrying again had not entered her mind – but the union with Borghese held out an alluring prospect. She felt no love for him – that finest of emotions she had yet to experience – but he was handsome enough and had style. She would be a real Princess with armorial bearings on her carriage, and have a coronet to wear. What a triumph that would be over her sisters and, especially, over Josephine who, although the wife of the most commanding figure in Europe, was still plain Madame! There would be a new life in Rome, another social world to conquer with her beauty and magnificent dresses. As Princess Borghese and the sister of Napoleon she would instantly enjoy wealth and position and the homage of the great. And the fabulous Borghese jewels – who could wear them more becomingly than herself? Altogether the temptation was much too strong for Pauline to resist. The news of her acceptance soon spread . . .

Josephine, in a letter to her daughter Hortense in July, wrote:

> You doubtlessly know that Madame Leclerc is going to marry; Prince Borghese is to be the husband. Two days ago Bonaparte heard from her, saying she wanted him for her husband and that she felt she would be very happy with him. She asks Bonaparte's permission for Prince Borghese to write to him to ask for her hand. Joseph and M. Angiolini seem to have been the matchmakers. . . .

These two arranged the marriage contract as well, and signed it on behalf of the principals. Pauline had done well for herself financially too; flighty and impulsive she might be, and with her mind often on dresses and beauty treatment, the adulation of men and the vanities of life, but she was certainly not stupid. From Napoleon she received a dowry of half-a-million francs (things were evidently more than a dozen times better with the family than at the time of her first marriage!), to which diamonds to the value of three hundred thousand francs were to be added later. If Prince Borghese predeceased her, the dowry was to be returned and she would receive an income of fifty thousand francs a year from her husband's estate, the use of apartments in the Borghese palace in Rome and the cost of maintaining two carriages.

Pauline, having made up her mind, was impatient. The banns were published at Mortefontaine in August and the wedding was arranged to take place five days after the contract was signed. But then a hitch occurred, or rather an obstacle was placed in the path of the young couple and their supporters. As one French biographer has dryly observed: 'They had forgotten Leclerc.'

Pauline was still officially in mourning for her late husband, and Napoleon refused to allow her to re-marry until at least a year had elapsed since Leclerc's death on 2 November. The First Consul was at St Cloud, working day and night on diplomatic affairs with Spain and Russia and on the war with Britain, but he found time to make it quite clear to his family that the social code he had given to the nation could not be violated, especially at this early stage, by his own sister.

But the Dowager, of whom the Prince stood in some awe, had already announced the wedding to Roman society and sent her younger son to Paris; the Pope had been informed and had expressed his delight; and, what mattered most of all, Pauline had fixed the happy day and was not the kind of person to postpone it for two or three months. On the other hand, she dared not oppose Napoleon publicly, nor did she wish to. So a compromise was found. Pauline's wedding to Leclerc would have been purely a civil affair if Napoleon had had his way and Letizia had not insisted on the religious ceremony. Now it was agreed by all concerned – except Napoleon, who was kept in the dark – to hold the church wedding at once, and the civil ceremony could follow later. To the Borghese family, and to Letizia, the religious ceremony was the only one that mattered.

The wedding party gathered at the château of Mortefontaine, an appropriate setting for the event. Joseph had spent as much as the purchase price, a quarter-of-a-million francs, on improving the property, building an orangery and a theatre, and laying out the park in the romantic style, with a profusion of grottoes, columns, little temples and mock ruins.[3] Letizia was present, and Lucien too; he was again in disgrace, having married for love a second time instead of complying with Napoleon's 'system' and marrying the widow of the King of Etruria. The wonder is that the purpose of the gathering, if not the gathering itself, was kept secret from Napoleon. His police service usually had an eye on the activities of his family, especially of Lucien and Pauline, for he could never be sure that their behaviour corresponded to his desires. But he had recently suppressed the Ministry of Police, that being the simplest way of getting rid of the Minister, the arch-plotter Fouché, and the service was functioning in a loose and semi-official manner. There was also the probability that he was too immersed in higher things to bother with any reports of family junketings at Mortefontaine.

Pauline was married to Prince Borghese by Cardinal Caprara on 28 August 1803. They made a handsome couple as they received the congratulations of the select company on that summer's day in the Île de France. Obviously, they could not leave for Rome until the civil ceremony had taken place nor live together openly as man and wife. So the amusing situation arose of Pauline's reputation as a promiscuous woman coming to her aid and giving her cover for being seen often in the company of her legitimate husband – legitimate in the eyes of the Church at least. It was not until the end of October, when the First Consul and Josephine gave a dinner of nearly two hundred covers in honour of Pauline and Borghese and their wedding due to take place a fortnight later, that the First Consul was informed, perforce, of the previous religious ceremony. He showed his disapproval and resentment at his sister's disobedience by going to inspect the army camp at Boulogne just before the civil wedding was held, at Mortefontaine again, on 6 November.

Pauline had made good use of the intervening two months by completing her preparations for taking Rome by storm. Dressmakers came to the Hôtel de Charost with armfuls of gowns and lingerie and materials, and a small army of seamstresses spent long hours there trimming and altering; Pauline's frequent sudden changes of mind made the place seem like a madhouse at times and drove tradespeople and servants distracted. She had lessons in deportment from a dancing-master, and jewellers and designers were called in to reset some of the Borghese diamonds, emeralds, rubies, cameos and strings of pearls, now destined to add lustre to her beauty.

She still had much to learn, and suffered another defeat at the hands of a woman on the occasion of the formal visit she and her husband paid to Josephine soon after their civil wedding. Pauline was in triumphant mood, a little too much so; she thought to impress Josephine and make her jealous by a parade of flashing jewellery and the title of Princess. She knew her beauty could dim that of Josephine – who, as everyone was well aware, had turned forty – and the fashion style of the time, inspired by the form-fitting light draperies of Greek statues, suited Pauline to perfection. There remained the colour and material of her dress to be decided, and after due consideration she chose green velvet – and swore all concerned to secrecy. In the coming clash of feminine personalities she would need all available weapons.

And clash there was. Pauline and her Prince arrived at the palace of St Cloud in a six-horse carriage with liveried outriders.

At the door of the reception room a chamberlain announced them: 'Monsignor the Prince and Madame the Princess Borghese.' And Pauline, sparkling with diamonds and wearing her green dress, stepped into a room furnished and draped entirely in blue. At the far end, savouring this destruction, sat Josephine in a simple gown of white muslin with no ornamentation but a golden girdle. She had learnt of her sister-in-law's dress plans and turned them to her advantage with a brilliant and cruel stroke.

Pauline knew better now than to give any sign of her mortification and inward fury. Josephine, with a slightly ironic smile, complimented her on her dress; and the two kissed each other as though there was no hate in their hearts.

A few days later, on 14 November, the married couple set out on the long drive to Rome, Pauline having received from Napoleon, who could not remain angry with her for long, a friendly letter of good counsel:

I shall be away for a few more days. However, the bad season is approaching and the Alps will soon be covered in ice. So start on your journey to Rome. Be sure to show sweetness and kindness towards everyone, and great consideration for the ladies of your husband's family. More will be expected from you than from anyone else.

Above all, see that you conform to the customs of Rome. Never decry anything or say 'We do this or that better in Paris'. Show respect and devotion towards the Holy Father, to whom I myself am much attached.

What I should best like to hear about you, is that you are good. The only nationality you must never receive in your house is the English, so long as we are at war with them; in fact you should never have them in your company.

Love your husband, make your household happy, and above all do not be frivolous or capricious. You are twenty-four years old, and ought to be mature and sensible by now. I love you and shall always be glad to hear that you are happy.

He signed himself, regally, 'Bonaparte'. It was a letter which proved how well he knew Pauline (except that he had mistaken her age; she was only twenty-three), which meant he must have been dubious of his advice being followed. On one important point it certainly could not be followed: Pauline found herself unable to love her husband. Though that is putting it the wrong way round.

Prince Borghese, she had found, was a peaceful soul – even in bed. He was pleasant enough, showed her constant respect and affection, but all his passion seemed to go on horses and carriages. He had the fine appearance of a man, but little more. She openly expressed her resentment and distress to close friends. When Laure Junot was surprised at being invited to join Pauline and her husband in their carriage on a ride back to Paris from St Cloud, saying they were in the midst of their honeymoon, Pauline exclaimed: 'A honeymoon with that imbecile? What on earth are you thinking of?'

The story circulated that Borghese was impotent, but this appears to be an exaggeration. His fault in Pauline's eyes was in not being a sexual athlete. By day he was a dull person, unable to entertain or interest his fickle but exacting wife. Altogether she was not looking forward to the two or three weeks' journey to Rome in his close company.

Chapter 6

The Princess is unhappy

It was the beginning of a series of long journeys that Pauline was to make in France and Italy. Such journeys were possible only for the great of the land and their many servants and hirelings, but so arduous and tedious were they that it is difficult to believe that the great were envied, in this respect at least, by the mass of people who spent nearly all their lives in one small area. A description of long-distance travelling at the end of the eighteenth century has been given by one of the nobility, Madame de la Tour du Pin, and there is no reason to believe that the journey of Pauline and Borghese differed from it in essentials:

We travelled in a large berlin with six horses: my uncle and my grandmother in the back, myself on the seat on front of them next to a secretary of one of the priests on my uncle's staff, and two servants on the front seat. At the end of the day's journey these servants were usually far more tired than those who had ridden horseback all the way, for the seats were not set on springs. A second berlin, also drawn by six horses, carried my grandmother's maid and mine, two footmen and, seated on the cross-bench, two servants. There was also a post-chaise with our butler and chef. We took three couriers with us, one riding half-an-hour ahead of us and the other two with the carriages.

We travelled with eighteen horses, and an order would be sent through the administration to reach the posting stages several days ahead of us to ensure that fresh horses would be ready. We drove for long hours every day, leaving at four in the morning (in summer) and stopping only for a meal. (But the day's journey would end soon after sunset, for the gates of towns were closed when night fell.) The first courier would arrive an hour ahead of us to ensure that the table was ready, the fire lit and some good dishes prepared or given at least a

finishing touch by our own chef. He travelled with bottles
of meat jelly and sauces prepared in advance, as well as everything else needful to make the bad inn meals palatable. The
first courier would leave again as soon as we arrived, and when
we stopped for the night we would find, as in the morning,
everything in readiness for us.

There were bands of highwaymen operating in more than
half of the *départements* created by Napoleon for administrative
purposes; most of these brigands were deserters from the army.
People travelled in company as much as possible, as a safety
measure. But those of high position and influence could rely on a
picket of cavalry being detailed by the Préfet to escort them
through any dangerous stretch, as they passed from one
département to the next. Bad roads, however, were a hazard to all;
the mightiest in the land could be, and sometimes was, pitched
out of his carriage into a ditch. And in the rainy season, which
was the time when Pauline and her husband were travelling, the
occupants of even the most splendid coach had to scramble on
to the seats when fording a river, as the water came lapping
over the floorboards.

Pauline always found travelling by coach most uncomfortable,
and on long journeys she insisted on short stages. But in her
present circumstances she had no wish to prolong the journey
more than was absolutely necessary. There was one great consolation – she was travelling south, *vers le Midi*, to light and colour
and vivacity. Pauline was essentially a child of the Mediterranean,
and except for a brief stay at Toulon, ill and dispirited, it was
seven years since she had been in the Mediterranean region. And
she would be speaking and hearing Italian again, that lilting
language made for lovers!

The Alps were crossed by the St Bernard and then it was
Aosta . . . Milano . . . Bologna . . . Firenze. Sixteen days after
rumbling out of Paris, they came over the Apennines and saw
Florence spread below them in the wide Arno valley. Borghese
owned a palace there, and Pauline persuaded him to let her rest for
a few days. She met the Florentine nobility at a banquet in the
Pitti palace, and the honours accorded Napoleon's sister were
those usually reserved for royalty. The widowed Queen of

Etruria, Maria-Luisa, received the Borgheses. The Queen was as plain and misshapen as the Princess was pretty and graceful, but as frequently happens in such cases the two took a liking to one another. Altogether Pauline had not had the rest she expected when the journey to Rome was continued. For three days the carriage rattled past the endless vineyards and olive trees of Tuscany, and on 8 December crossed the wild waste of the Campagna. By the 9th Pauline was at the vast Borghese palace in Rome.

Her mother-in-law welcomed her affectionately, and one of the first to call to pay his respects was the Papal Secretary of State, Cardinal Consalvi, who brought a message that the Pope wished to give her audience as soon as possible. Pauline pleaded fatigue from the long journey and asked for a few days' respite; but her real reason for delaying tactics was that the coach carrying luggage and her best gowns had not yet reached Rome. When she was ready to be received, Cardinal Fesch and the Dowager Princess presented her to Pius VII, who was enchanted by her (he was a man, after all). At the end of the interview he gave Pauline a beautiful rosary and a superb cameo.

Two great receptions were given for her in the Borghese palace, and to them came the nobility of Rome, the diplomatic corps, members of the Sacred College, and titled foreigners. All were captivated by the gay and lovely new Princess. But soon, very soon, the novelty of her surroundings and social life began to pall. The Borghese palace was a magnificent seventeenth-century residence built in the shape of a spinet and had a huge arcaded courtyard adorned with statues, but was more like an art gallery than a home. The walls were covered with pictures, many of them unframed, but furniture was sparse, the vast rooms were damp and cold, and there was no bathroom . . . Pauline missed the comforts of her 'love-nest' in the Faubourg St Honoré. She became irritated by the stilted code and rigid conventions of Roman society and was irked by the tedious ceremonial of reception days. She was soon longing for the faster pace and gayer, freer scene of Paris. By the end of February she was putting out feelers for a return to the French capital, writing artfully to Murat:

. . . You really are settled in Paris? I do hope that is giving you all the happiness you deserve, what with your goodness and your devotion to my brother. You have said goodbye, then, to beautiful Italy? I too should like to leave it for a while, to see all my relations again and that dear France on which one's thoughts dwell in spite of oneself! I don't know, but I think that the air of Rome does not suit me very well. I am always catching colds. My little Camillo has just been obliged to journey to Naples on unavoidable business . . . Please give Caroline an affectionate kiss from me. I hope we shall all meet again in France soon. . . .

Nothing came of this ploy and Pauline began to make life difficult for all around her, a matter at which she was adept. She was more than ever discontented with her husband and complained to her uncle, Fesch: 'I'd far rather have remained Leclerc's widow with an income of only twenty thousand francs than be married to a eunuch.'

The officious Fesch reported to Napoleon on her behaviour, and the First Consul wrote to her in a stern and formal manner:

Madame and Dear Sister,

I learn to my sorrow that you have not had the good sense to conform to the manners and customs of the city of Rome, that you have shown disdain for its people and that your eyes are constantly turned towards Paris. Although fully occupied with important business, I am taking time to let you know my wishes, in the hope that you will abide by them.

Love your husband and his family; be obliging and amiable, and accept the ways of Rome. And do not count on me for help if, at your age, you let yourself be governed by bad advice. As for Paris, be assured you will find no support here, for I shall never receive you without your husband. If you fall out with him, it will be entirely your own fault, and then France will be forbidden you. You will lose your happiness and my friendship.

This letter, dated 6 April, was sent by hand of Fesch, to whom Napoleon wrote a covering note: 'I don't believe half of what you say in your letter . . . but I have let her know my views clearly and precisely, and I hope she will act upon them . . . Tell her from me that she is no longer beautiful and will be less so in a few years . . . Her husband ought to remember the way she has been accustomed to live in Paris, and allow her something of the freedom the women of our country have. . . .'

If Fesch passed on the gibe about her being no longer beautiful, she would have known it to be some brotherly teasing, and which took the sting out of his formal letter. However, Napoleon had done his best; but Pauline had already made up her mind to get away from Rome and the Borghese family, for a time at least.

On 27 April the French envoy in Florence wrote all innocently to Talleyrand, the Minister for Foreign Affairs: 'I have just learnt from Madam the princess Borghese that she is coming to Florence in two months' time. I beg you, citizen minister, to acquaint me in what manner the First Consul wishes her to be treated at Florence, and whether it is his intention that I should give fêtes on her behalf. If so, I beg you to be kind enough to provide the expenses.'

In the meantime, Letizia had arrived in Rome accompanied by her old friend from Marseilles days, Madame Clary, and they were soon followed by Lucien, his two daughters and his new wife, Alexandrine, who had been divorced by her first husband. Letizia stayed with Fesch at the French embassy, the Falconieri palace, in the centre of Renaissance Rome; and Lucien, who had more or less gone into exile, bought a property out at Frascati. He had acquired a fortune in diamonds and pictures while ambassador in Madrid, where he had been successful in preventing Spain from forming an alliance with England.[1]

Pauline was cheered by seeing her mother and Lucien again, and from them heard all the family news. The youngest brother, Jerome, was in Napoleon's bad books for having married an American girl while on leave from his ship; Letizia was grieved by the break between Napoleon and Lucien, and the latter was incensed by the manner in which his brother was betraying republicanism to the point of – and this was the momentous news for Pauline – manoeuvring to have himself proclaimed Emperor of the French. Did she fear for him and wonder whether his ambitions were over-reaching themselves or was she filled

with admiration and thrilled at the prospect? At all events, when
news reached Rome that Napoleon had indeed been proclaimed
Emperor,[2] Pauline continued with her plans for going to Florence;
she had troubles enough of her own, having quarrelled with her
mother-in-law and started to live apart from her cold and listless
husband, and was afraid of the situation reaching the ears of
Napoleon, it being far removed from what he had hoped.

On the pretext of her frail health she announced her departure
for the baths at Lucca. In any case, summer in Rome was
dangerous, for when the sun was hot a fever-laden air steamed
off the marshes, and then it was unsafe to be within twenty miles
of the city. Coaches and carriages piled with luggage rumbled
out of the gates, and Pauline's gilded coach was among them.
She had left her son with Lucien at Frascati and was looking
forward to a gay time, free from all restraint at last, and perhaps
to recovering her sense of fun.

First she went to Florence, where she was again received by
Queen Maria-Luisa with great distinction in public and much
friendliness in private. She created a sensation when she drove
out in a splendid carriage to the Cascine park, the city's rendezvous
of fashion, with her Negro servant Paul, dressed like a Turk,
standing behind her. And she created a greater one by commis-
sioning Antonio Canova to carve a statue of her 'almost naked'.

Canova was then in his late forties and at the height of his
fame. He had made the authorised statue of the previous Pope,
Pius VI, and had sculptured the tombs of the two preceding
popes, and was greatly in demand by the Italian nobility, especially
the fairest of the women, for statues or busts of themselves. His
work was stylised by his admiration for the statues of antiquity,
and he proposed to represent Pauline as Diana the Huntress.
But when she learnt the legend attached to this goddess, she
refused.

'Diana asked her father, Jupiter, to endow her with eternal
virginity,' said Pauline. 'If I were represented as that goddess,
everyone would have fits of laughter.'

So it was decided to represent her more appropriately as
Venus, and the chosen pose was lying nude on a couch, partially
covered by a thin veil, with her right hand concealing . . . her ear,
the one imperfection. The original intention was that Pauline

would pose only for the face, but when Canova gallantly expressed doubts about finding a model with such harmonious lines as the Princess, she had no hesitation in deciding to be her own model. The thought of appearing with some slight imperfection, even in marble, was more than she could bear.

One of her lady friends later expressed astonishment at her daring to pose in such a state of nudity. 'But why not?' said Pauline in her serious little way. 'There was a good fire in the studio.'

Canova made a plaster cast and the statue was completed after Pauline had left Tuscany. In February 1805 it was mentioned among the works in the sculptor's studio: 'No. 7. Her Imperial Highness, Madam the Princess Borghese, almost naked, reclining on an antique couch.' It was sent to join all the other Venuses in the gallery of the Borghese palace in Rome, but the Prince had it locked away, and in later years a special authorisation was needed by art students wishing to view it.[3]

Pauline left the heat of Florence in early July and went at last to Bagni di Lucca, in a cool, shady valley nearer the coast. This was the beginning of what became an important element in her way of life, a periodical visit to one watering-place or another, to drink the waters and take medicinal baths. The exact nature of the disorder for which she was seeking a cure is not known; it was not the custom in her day to reveal such details, especially of female ailments, always supposing that they were within the scope of the medical knowledge of the time. Her ailment probably had its origins in the complications following the birth of Dermide. Her habit of reposing on a chaise-longue, for much longer periods than the prevailing fashion required, and the distress she suffered on long coach journeys, suggest that she was subject to some kind of internal disorder. One of the foremost gynaecologists of the day later diagnosed her condition as a chronic inflammation of the womb, accompanied by general prostration and exhaustion. However, she had not yet reached that stage – for which there were additional sexual causes – and was able to enjoy the social life which was the chief reason for the idle rich gathering at Lucca or any other spa. Such places were the equivalent of the seaside resorts which became fashionable two or three generations later, and taking the waters was as much an excuse for spending the summer in pleasant surroundings and with lively company as sea-bathing was to become.

Pauline's mother was already at Lucca, one of the few who really needed a cure, for the climate in Rome had brought on the malaria she had suffered from in her younger days, and in addition she was depressed by the break between Lucien and Napoleon. Pauline saw little of her; the Princess went everywhere and received all the members of the diplomatic corps in Florence, who had deserted their posts to come and pay court to her; while Letizia led a quiet, almost retired life. She was still very careful with her money, although she was receiving a large allowance from Lucien as well as from Napoleon; she deposited her savings judiciously with bankers in Naples, Rome, Paris, and even in London, and summed up the family's situation with her immortal phrase, 'Let's hope it lasts.' Pauline, of course, never gave a thought as to whether it would last or not; she lived only for the present.

She was just beginning to recover her spirits when news was brought to her of the sudden death of her son. Dermide had been seized by a fever followed by violent convulsions on 11 August, and died within forty-eight hours. Pauline's grief was shattering. 'My poor little boy,' she wept. 'If only I had been with him . . . I would have nursed him as I nursed his father. Why was I not told that he was ill?'

There had been no time. Even if she could have been informed on the day the child fell ill, she would not have been able to reach him before his death; Rome was a day and a half from Lucca by post-chaise, the fastest means of travel for her. It was poor consolation for losing the only tie with what had been a comparatively happy period in her life. Now she was saddled with a most unsuitable husband and required to live in a milieu which she found frustrating and unsympathetic. Pauline would not have been herself if she had accepted the situation philosophically.

She returned to Florence, where the Queen of Etruria showed her every sympathy. But the part of a grieving mother was too wearisome for Pauline to play for long, especially as she had discovered that as Dermide had not reached the age of seven she was not obliged to wear mourning. And she now had a telling excuse for wishing to return to Paris. She wrote to Napoleon deploring her state of health, as usual, and saying that she wanted to bury her son's body beside his father at Montgobert.

On 29 September the French ambassador in Florence wrote to Talleyrand: 'Her Imperial Highness is intending to leave tomorrow for France. Her health has been very unsatisfactory ever since her son's death, and for that reason she can only make the journey by easy stages. She is thinking of going to her estate at Montgobert.'

Napoleon had soon given Pauline permission to return to Paris, not so much out of compassion for her or because he had relented over her behaviour in Rome, but because he required the presence of his family at the impending momentous ceremony – his coronation as Emperor of the French.

Chapter 7

Her Imperial Highness takes a lover

When Pauline arrived in Paris in the autumn of 1804 she was at once drawn into a first-class family row.

Under the new monarchical constitution of the Empire, the hereditary succession was based on the principles of the Salic Law: as Napoleon had no children by Josephine, the crown was to pass to Joseph and then Louis, and their heirs. Jerome and Lucien had been excluded from the succession by Napoleon because of their rebellious conduct in making unsuitable marriages. Jerome later toed the line and Napoleon had his marriage to the American girl, Elizabeth Patterson, annulled so that he was available for a political match. But Lucien remained adamant, and although his marriage was prolific in progeny it was barren of preferment. Joseph and Louis were raised to the rank of princes, and when Caroline and Elisa realised that their sisters-in-law would be princesses, but not they themselves, and that the children of their sisters-in-law would have princely rank, but not their own, they bitterly assailed Napoleon for his neglect of them. He gave vent to his feelings in a delightful phrase: 'To hear my sisters talk, anyone would think I had defrauded them of their rightful heritage from our late father, the king!' Pauline, a princess in her own right, looked on with a little amused smile. She benefited, nevertheless, from her sisters' tears and reproaches, for Napoleon gave way to them and announced officially that in future 'the sisters of the Emperor will bear the title of Imperial Highness.' So Pauline found herself a French as well as an Italian princess.

The storm of protest from Caroline and Elisa was the least of Napoleon's tribulations. A national referendum had approved the new constitution by an overwhelming majority – by three million votes to three thousand – but the greatest opposition to the Emperor, certainly the most vehement, came from his own family. Josephine, knowing she could never have another child, pressed him to change the order of succession by recognising the son of her daughter Hortense and Louis as his adopted heir. Joseph hotly opposed this as encroaching on *his* rights. Then the Bonaparte sisters combined against Josephine; and in this Pauline, who could not forget the humiliations she had suffered from Napoleon's wife, was the most active. At the time, it was still undecided whether Josephine was to be crowned and anointed Empress. She ardently wanted this, as a powerful counterweight to the threat of divorce, especially as the Pope was to perform the ceremony. Pauline and her sisters tried hard to convince Napoleon that now was the time to carry out this oft-repeated threat, throwing at him all the infidelities and extravagances of which Josephine had ever been accused. Josephine did not help her cause when, unexpectedly entering the room where the sisters were fiercely assailing Napoleon, she retaliated by accusing Pauline – knowing her to be the chief enemy – of incestuous relations with Napoleon, as a reason for his being so indulgent towards her. It was too preposterous; Josephine had obviously lost control of herself in her frenzied anxiety. But it almost precipitated the divorce. Napoleon relented when he saw his sisters exchanging triumphant looks while Josephine sat weeping, her violence spent. Not for the first time in their married life, he turned to comfort his wife when she was attacked by his squabbling, vindictive family.

In public the Bonapartes naturally presented a united front and the Coronation in the cathedral of Notre Dame went off well, except for one small incident in which Pauline was involved. Did her thoughts on that great day go back to her arrival in France little more than a decade before, when her brother the Emperor had been an obscure captain without employment? The contrast between their position and fortune then and now could hardly have failed to impinge upon her mind.

Several people in the Bonapartes' circle wrote of the Coronation and the preparations for it with feelings almost of awe. One of Josephine's ladies-in-waiting, Comtesse Claire de Rémusat, wrote:

> The Empress called in the greatest artists and artisans of the day to confer with her on the design of the official costume for the court ladies as well as of her own: the long mantle to cover

our dresses, the gold or silver embroidered lace or tulle ruff
rising high from the shoulders to frame the neck and face . . .
At this point, we ladies of the court suddenly discovered a sad
lack in our education, that of making a proper obeisance. And
as suddenly we called in Despréaux, the dancing master to the
former Queen, to give us a course in approaching and curt-
seying before a throne. Next came rehearsals of the intricate
coronation ritual, with the court painter David to direct the
principal figures in their movements, designing the living
tableau of the rite as he would later put it on canvas. It still
seems a dream, one of Oriental splendour straight out of
The Arabian Nights.

Laure Junot wrote:

It is impossible to imagine the excitement, the gaiety and
the revelry that prevailed in Paris at the time. The streets were
thronged from morning to night with a joyous, hustling,
bustling multitude, some rushing to try to secure tickets for
the ceremony, others to engage windows along the route of
the procession . . . Before daybreak on the second of December
[the date of the Coronation] all Paris was awake and stirring,
hundreds never having gone to bed.

At nine o'clock the great golden coach, drawn by eight bay
horses and surmounted by a crown and four spread-winged
Imperial eagles, passed through the gates of the Tuileries,
the Emperor and Empress seated on its white velvet cushions.

Josephine wore a gown and short cape of white satin embroidered in gold and silver, and her scarlet velvet train was carried
(under protest) by the Princesses Caroline, Elisa and Pauline.
They passed down the nave of the cathedral whose walls 'were
hung with glowing tapestries and adorned with flowers; the
vaulted roof re-echoed the chant of the priests. All the representatives of France were assembled: the military in their bright-hued
uniforms, senators in plumed hats, the clergy in their robes, and
young and beautiful women glittering with jewels . . .'

After the Empress had risen from her knees to move back
to the throne (Napoleon having placed the crown upon her

head), the three Bonaparte princesses allowed the full weight of her ermine-lined velvet train to fall against her, with the result that the Empress almost staggered as she mounted the steps of the dais. The Emperor's eagle eye caught the byplay and he hissed a low but effective warning, so that his sisters quickly picked up the Empress's train again.

This incident was recorded by Claire de Rémusat, who had no love for the Bonaparte sisters. But it allows Pauline to make one of her few, brief and incidental entries into History – or rather, as the French say, *la petite histoire* – in a manner typical of her.

All Napoleon's family were present at the Coronation except Lucien and Jerome – and Letizia, who had been invited but had lingered in Italy with Lucien, hoping for a last-minute reconciliation between her Luciano and her Napoleone. She eventually reached Paris seventeen days after the Coronation, but was given a prominent position at it by the court painter David in his official representation of the ceremony. By then she too had composed her differences with her august son and begun to understand his 'system' which had to prevail over everything, even his family – especially his family. Then Napoleon arranged her position with a few swift decrees – her rank, her household and armorial bearings, her allowance from the civil list. Her title was difficult to choose, but by a clever little phrasing Napoleon found the means of proclaiming that she had indeed given birth to him and yet making it quite clear that he was the founder of the dynasty. Letizia became *Son Altesse Impériale, Madame, Mère de l'Empereur*; more shortly, she went down to history as *Madame Mère* or *Signora Madre*. Napoleon wanted to give her one of the royal palaces as a residence, but she protested at this and instead bought from Lucien his town house in the rue St Dominique.[1]

The one member of the family who did not derive any benefit from Napoleon's elevation was Pauline. The one thing she did ask of him, to rid her of Borghese, she would have obtained in any case. Borghese had followed Pauline to Paris for the Coronation; when he spoke of returning to Rome, Pauline was up in arms at once, for she would be obliged to go with him. Napoleon, who could not remain angry with his favourite sister for long, turned his great mind briefly to her marital problems and found a solution. Borghese was given French nationality, which absolved Pauline from having to live in Italy, and Napoleon commissioned him a colonel in the mounted Grenadier Guards, which were encamped at Boulogne. As some compensation for the cavalier way in which he was being treated, Napoleon gave him the Grand Cross of the recently-created Legion of Honour and one of the Orders of the Golden Fleece received from the King of Spain. Borghese was delighted, not only with the decorations but especially at the opportunity to lead a virile life among horses and hard-drinking, hard-riding soldiers. Napoleon was satisfied because the proprieties were being observed; his sister's alliance had the appearance of unity. And Pauline could put up with the inconvenience of being Borghese's wife so long as he was at a distance from her, she had a share in his magnificent income, wore his family's splendid jewels and bore his princely name.

In return, Napoleon insisted on Pauline conforming with her new position as an Imperial Highness. The masterful brother she had found on her return to Paris had little of the appearance of the thin, lank-haired, intense young lieutenant she had idolised at first sight at the age of six. He was already developing, at thirty-five, the paunchy figure of his many portraits, and his features were stamped with power and decision. But his feelings towards Pauline were the same as they had ever been, warm and affectionate, while she still admired and respected him. Though she had no interest in politics, the will of the Emperor was something she accepted. And it was his will that she should have a household and her own court. Pauline had no say in the appointments; they were made by Napoleon or the grand marshal of his own household, Duroc, and – as when establishing Madame Mère's household – with an eye to wooing the aristocratic families of the Faubourg St Germain.

Pauline's chamberlain was Monsieur de Clermont-Tonnerre, the impoverished head of an illustrious family in the Dauphiné. Genial in disposition (fortunately, for he was going to need it), he had a gift for a neat turn of phrase, and his social qualifications were of the best. The chief equerry was Louis de Montbreton, a lively, versatile gentlemen capable of creating an agreeable atmosphere (and, as it happened, of paying court to Pauline).

The two ladies-in-waiting, Madame de Bréhan and Madame de Barral, were both attractive and distinguished; but the *dame d'honneur,* Madame de Champagny, was plain in appearance and lacking in any dress sense. Pauline soon pronounced her an awful bore. The person Pauline came to like best in her household was a junior member, Mademoiselle Millo, the *lectrice* or reader. She was intellectually the most brilliant of the ladies and was the author of a popular historical novel, *Foscarini, ou les Patriciens de Venise.* She could turn easily from discussing serious subjects knowledgeably to making light conversation on dress and the amusements of the day. Other posts in Pauline's official establishment included a physician, Doctor Peyre, an almoner and two chaplains, a secretary, a chief steward and a pharmacist.

This somewhat disparate and – one must hope – adaptable company joined Pauline at the Petit Trianon in the grounds of the palace of Versailles, where she was spending the summer of 1805, her doctors having prescribed country air for her. Napoleon had allocated to her as a summer residence this charming villa built by Louis XV, and at the same time had given his mother the Grand Trianon; but she never used it. Pauline, though, was as enchanted as Marie Antoinette had been with this summer residence; she gave smart little parties and entertained herself and her guests by having the fountains and a military band play. And from there she put in hand improvements to her town house, the Hôtel de Charost, preparatory to leading Empire society during the winter season.

In late September Napoleon left St Cloud to take the field against the Austrians and the Russians, having already moved his armies from the Channel ports to deep within Germany. Borghese was with his regiment several hundred miles beyond the Rhine, a matter of great satisfaction to Pauline. She arranged with Cambacérès, the Arch-Chancellor, to be informed the moment official dispatches arrived from the front, but this was because she feared for Napoleon's safety. Meanwhile she took up residence at her town house and gave receptions and balls, keeping up morale on the home front while her brother was fighting and winning battles.

The members of her household were keen to prove their abilities in this their first season – keen to keep their posts, too, for with the continuous splendid news arriving from the Grand Army, and the extension and consolidation of the Empire, there was now much competition for places in the households of any of the Bonapartes. Pauline used the first floor of her house for small gatherings of her intimates, and the ground floor for official receptions. She would receive her guests in the central room which looked down the length of the garden; this room had gilded Ionic columns, was decorated in white and gold, and furnished in the austere Empire style. Pauline would be sitting, or more often reclining, on a settee decorated with gilded leaves, sphinxes and griffins, and wearing a low-cut evening dress in one of the fashionable court colours, gold or green or pink. Green was her favourite colour; her livery was green and her writing-paper was green-bordered. When guests had paid their respects to Her Imperial Highness they passed through into the salon where there was music or into the next room where there was a long supper table.

It was not Pauline's idea of an exciting evening, but she was playing the part expected of her and performing with grace and distinction. Most of the day was spent in preparation for her public appearance. At ten in the morning a maid drew the curtains of her spacious bedroom on the first floor, and the Negro servant, Paul, prepared her bath, the necessary five gallons of milk having been delivered as usual. The bathroom adjoining the bedroom was small and had a low ceiling, and the bath stood in an alcove. Pauline had a mania for baths, and she liked whenever possible to have a bath in milk for the sake of her complexion and the texture of her skin. But milk leaves a disagreeable odour; so Paul would go up a back staircase to a small room above the bath and, at the appropriate moment, pour clear water down through a specially-made opening in the floor. This primitive form of shower washed the milk off the bather below. However, before this moment arrived, Pauline would have a long relaxing soak in the carefully heated water and forty pints of milk, and sometimes permitted a few favourite admirers to be present until Paul was summoned to lift her out and carry her back to the bedroom. She felt nothing but pride in revealing the beauty of her body to admiring eyes.

Her indolence led to her being carried to her bath by Paul

as well as from it, especially when she was genuinely indisposed. This was too much for some of her friends, and they protested that it was not decent for a Negro to be brought into such intimate contact with her person.

'But a Negro is not a man,' said Pauline artlessly. 'Or are you shocked because he is young and unmarried? Well, I can soon arrange that.'

She thereupon sent for Paul and one of the kitchen-maids and told them she was going to make them happy – they were to be married to one another. The maid protested, but Pauline's impulses had to be carried through. 'I will see my almoner about it,' she said. 'You must be married within the week.' And so they were, and Paul resumed his duties with the conventions properly observed – at least in the eyes of the irrepressible Pauline.

After her bath she sat before the mirror in a chemise while a trained maid arranged her dark hair in the style chosen for the day, and she herself applied her make-up with deft fingers – the almond paste, cucumber salve and *lait de rose,* each with its particular function, and a special Oriental preparation for darkening her eyebrows and lashes. Attar of roses was then sprayed over her exquisite body, a garment or two put on, and she appeared in the ravishing *déshabillé* in which she received morning visitors.

This morning levée took place downstairs in the end drawing-room next to the state bedroom. Pauline never slept there; the elaborately-carved bed with a golden eagle atop the baldachin was for ceremonial purposes. The most important people Pauline saw in the course of the morning were, to her mind, those from the busy little world of dressmaking, millinery, perfumery and allied trades. It was a long and solemn business, from the selecting of shoes and gloves to the approving of material for a dress to be made by *la petite* Leblanc, whom Pauline preferred to the more famous and expensive dressmaker, Leroy.

The hours spent in the bath, before the mirror and in the hands of her dressmakers had their desired effect when Pauline appeared at a ball or a reception later in the day. At twenty-five she was at her peak; and the memoirs of the period are unanimous in recording the extraordinary effect of Pauline's beauty during her year or two in Paris at the beginning of the Empire.

Arnault named her 'the prettiest at this period so plentiful in pretty women'. Beugnot, one of Napoleon's chief administrators, wrote: 'This princess is a typical French lissom beauty, enlivened by gaiety.' General Thiébault asserted with military forthrightness that she was 'a most magnificently-made creature, with the most seductive ways, and the prettiest figure that nature has ever made; and one that is no stingier in displaying its charms than Heaven has been in endowing it.'

Even women acknowledged her faultlessness, though not without a hint of jealousy or a touch of criticism of other attributes than her beauty. The Polish Countess Potocka, who came to Paris for the Coronation, wrote of Pauline:

> She represented the type of classic beauty such as is seen in Greek statues. In spite of all she has done to hasten on the effects of time, with a little artificial assistance she still bore off the palm. Not a woman would have dared to contend with her for the apple which Canova adjudged her after seeing her – if tales be true – unveiled. In addition to the most delicate, and also the most regular, of features imaginable, she possessed a figure whose lines were admirable – admired, indeed, too frequently.

Laure Junot stated 'it is impossible to form an idea of the perfection of the beauty of this truly remarkable woman'. And Georgette Ducrest, who belonged to Josephine's circle, which naturally viewed Pauline with disfavour, admitted that she was 'unquestionably the loveliest woman I ever saw. Neither jealousy nor envy . . . has ever succeeded in discovering the slightest blemish in that beautiful countenance . . . Happily for women of lowly minds, they had an ample field for revenge in dwelling upon her temper and conduct.'

Yet all this praise fails to bring Pauline to life. The people who attempted pen-portraits of her seem to have been baffled by her beauty. Nor are the existing portraits on canvas any more helpful; and Canova's masterpieces in marble only immortalise her physical perfection. Was her voice seductively husky or was it high-pitched and jarring to the ear? What was the effect when that lovely face became animated, when her amused, tantalising little smile hovered on her lips and when, as she gestured, her bracelets tinkled away as though announcing a caress?

In all likelihood, very few people apart from her near relatives knew her well. And no one, at this time in her life, had awakened her full potential. She was a beauty still awaiting complete maturity, still to be brought completely alive by passion. That great and deep experience was not far off.

Empire society lived and loved hard, ate and drank deep. It was indeed a short life and a merry one, for it lasted barely ten years. But when Napoleon returned to Paris early in 1806, having more or less supplanted the Habsburgs and sent the one hundred and twenty flags captured from the enemy to be hung in Notre Dame, it did seem that the Empire was solidly established. To emphasise this to the French people, Napoleon issued orders for military parades, firework displays and public balls to be held in Paris and all the provincial capitals, where the Préfets were his representatives and the leaders of local society. To recompense his generals and to keep his chief supporters happy, he distributed titles and allotted revenues. And he disposed of various conquered kingdoms and principalities to members of his family in accordance with his system and because it was the best way to keep them quiet. Joseph became King of Naples and Louis King of Holland. Murat was created Prince of the Empire and Grand Duke of Berg and Cleves, so that Caroline achieved her ambition to become a reigning princess. Elisa clamoured for a territory outside France, knowing Napoleon's contempt for her husband, and she was made Duchess of Lucca and Princess of Piombino. Pauline asked for nothing; but Napoleon, not wishing her to feel slighted, gave her the duchy of Guastalla.

She was childishly delighted to read the decree which appeared on 30 March 1806: 'The duchy of Guastalla being at our disposition, we do hereby dispose of it in favour of our well-beloved sister Pauline to enjoy it in full ownership and sovereignty under the titles of Princess and Duchess of Guastalla.'

However, knowing the regions assigned to her sisters, Pauline was puzzled that she had never even heard of Guastalla; and when thanking Napoleon, asked him where it was.

'It's a village in the States of Parma and Piacenza,' said her brother, then hastily added after a glance at her face, 'a town, a borough.'

'A village!' exclaimed Pauline indignantly. 'What do you expect me to do with that? You've made Annunziata' (Pauline had an irritating manner of calling her sisters by their baptismal names when annoyed with them) 'Grand Duchess of Berg and Cleves, real States with ministers and regiments, but all I, her elder, will have to govern is one wretched village with a few miserable pigs!'

Napoleon, who was probably wishing he had left well alone, tried to conciliate her. He had nothing better left to give her for the moment. This little pawn on the Napoleonic chessboard was in fact only fifty square miles in extent and had a population of less than ten thousand. He proposed that she should keep the title but cede the duchy to the kingdom of Italy in return for a monetary consideration greatly in excess of its revenues. This arrangement pleased Pauline, who could always use money. And she had shown once again that she had some sense in her head and could at times prevail over her imperious brother.

'You will find herewith,' the Emperor wrote to Pauline on 24 May 1806, 'the decree I have had drawn up relating to the cession of your duchy of Guastalla to the kingdom of Italy. You will see that my Italian treasury will pay you six million francs, of which one-and-a-half million is to be paid in July and the balance within three years . . . See that your man of business takes up this matter at once.'

Pauline used some of this huge windfall to set in hand extensions to the ground floor of the Hôtel de Charost, so that she could give even more splendid balls and receptions. Two large rooms were added to the garden front of the house, one projecting from either end, and the kitchens were enlarged. Pauline left Paris in the meantime, to take a cure at Plombières-les-Bains in the Vosges, which was the fashionable spa that year. She badly needed the change of air and the curative properties of the waters to set herself up again for another Paris season.

She took the road in July accompanied by the chief members of her household and a number of servants; the luggage included her special bathtub for her milk ablutions, also a sedan chair and a well-cushioned litter, for her to be carried in one or the other

Prince Camillo Borghese

by F. Gérard

Napoleon crowning Josephine (December, 1804)
Her train-bearer (*right*) is Pauline
by J. L. David

when tired of the coach or when road hazards required the passengers to walk, and for her use while at Plombières. She was developing an infuriating habit of putting her entourage to extraordinary trouble to satisfy her sudden whims; it was her way of preventing boredom – in them as well as herself. The 250-mile journey took the small cavalcade through Bar-le-Duc, the capital of the Meuse *département*, where a brother of Pauline's first husband was the Préfet. She sent a courier on ahead to inform him that she graciously intended to spend the night at the Préfecture and to give him detailed instructions about her bath on arrival.

Monsieur Leclerc, somewhat bewildered, went to great lengths to prepare for Her Imperial Highness and her retinue, including sending men out to scour the neighbourhood for the necessary extra gallons of milk. As soon as Pauline arrived, her bath-tub was carried to the apartment prepared for her. Leclerc conducted her there, saw with relief that all was as requested, and said, 'Everything is ready for your bath, Your Highness.'

'And my shower afterwards?' asked Pauline, looking round the room.

'Your shower?' muttered Leclerc, nonplussed. 'I'm afraid we have no shower apparatus.'

'It's quite simple,' said Pauline ingenuously. 'Just make some holes in the ceiling, above the bath. Forgive the trouble I am causing you, but my health makes it all absolutely necessary.'

She continued her journey next morning after giving Leclerc a gracious word of thanks and leaving his best bedroom, now with a perforated ceiling, still smelling of sour milk.

At Plombières she conceived the idea of journeying about the mountainous neighbourhood in a large palanquin. She had one built specially, modelled on ancient Italian vehicles of this type, and her equerry, Monsieur de Montbreton, was given the unenviable task of training four mules to draw it. For a month he struggled gamely to carry out his capricious mistress's wishes, then had to confess his inadequacy. Regretfully, Pauline was obliged to abandon the project.

When she left Plombières early in September to return to Paris her health and spirits were much improved; she was, indeed, noticeably radiant and had become more agreeable. She also had an addition to her entourage in the person of Count Auguste de Forbin.

Pauline arrived back in Paris to say goodbye to Napoleon, who was about to take the field against Prussia. She had also, for form's sake, to say farewell to Borghese, who had been promoted major-general and was off to war again. There had been one or two stormy scenes between him and Pauline earlier in the year, when he had objected to her receiving certain gentlemen much too often. She had made it plain that she had not the slightest affection for him and meant to go her own way. Borghese, who was all for a quiet life, accepted the situation philosophically and sought female consolation elsewhere, with someone much less exigent than Pauline. But they appeared together on formal and official occasions, conforming with the Emperor's wishes. Pauline had little to suffer in this respect on her return to Paris, for her husband and Napoleon left the capital in late September to join the French armies in southern Germany. She just had time to persuade Napoleon to appoint Monsieur de Forbin principal chamberlain to her household.

Auguste de Forbin was a year older than Pauline and came of an ancient Provençal family whose properties had been confiscated during the Revolution. He had seen his father and uncle killed in the streets of Lyons during the Terror, and he and his mother had narrowly escaped a similar fate. In his late teens he had gone to Paris to study painting under David, then had served two years in the army. He developed into a fine figure of a man, tall, strong and handsome; he had a round, pleasant face which reflected an easy-going attitude to life, and with his distinguished appearance, his proud and easy manner, he had the air of a perfect courtier of the *ancien régime*. He was a dilettante, painting a little, writing light verse and prose with ease; gifted with a versatile mind, he could talk amusingly and was adept at all the social accomplishments of the time. Women raved over him, and many had granted him their ultimate favours. When he first met Pauline, on a wet summer's day at Plombières, he was heavily in debt.

She fell deeply and passionately in love for the first time, and with a man who was quite equal to satisfying her. And Forbin, although his emotions were not so deeply engaged, was genuinely fond of her and prepared to impart to her the refinements of life which came naturally to him. He was in fact an ideal lover and companion for Pauline, who was aware of her lack of culture but willing to be taught only by someone she loved and respected. Under his influence much of the hoyden in her disappeared; she matured mentally and her character softened. It was a great and ripening episode in her life.

Of course she paid nearly all his debts, and Pauline's circle gazed admiringly at her new chamberlain's splendid horses and carriage – and whispered to one another behind their hands. But Forbin earnt his keep; he took his official duties seriously and brought a firm hand to bear on what had been an erratically governed household. While Pauline was spending the morning in her customary idle, but to her important, manner, Forbin would be issuing the orders for the day, checking accounts, inspecting the stables, receiving callers and arranging appointments with Her Imperial Highness. She would appear at midday, radiant in an exquisite morning gown, and take Monsieur de Forbin's arm for a stroll round the garden before joining her ladies-in-waiting and the gentlemen of her household for luncheon. Afterwards, she and her chamberlain would withdraw to one of the first-floor rooms where he read aloud one of the latest books – Madame de Staël's *Delphine* it might be – or talked to her about poetry, music and the arts in general, but usually ending with her in his arms.

That winter of 1806 everybody remarked on the happiness and high spirits of Pauline. Josephine went to join the Emperor in Germany, so Pauline and Caroline had the role of leading hostesses (Elisa was living in Tuscany) and entertained on a grand scale.[2] But the combined strain of the social activity and the near-delirium of her new-found happiness was more than Pauline's constitution could stand. In addition she became fearful that her affair with Forbin would reach the ears of Napoleon. Although he was far away in Poland, one never knew what reports the reinstated Fouché and his secret police might be sending him. And Forbin had been indiscreetly ardent in the presence of others on several occasions; in fact this affair was the talk of the town.

Early in the spring, Pauline's health really broke down.[3]

Chapter 8

Summer idyll in Provence

Doctor Peyre, Pauline's physician, was seriously alarmed by her condition and, knowing that she took little notice of his advice, persuaded her to be examined by Doctor Jean-Noël Hallé, the foremost gynaecologist of the day and physician-in-ordinary to the Emperor. The report that Hallé made is highly significant and its implications explain much that would otherwise be obscure in Pauline's life. More than anything it reveals that her long quest for health and love could never be wholly successful; that she could gain the one only at the expense of the other. Such was the tragedy of her life.

The report from Hallé that Pauline's physician read on 20 or 21 April 1807 was as follows:

My dear colleague,

I have thought very carefully about the condition of Her Highness and the state of hysteria we found her in yesterday.

The womb was still sensitive, though a little less so. The ligaments still exhibited signs of the painful inflammation for which we prescribed baths last Thursday.

The spasms in her arms were due to hysteria, as were the pains in her head. Her general state is one of prostration and exhaustion.

The inflammation is by no means usual. The present condition of the uterus is caused by a constant and habitual excitation of that organ, and if this does not cease a most grievous condition may result.

That is the source of her trouble, and I hinted at its causes when speaking to the Princess last Thursday. I blamed the internal douches and spoke in a general way of possible causes of an irritation of the womb. I thought I made my meaning clear, but am afraid I may not have done so sufficiently. I don't know for sure, I can only guess, with the means available to us; but what I have said about the nature of the symptoms which you and I saw, and which you have seen far more often than I, is more than sufficient to give the key to the riddle.

The douche and its tube cannot always be held responsible. One is bound to assume a continuous cause for such exhaustion in the case of a pretty and impressionable young woman living apart from her husband. Whatever the cause, it is high time to exclude it. I have seen many a woman fall victim to similar weaknesses, and they all began the same way. It is clear that unless she takes prompt action it will soon be too late.

I can't say more than that. But we must certainly try to save this young and attractive woman from ruin. If there is someone encouraging her failings and is a party to them, he would not blame himself, whoever he is, but we should be blamed for having noticed nothing or permitted everything. I've no wish to pass for a fool nor to be accused of base and stupid complacency. But quite apart from that, there is the necessity of saving this unfortunate young woman whose state affects me deeply; and I am not without hope for her.

Act quickly then, my dear colleague, for there is no time to lose. Make use of my letter as you think fit, and enable me to speak openly and to the point. If we cannot speak frankly and professionally, we would do better to withdraw.*

In brief, Pauline was suffering from salpingitis – inflammation of a uterine tube – and the medical science of the time could do little about it. But a modern psychologist could hardly have resumed the case better. Hallé's position in Court circles gave him an insight into Pauline's private life; though he would have undoubtedly heard from Peyre about the unsatisfactory nature of her marriage to Borghese and the love affair with Forbin. He had that man in mind when he wrote, 'if there is someone encouraging her failings and is a party to them, he would not blame himself . . .' He realised the passionate nature of Pauline; but passion was the one indulgence that her state of health would

* Levy, Arthur, *Napoléon Intime*, Plon, Paris, 1893, pp. 317–19. This letter was communicated to Levy by a descendant of Hallé. It is here reproduced in full for the first time in English.

not allow. In short, he strongly advised that Pauline must mend her ways and lead a quiet life.

This was the last thing Pauline was likely to do just then, even if she could; and Peyre knew it. The Emperor was away campaigning against the Russians, so Peyre went to see Pauline's mother. The family, Napoleon and Letizia in particular, were often sceptical about Pauline's illnesses, and with reason; but on this occasion Letizia was seriously alarmed. She spoke severely to her daughter, threatened to reveal the affair with Forbin to Napoleon if she did not give him up and go to take a cure, as Peyre had strongly advised, at Aix-les-Bains. Pauline promised to do both these things. Cambacérès wrote to the Emperor to obtain permission for Pauline's journey, and this was given, though reluctantly: 'Doctors advise their patients to go to these watering-places simply to get rid of them. I think it much better for her to regain her health at home instead of rushing about the country in search of it. . . .'

Pauline had no intention of giving up Forbin. She was infatuated by him; her passions were fully aroused and had command of her. It was the Fréron affair all over again, except that now she was independent and free – more or less. All she wanted for the moment was to get away from these interfering people, and for that she would have promised anything.

Early in May Pauline left Paris accompanied by several members of her household including Doctor Peyre – but not Forbin – and having promised her mother to visit uncle Fesch at Lyons (he was the Archbishop there) on her way to Aix. Letizia was suspicious of her eagerness to get away. 'Her constant suffering rends my heart,' she wrote to her half-brother, 'and I am very anxious about her in other ways.' Letizia privately charged Monsieur de Montbreton, the only person she trusted in Pauline's household, to send her full reports of what went on at Aix.

Pauline did visit her uncle, who gave her some moral lectures, and she did go on to Aix, with an addition to her entourage in the person of Monsignor Isoard, whom uncle Fesch had detached from his staff as a kind of father confessor. But once at Aix Pauline proceeded to carry out her own plans. She sent off disarming letters to her mother and to her uncle, then persuaded or intimated to Montbreton and Madame de Bréhan that Aix was best for them but for her own maladies a spa further south was necessary. And she wrote to Forbin to tell him of her new destination. Aix was much too frequented for the lovers, but Gréoux-les-Bains in Provence was a small, little-known and secluded place in the foothills of the Alps, difficult of access by carriage. Pauline set off accompanied only by her favourite attendant, Mademoiselle Millo, and a few servants – and, perforce, Doctor Peyre and Monsignor Isoard. They would be bound to report on her behaviour to her family, but Pauline was past caring. Her only desire was to reach Gréoux and there rest and recover her health while enjoying a summer idyll with Forbin. The two things together, alas, were not possible; though Pauline did not know it or refused to admit it.

Pauline arrived at Gréoux in late May, travelling down the Rhône valley to Avignon and then along by the Durance until the road became a rough track, when she had herself carried in a litter for the rest of the way; her small party proceeded on horse-back and in a mule-cart.

When within a couple of miles of her destination Pauline would have had a sudden view of the great castle built by the Knights Templars atop a hill, with flat-roofed houses clustered tightly around the slope, all pink and white against the deep blue sky, the whole set in a circle of higher hills covered with trees and bushes of all shades of green.

In Gréoux she took rooms in a hotel and sent off letter after letter to Forbin, who was still in Paris. Only one of those letters has survived, written in her scrawling, nervous hand on four sheets of the green-bordered paper she used. As it is the only love-letter of her mature years known, and also throws some light on her situation and the way her thoughts ran, it is worth giving in full. It is dated 'Gréoulx, June 10, one o'clock.'

Beloved,
    No letters from you this morning. I am most anxiously awaiting one, as you said in your last that you had a fever. I hope nothing will come of it and that my beloved is already well again. This morning I went to the baths and also drank four glasses of the spa water, which went down well enough and

seemed to do me good, but on coming out of the bath I felt rather weak; however, I am sure my health is much better.

You wrote to M—— that you would soon be going to Aix, that you had been ill but under Mme Derville's tender care and nursing had greatly improved. What a lucky woman she is! To be able to look after you, to confess her feelings towards you – how I envy her. But I who love you, who have given you so many proofs of my love, I have to keep a check on myself and hide my feelings. Oh, are you not my husband? Has mine deserved that title, so sweet, so sacred? No, he has not, for if so you would not be my beloved. So you must return love for love and believe that everything I do is for our good.

I have thought it all over and am more sure than ever that all those around us fully believe that it is over between us, so we can be easy in our minds. The doctor was the one who revealed everything, not through malice but because he is a coward and a fool. My mother and uncle know everything; you cannot imagine what I went through at Lyons, the tears I shed at finding ourselves discovered. Mme de B—— [Bréhan, lady-in-waiting] took the opportunity to protest about the way you behaved in her presence, and said she was not the kind of person to put up with our forgetting ourselves in front of her as we had done in Paris. You can understand how I suffered, considering I am kindhearted and had taken her into my confidence. As for M. de Mon—— [Montbreton], you know better than anybody how he has behaved. He has been the cause of our separation and of a deal of trouble, and has betrayed my trust in him in a way that is very hard on me. Mlle D—— [Dormy, lady-in-waiting] is a good girl, but she cannot be trusted. Mme Du—— [Ducluzel, housekeeper] has no love for you. Ad—— [Adèle, chambermaid] is a tattler. Mme de Ba—— [Barral, lady-in-waiting] is neither a good friend nor a bad enemy. She just does not wish to be of help to us. M. and Mme de St M—— [Saint-Maur, private secretary] do not count. So I only see Minette, Emilie and Nini [the maids].

The greatest caution will be necessary, even sacrifices and denials, if you are not to lose me. I will let you know how you are to behave. You will have to put up with it and believe that I suffer more than you from these restraints, which will save us from much annoyance and even from losing each other altogether. Besides, if my husband comes, we shall certainly have to resign ourselves to that. So I am only providing against events. Goodbye for now; I am going to have a little rest, as I have never written for so long before, but you know how I do the impossible for you, for you alone. I will write again this evening.

Nine-thirty.

I have been out, the weather was so lovely. A carriage road is being made, and we went and watched the workmen. It will be wide enough for two four-horse carriages to pass. But I felt sad, for neither this nor any other distraction can drive thoughts of you from my mind. Mme —— has a fever, so I am alone with the doctor and Isoard, who is here at my uncle's request. He is a kindly soul but as stupid as the rest of them. I have arranged for you to come to the baths and stay all the time I am there. Mme Du—— will be there too, and the doctor and Isoard, but don't let that frighten you. I have arranged it that way so that my dear one can come as well. I am only afraid that the heat may make it uncomfortable for you. No matter who else may be present, I shall have eyes only for you. How this solitude will please me when you are here! May it last a long time, and may we never, never be separated!

If we are careful, we can always be happy. I am waiting impatiently for news of your fever. Tell me what you are doing. Bring your painting things with you, so that you can do some pretty sketches for me. My pavilion is nearly ready. I am having flowers planted all round it, and making it as comfortable as possible for my beloved.

By the way, I forgot to tell you that my husband has been made a General. He writes me charming letters full of affection – where it all comes from, I don't know. But now I must stop, for so much writing tires me. The baths, too, make me a little weak. *Addio caro, sempre caro amico, amante caro, si ti amo ti amaro sempre.* Tomorrow I will write to tell you just how you are to manage here, and I will do my very best to arrange things well. I am going to try and sleep now, but I dream constantly of you, especially lately. *Si ti amo di piu, caro idolo mio.*

Ti mando dei fiori che sono stati nel mio sino, li ho coperto di baci.
[I send you some flowers, covered in kisses, which have lain
in my bosom.]

Pauline ended in passionate Italian, just as she used to when
writing to Fréron; but those earlier letters had a more mature
style and tone, which supports the belief that they were written,
or drafted, by Lucien.

It was not exactly a letter likely to bring Forbin post-haste from
Paris. What, one wonders, did he make of this petulant letter
from a spoiled young woman who was madly in love with him?
He was not a man to be treated so imperiously, but he was fond
of the young woman; and she was rich and the sister of the
Emperor. He was a younger son, and although the family had
recovered its property (three vast châteaux in Provence alone, all
in need of repair) the feudal dues and other income no longer
existed and the head of the family was in no position to help
Auguste financially. Moreover, he was still Pauline's chamberlain
and being handsomely paid for his services. So he went to
Provence in July, and there indeed ensued a summer idyll under
deep blue skies, amid the lavender-scented hills.

Pauline had taken rooms at the newly-built Hôtel des Thermes,
close to the baths, at the lower end of the village. The owner of
both establishments, a Monsieur Gravier, was delighted at
having such an illustrious client and could not do enough for
her, and it was probably he who suggested an ideal spot in which
to build the pavilion mentioned in her letter to Forbin. It was
in the midst of a wood about a mile from the hotel, in the Domaine
de Laval, a property owned by a Monsieur de Montesan who was
a friend of Gravier's. Pauline had followed the work in progress,
being carried to the site in a sedan chair over a path along the
aptly-named Ravin de Paradis – not a ravine but a wide dip
between the hills. When completed, the pavilion or *casino* was a
circular stone building with a domed roof, about twenty-five
feet high and twelve feet in diameter. There were no windows,
but it had a high, double door. A narrow frieze of intertwining
brown leaves ran round the wall at head height and another,
similar, band ran where the wall began to curve to form the roof.
It was a simple but delightful little building in the eighteenth-

century style of the Île de France, a most striking sight in the heart of a wood in Upper Provence; not large enough to live in but enough for lovers' meeting in comfort. It stood on the flat top of a mound and hard back against the rocky slope of a steep hill. A flight of stone steps had been made to lead down to a clearing in front of a natural grotto in the hillside. A huge, smooth stone slab was set up as a table inside the grotto, with stone benches behind; and outside, a few yards from the grotto, there happened to be a young oak tree which spread some shade over the little plateau.

Pauline and Auguste could make love in the *pavillon de rendezvous* far from prying eyes, in the midst of nature and to the shrill cries of cicadas, then descend to the grotto for a picnic out of the heat of the sun or sheltered from rain, with a view of the high wooded hills on the other side of the Ravin de Paradis. Then perhaps Auguste put up his easel – if he had indeed brought his 'painting things', as bidden – and arranged cushions for Pauline to recline under the oak tree.[1]

A more romantic spot would be difficult to find, or to conceive. For Pauline to have arranged such a setting was proof that she had acquired good taste, despite her lack of formal education, or that it was innate. And these dispositions to 'provide against events' showed that she had a romantic mind and was still basically a child of nature as when running wild at Ajaccio. Her romanticism had been suppressed when a girl, at the time of the Fréron affair, and then by her arranged marriages; but now, in this remote little spa and free to be true to herself, she was able to give expression to it.

The amount of time that Pauline devoted to taking the cure – the ostensible reason for her being at Gréoux – was probably not very much, despite the evidence of her letter. For one thing, the baths were underground (as they still are today), for the waters were known to lose much of their efficacy if exposed to the light; this, and their high temperature, made taking the cure an uncomfortable and exhausting business: hence Pauline's references to the heat and feeling a little weak on coming out of her bath. (Doctors today prescribe a limited period in the bath and insist on the patient resting in bed afterwards.)[2]

Auguste, too, was supposed to be taking the cure. He stayed

at the same hotel as Pauline for a while, then went to live at one of the Forbin châteaux, La Verdière, handily situated about twelve miles south of Gréoux, and rode over to the spa to meet Pauline. Perhaps he grew tired of the 'restraints', the 'caution . . . even sacrifices and denials', but the fact is that he eventually took Pauline back with him to stay at La Verdière, a vast and ancient building, more fortress than château, perched above the hill village of St Roch and having magnificent views from the upper terrace. There she was given a bedroom which had a narrow, secondary staircase leading down to a small boudoir where much of the space was taken up by a *causeuse*, a sofa for two. And at La Verdière a subtle change in relationship probably occurred: instead of Auguste being her chamberlain and lover, she became his guest and mistress. After all, the Forbins had been governors of Provence ever since its union with the French realm in the late fifteenth century, and during three centuries the family had given France several men who were prominent as ambassadors or naval commanders. There among the family portraits of aristocratic lineage Pauline would be put in her proper place.

Perhaps that is how it was. Yet the existing portraits of Auguste de Forbin do not give an impression of haughtiness or even of authority; he looks a happy-go-lucky type with nothing of the snob about him. And Pauline was not a woman to be impressed by past glories. She lived very much in the present; her family ruled the roost, and she herself had only to take up residence with her husband in Turin to queen it over all Piedmont and half of Lombardy. No; she had lovers, but she was certainly never any man's mistress. It is more likely that she, too, grew tired of the restraints and the caution and, the dominant one of the two, pressed Auguste into arranging for a visit to his family home, where the very nature of the buildings ensured absolute privacy.

From La Verdière the two went to the Forbin château of La Barben, some fifty miles to the west, between Aix-en-Provence and Salon. This, too, had been originally a fortress and was still difficult of access; with sheer rock on three sides, the only entrance was a steep slope with a fortified gatehouse. The château itself, built within the fortifications, was more elegant, better furnished and more comfortable than the rather grim and austere La Verdière.[3]

Pauline, as restless as ever, decided to return to Gréoux in late August. She and Auguste made a leisurely journey from La Barben, sampling the waters at Aix-en-Provence on the way. Then she took up her cure again at Gréoux, under the severe eye of Doctor Peyre.

Borghese had not put in an appearance, as Pauline had feared at one time; Napoleon's swift and victorious campaign against the Russians had retained him in the field. But while his wife and her lover were reclining in the shade of an oak tree on several hot July days, he was galloping furiously across Europe. Napoleon had taken a liking to this brother-in-law, who had conducted himself bravely at the battle of Friedland; in addition to promoting him full General, Napoleon gave him the important and popular mission of taking to Paris the news that peace had been signed between France and Russia. This mission would draw public attention and acclamation upon Prince Borghese and therefore upon Pauline – Napoleon, as was often the case, had an ulterior motive. Borghese set off with great enthusiasm to carry dispatches to Cambacérès. Soon afterwards, the clauses of the treaty of alliance between the Tsar and the Emperor were agreed and signed, and Napoleon's best official courier, the famous Moustache, was sent with a copy to Paris. Fast though Borghese rode, the more hardened Moustache rode faster; and at about a hundred miles from Paris the latter overtook the Prince. Dismayed and angry, Borghese offered the other twenty thousand francs to let him have an hour's lead; but Moustache, very conscious of his duty and proud of his reputation, refused. And although Borghese made strenuous efforts, having himself lifted in the saddle from one spent horse to a fresh mount, his dispatches were out-of-date when he staggered into the Tuileries and handed them to Cambacérès.

His wife was meeting with setbacks too. She found that Forbin's love was waning. He had had enough of this ailing, capricious woman; and now that the husband was back in France, and the Emperor too, he judged it wise to bring the affair to an end. Pauline's health, inevitably, was not improving; and Doctor Peyre was furious with her. He knew that while she had a lover she was caught in a vicious circle; her particular ailment acted as an irritant to her naturally passionate nature, it excited her sexual appetite; and by appeasing that, she was undermining her health and morale, bringing about 'a most grievous condition', as Hallé had predicted.

Perhaps Peyre spoke confidentially to Forbin, and this may have been the deciding factor in his leaving Pauline; he was, after all, a gentleman of taste and discretion. Or it may have been some small incident – for instance, when Pauline threw a book at his head – which finally decided him. At all events, in September he packed his bags and travelled north. He went to Fontainebleau, boldly asked to be received by the Emperor and requested active service with the army. During the next two years he took part in the Spanish and Austrian campaigns. He never saw Pauline again. It was not until he was in his forties, in the calmer times of the Restoration, that he found his proper place in life and developed his talents to the full. He was appointed director of the Louvre (which still contained much Napoleonic loot), he wrote books on art and architecture and a novel, *Charles Barimore,* and he became an established painter of landscapes. But he is chiefly remembered as the man who was loved by Pauline Bonaparte-Borghese.

She was all the better in character for having come under his influence, and he had broadened her mental horizons. And she was all the better in health after he left her. The waters at Gréoux were doing her much good, or at least the dry, mild climate and the enervating air were, and she stayed on there until late October. The idea of returning to Paris did not greatly appeal to her, much as she liked the pomp and brilliance of the winter season. Her husband was living in the Hôtel de Charost; the long journey back would be very trying; and she would come under supervision from her family. On the other hand, there was the call of the Mediterranean, so near. Pauline decided to spend the winter quietly at Nice, and Doctor Peyre could but approve and be thankful.

Chapter 9

The return of Borghese

By late November Pauline was installed with some of her household in a large, fine villa at Nice. It belonged to a Monsieur Vinaille but had been requisitioned by the Préfet for the Emperor's sister; the gardens, planted with orange and lemon trees, extended down to the sea. Nice, for a long time the one port of Savoy, had become part of France and was included in the Alpes-Maritimes Département, like the Principality of Monaco a few miles along the coast; although quite small compared with modern Nice, it was an important place, especially since Napoleon had built the Corniche road to enable his troops to advance more rapidly into Italy, if need required, than when he had conducted the campaign which set him on his triumphant way. Pauline soon settled into a quiet, orderly routine, even having set hours for meals with her household. She had breakfast alone in her bedroom, then received in the drawing-room such local authorities and visiting notables as wished to be presented to her, for she never forgot – publicly – or allowed others to forget that she was a sister of the Emperor. In the afternoons she went for drives by the sea or up along the Corniche to enjoy the marvellous views; that glorious coastline had not yet been desecrated by the hand of man. In the evenings there was music or card-playing.

This calm and regular life, following after her cure at Gréoux, greatly improved Pauline's health. Her entourage, especially Doctor Peyre, wondered if she had indeed changed her ways. But it could not last. As her spirits rose, so did her effervescence begin to seek outlets for enjoyment. At first these were innocent enough. She arranged a special courier service from Paris which brought her the latest fashions, gowns and hats and the trinkets of all kinds which were so dear to her. On learning that Napoleon was in Turin (he had been on a political tour of Italy and had also had a meeting with Lucien at Mantua, an unsuccessful attempt to win his erring brother over to his system) Pauline thought it would make a pleasant break to visit the Emperor, perhaps spend Christmas with him; it was more than eighteen months since she had last seen him. But that outlet was closed to her. 'How can you think of coming to Turin by the roads you would have to travel over?' Napoleon replied on 20 December. 'Stay all winter at Nice and get well, so as to be able to come to Paris in the spring.'

She was already well again; so much so that she had a physical need of someone to take the place of Forbin. There was no gallant young man in Nice who took her fancy. Then she remembered that in Paris there was a very presentable member of her household, a concert-master who was drawing a handsome salary of 750 francs a month. She sent for him to come to Nice at once.

Felice Blangini was a year younger than Pauline, having been born in Turin in 1781. He was a competent musician, singer and composer, and had achieved some success in Paris in 1806 with his opera *Naphtali*. He then became a fashionable teacher of music and was taken up by several leading hostesses including Caroline Murat, to whom he dedicated some nocturnes. Pauline had singing lessons from him (this was at the time when she was experiencing Forbin's guiding hand) and then attached him to her household, happily just forestalling Josephine who had the same intention. One day she handed him some verses she had written and instructed him to set them to music by the following morning. Blangini must have been inspired, for he wrote later that it became one of the most popular of his compositions.

He set off from Paris with some trepidation. He was a very timid young man, and from what he had seen and heard of Her Imperial Highness he found it difficult to believe that his presence was required solely to conduct musical evenings. He arrived at the villa Vinaille on a wet January night and was given a comfortable room on the ground floor with a view of the gardens and the sea beyond. He at once found that his services were greatly in demand – as a musician. The villa vibrated all day long to the strains of Blangini accompanying the Princess at the piano. The household was treated to a positive orgy of Blangini and all his works; he and Pauline played duets together incessantly and sang all the songs and ballads he had ever composed. When Pauline became enthusiastic, she never did things by halves;

but her enthusiasms rarely lasted for very long. Blangini soon found, too, that his misgivings had not been unwarranted. The Princess was vibrating to the charms of her musician as well as to his music. Before long, it was clearly evident to the household that he had become the successor to Monsieur de Forbin: music had supplanted painting among Pauline's mobile enthusiasms.

His life ceased to be his own. When he did manage to escape from the villa for an hour or two, Pauline had him followed by a footman with orders to approach him, if he dallied over-long, and say that Her Imperial Highness required his presence at once. When she went for a drive in her open carriage emblazoned with the Imperial arms, she took Blangini with her. The poor man – though in some respects he can hardly be pitied – was terrified that reports of Her Imperial Highness's latest affair would reach the Emperor, if not her husband.

A much closer person to take a dim view of Pauline's behaviour was Doctor Peyre. He could not have been surprised when one night he was roused by the imperious ringing of the Princess's bell, the banging of doors and the clatter of hurrying footsteps. Pauline was in pain and the whole household was being alerted. Peyre slipped on his dressing-gown and went along to her bedroom. From the corridor the sleepy-eyed servants and members of the household could hear the doctor's voice raised in sharp remonstrance. He probably said things which he would have refrained from uttering in the judicious light of day, or would have at least couched in tactful terms. As it was, Her Highness's vanity was wounded and her temper roused. She replied so vigorously that Peyre left her room in a fury. When morning came, he packed his bags and moved out. He was a good doctor but a poor courtier.

It was soon after this incident that Pauline made her sentimental visit to the Château Sallé at Antibes – 'a pilgrimage', Blangini called it in his naïve *Souvenirs*, for he had to accompany her. So did a number of other people. Pauline's natural impulse to return to a place, so close at hand, where she had spent many happy weeks with her mother and sisters gave her an opportunity to indulge her sense of fun and farce, which had been somewhat dormant for a time. Perhaps it was awakened by the coming of spring to the Côte d'Azur; there was warmth in the sun again, the flowers were blooming and making a riot of colour, the lemons and mandarines were almost ripe. At all events, instead of a quiet drive in a carriage the ten miles or so to Antibes and a visit incognito to the empty Château Sallé, Pauline made a spectacular progress along the coast in a flower-bedecked galley powered by two rows of white-clad oarsmen, and she informed the commander at Antibes of her coming. The galley had a pavilion amidships for Pauline and her ladies; Blangini made the inevitable comparison of Cleopatra advancing over the waves to meet Mark Antony. Her Imperial Highness was greeted by a salute of twenty-one guns on arrival at Antibes, and a throng of people was at the quayside to enjoy the colourful and unusual sight. The commandant conducted Pauline and her entourage to his residence where a grand dinner was given in her honour, followed by a public reception and ball.

Next morning Pauline visited the scene of a happy period of her girlhood, and she became the carefree, vivacious Paulette again as she darted from one room to another of the deserted château.

'That was my mother's room, and this is where I slept,' she cried gaily to her ladies and escort. 'My sisters were over there, on the other side of the hall. And here is the room which my brother Napoleon had when he came to stay with us for a day or two!'

Her joy was evident to everyone. Yet how much better it would have been if she had gone there discreetly, with just one or two attendants, instead of giving a number of gaping officials and local notabilities an opportunity to comment between themselves on the Bonapartes' change of fortune and remind one another of that family's obscure origins. But such a thought would never have occurred to Pauline. For all her faults, her very human faults, she was no snob; and with her odd blend of naïvety and sophistication, she sincerely expected everyone to understand and share her pleasure in this step back to a time when life was simple and uncomplicated.

On the following day Pauline and her party returned to Nice by water, and she prepared to settle down again, for a time at least. She made no plans to return to Paris. But suddenly life became very complicated indeed. An Imperial courier arrived from Paris with official instructions for Pauline. There were copies of the Senate's decision, on the recommendation of the Emperor, to transform the Transalpine Provinces into a special Department-beyond-the-Alps under a governor-general ranking as a Grand Dignitary of the Empire; and of the Emperor's appointment of his brother-in-law Prince Borghese to this post. Pauline gave a shrug of her pretty shoulders; she could not care less what happened to Borghese – until she read on and learnt that the Emperor had directed him to call at Nice and take his wife with him to Turin, where they were to reside together at the former palace of the King of Sardinia and hold court in the name of the Emperor of the French.

This move of Napoleon's was one outcome of his Italian tour; he had decided to put more animation into Turin and restore something of its former brilliant court and social life, and to remind the Piedmontese of 'our desire to be more closely informed of their concerns and our constant thought for even the most distant parts of our Empire', as his proclamation put it. At the same time, this was a move to end the scandal of the continued separation of Prince and Princess Borghese and to compel them to live under the same roof for at least a few months of the year. Reports of Pauline's indiscreet love affairs had reached Napoleon and he had decided to call her to order.

Napoleon had drawn up in the minutest detail the size and character of the household, had fixed the budget and named the sums allotted to each item. There would be a grand marshal of the palace; the Prince was to have six chamberlains, four equerries, four aides-de-camp and a secretary; for the Princess, six chamberlains, a lady of honour (the Dowager Marchioness Cavour), twelve ladies-in-waiting and four equerries.[1] Every Sunday the Prince and Princess were to hold a formal reception in the state apartment, and once a week the Princess was to receive in her private apartment. The public entertainments were set out in detail and everything was inventoried down to the number of horses in the stables and pieces of the dinner services. And the control of the purse was put in the hands of the governor-general – of Camillo, not Pauline.

She was furious, but she recognised Napoleon's mood and understood him too well to think of resisting his commands –

at least, not at once. A battle of wills was on, and Pauline faced
the situation with that hard core of determination which she
could call on when absolutely necessary. For the moment, she
submitted; but with the firm intention of getting her own way
in the end. She had one great advantage in that Napoleon's mind
was occupied with a thousand-and-one things, while she could
concentrate on this single matter.

She submitted, made no protest to Napoleon and awaited the
arrival of her husband. But this, of course, did not mean she was
docile; she proceeded to make life a great trial for everyone around
her, as she had done on previous occasions when things were not
to her liking.

Borghese reached Nice on 13 April, having warned his wife of
his arrival. She was not ready to start. He had a large staff with
him and a long baggage-train (somewhere among it were seven
Court dresses by Leroy and a magnificent purple, gold-embroidered riding-habit ordered by Pauline to dazzle the Piedmontese;
though it is difficult to imagine her on a horse). Pauline main-
tained that there was no room in her villa, and Borghese had to
rent one in the neighbourhood. However, having been given strict
orders by Napoleon, Borghese himself stayed at the Vinaille
villa; but he and Pauline had separate bedrooms, and she insisted
on some members of their households taking their meals with
them. And she revived her musical evenings; it was another
means of avoiding being alone with her husband. Mademoiselle
Millo sang, Blangini played the piano and Pauline flirted with
her husband's handsome secretary, Maxime de Villemarest.

Borghese's young secretary made a good living later in life
by ghosting various people's memoirs, including Blangini's.
That evening in Nice he was seeing Pauline for the first time and
found her beauty even more stunning than reports had led him
to believe. 'She was utterly feminine, *femme-femme*', he wrote
later. 'Though she looked languid and delicate, there was life
and energy pulsing within, and her personality made itself felt.
Her glance had an intelligence and a penetrating quality that gave
her features a certain resemblance to the Emperor's.'

Pauline must have fully recovered her health and spirits during
the winter at Nice and was in good form. Blangini had proved
to be a faint-hearted lover, despite experiencing all the protection

vouchsafed by the Imperial Venus; and the news of Prince Borghese's coming to Nice had completely turned him off. When
one of Borghese's aides-de-camp coldly informed him that his
name was not on the lists of personnel drawn up by the Emperor,
he announced his intention of returning to Paris. But Pauline
would not hear of it; she promised to create an appointment for
him in Turin at double his former salary. He would be the
resident gigolo, as it were; though he was not really her type and
she no longer had a great need of him. The quiet pastoral life at
Nice had ended and Borghese had brought with him several
dashing army officers, much more to her taste. But she was in
a mood to frustrate the desires and wishes of anyone.

Having caused all the delay she could, Pauline signified her
willingness to leave for Turin, provided the journey was made
in easy stages. The departure of the two households was an
amazing sight for the Niçois. There were eight large, lumbering
coaches with heaps of boxes, chests, cases and bundles under the
leathern tops of the *impériales,* a few baggage-waggons (one
containing Pauline's sedan-chair) and, for Pauline and her
husband, a well-sprung, well-cushioned berlin made by one of
the best carriage-builders in Paris. The convoy set off with much
cracking of whips and neighing of horses, looking more like a
hastily-equipped safari than the stately train of a viceroy on his
way to make a ceremonial entry.

It was the third week in April, a lovely time in the Nice region;
the sun was warm yet not excessive, the sky a deep blue and the
mountain views magnificently clear as the convoy wound its
way up to the Col de Braus and then down to the town of Sospel
in a wide valley, where a halt was made for the night. On the
second day the road was rougher and narrower and at times
dangerous, passing through gorges as it climbed up to the
6,000-foot Col de Tende, and the wind blew cold across the
mountainous slopes. The going was slow and was made even
slower by Pauline's behaviour. When everyone else got out of the
coaches and walked up a steep stretch, she called for her sedan-
chair, which had to be unloaded from the baggage-waggon.
But that did not suit her for long, and she started to walk, only
to remember that she was indisposed; and the long cavalcade
had to halt while she was settled again among the cushions in

the berlin. This comedy was repeated several times, while Borghese had to listen to her protests and complaints that the awful journey was killing her. He showed commendable patience and restraint, but was driven to the point where, to avoid a scene, he got out of the berlin when she got in and returned to his seat when she got out again. So he walked most of the last few miles to Tende.

Pauline probably did feel ill and uncomfortable; in her restless life she suffered innumerable hours of discomfort on the roads of France and Italy. But on this journey she seemed determined to tire and exasperate everyone around her. When the company reached Tende at about five in the afternoon, worn out and with appetites on edge, Pauline retired to her room at the inn, saying she was unwell. The others were about to sit down at table when loud groans and cries came from above. Servants ran to and fro. Her Imperial Highness had a colic, or so it appeared, and was demanding an enema made from a calf's intestines to alleviate her pains. Monsieur de Clermont-Tonnerre, her one chamberlain again, proposed a more easily available remedy, linseed oil for instance. But no, only a calf's intestines would do. It was no good pointing out that in a mountain village three thousand feet up, a calf was a rare animal – Pauline probably knew that already. Servants and equerries went off in different directions, and a couple of hours later a man returned leading the animal so desperately wished for by one and all. Pauline came downstairs to make sure she was not being deceived, the calf was slaughtered, its intestines boiled, and the enema administered to Pauline by one of her ladies-in-waiting. Her colic was miraculously cured, and at eight o'clock the weary and famished retainers were able at last to sit down to a meal.

The convoy crossed the pass next day and so left the Alpes-Maritimes and entered the Département of which Borghese had been designated governor. At the first village the mayor was ready with a flowery address of welcome. Borghese was about to reply when Pauline claimed that the duty fell to her, as she was a French princess and had precedence over him.[2] This was more than even Borghese was prepared to accept. He patiently explained that the Emperor had named him, not his wife, governor-general. He was supported by Clermont-Tonnerre, who added that the Emperor would be most annoyed if he learnt that she was interfering in public affairs. It was the one argument which could prevail over Pauline. She withdrew, much vexed, and the mayor – who must have been wondering what kind of couple had come to rule his country – received a pleasant little speech from the governor-general which had been written for him by Villemarest. It helped to improve the impression made on these villagers, the first of his subjects that the governor-general had met, and he was rewarded with acclamations as he proceeded on his way. With Pauline put firmly in her place and wanting only to reach journey's end now, the ceremonies and speeches at Cuneo and elsewhere went off well. And on 23 April 1808 the governor-general and his wife made their entry into Turin in an open carriage, she sitting on his left, escorted by a guard of honour and with church bells pealing, guns firing a salute and the crowds cheering. A round of elaborate entertainments, grand dinners, balls, receptions and gala performances at the Opera awaited them.

Turin was an agreeable town with broad streets and pleasant squares but Pauline was still determined not to live with Borghese or to remain in Turin, and she took as little part as possible in the official ceremonies, although it meant depriving herself of much of the pleasure, so dear to her, of displaying her lovely new dresses and being admired in them. She complained that the damp climate was ruinous to her health and pestered Borghese so much that for a while he moved the court out to Stupinigi, a palatial hunting-lodge a few miles south of Turin. She wrote letter after letter to Napoleon, saying how ill she was and asking to be allowed to go to a health resort, preferably Aix-les-Bains. Borghese refused to let her go without the Emperor's permission. She used her wiles on Villemarest, whose duties included reporting to the Emperor all that occurred, politically and otherwise, in the Département, and asked him to add appeals of her own. This astute courtier did as requested but carefully refrained from vouching for the accuracy of her statements.

It was Villemarest who was largely responsible for Pauline's one gracious effort to please the Piedmontese. On the eve of a grand ball at the Opera he went to her with a suggestion. 'Your Highness is aware how attached the people here are to their

customs and traditions,' he began tactfully. 'You will of course
open the ball, and I suggest that you call for a *manfrina*, one of the
popular rustic dances. To produce the right effect, the orchestra
could start by playing the opening bars of a French quadrille,
whereupon you would call on the conductor to stop and say
you wish for a *manfrina*.' It was the kind of idea that appealed
to Pauline. She played her part to perfection, and when she
called for the popular peasant dance the Opera rang with shouts
of '*Evviva la Principessa! Evviva il Imperatore!*'

Napoleon would have appreciated this stage-management; he
probably got to hear of it, to Pauline's pleasure. She realised
that his motives in imposing this way of life on her were political,
and she was too fond of him to bear a grudge – but that was no
reason for her to accept the situation. And he was not moved by
her appeals, whatever good reports he received about her.

'I have your letter of 18 May', he wrote to her from Bayonne
(where he was deeply engaged in power politics to bring Spain
within his dominion, and making one of his greatest mistakes,
as he later admitted). 'I approve of your going to take the
waters at the Val d'Aosta. I am sorry to learn your health is bad.
I suppose you are being sensible and that it is by no fault of
yours? I am happy to know that you are pleased with your
Piedmontese ladies. Make yourself liked; be affable with everybody. Try to be equable and make the Prince happy.'

Aosta was too near Turin for Pauline; and she was in no mood
to make anyone happy. Blangini was still with her household,
but she was too much engrossed with her illnesses, real and
assumed, to concern herself with him. He summoned up courage
to announce that he was returning to Paris, and Pauline sent for
him. He found her in her bath.

'My poor Blangini, how changed you are!' she exclaimed.
'But I, too, have suffered agonies this past month. Be patient.
I am going to take a cure at Aix. I have written to the Emperor
and to my mother, telling them that nothing will make me stay
in Turin any longer. I will get away on foot and in disguise if
necessary. I will not live like this. Go on to Paris, my dear
Blangini, and wait for me there. You will not have to wait long.'

She had convinced the doctors, including the court physician,
Doctor Vastapani, that she was dangerously ill. There was no

one for them to consult on her past medical history; by simulating convulsions, and as she was seldom free of her constitutional malady, the doctors were persuaded that a cure at Aix-les-Bains was indicated. But Borghese, despite their advice, still refused to allow her to leave the Département without the Emperor's permission. Pauline raged, saying that he wanted to kill her off. Those of her entourage who knew her best, such as Montbreton and Mademoiselle Millo, admired her play-acting but kept silent.

Then came an unexpected opportunity, and Pauline swooped on it like Napoleon detecting a vulnerable spot in an enemy position. Her brother Joseph arrived in Turin on his way from Naples to Bayonne. On Napoleon's instructions he had left his kingdom of Naples in the hands of a regent and was going to take over the Spanish throne which his younger brother had just wrested from the Bourbons.

Pauline poured out her woes to Joseph, though without telling him the whole story. She said how ill she was, and called in the doctors to confirm it. She was undoubtedly at a low ebb and Joseph, who had not seen her for two years, was deeply touched by her apparent sufferings. As head of the family, he waived Borghese's objections aside and before resuming his journey to Bayonne sent a letter to Napoleon by express courier:

> I have found Pauline here in a deplorable state. She has eaten nothing for eight days and cannot keep down even the lightest broth. Her doctors say she ought to leave the humid climate of Turin and go and take the waters at Aix in Savoy. Her husband hesitated because he had not received Your Majesty's permission for this. But I did not hesitate a moment to tell him to let his wife leave immediately and that I would assume all responsibility, for Your Majesty assuredly wishes his sister to recover.

On or about the same day as Joseph wrote this letter, Napoleon was replying to another of Pauline's appeals: 'Your present indisposition is only a touch of spring fever. . . . I see no objection to your going to the baths at Saint Didier, which is within the Département. But you are not to leave the Département without my permission.'

When this letter reached Turin, Pauline was already at Aix-les-Bains. Suddenly recovering her energy, she had started within twenty-four hours of receiving Joseph's permission, taking with her most of her French household and one of her Piedmontese ladies-in-waiting, Christina Ghilini; also in the party was Doctor Vastapani, by order of Borghese. To make sure of not being ordered back to Turin she dispatched letters to members of her family containing the most alarming accounts of her ill health; and Vastapani, who seems to have come under her charms or to have been taken in by her, sent grave reports on her condition to Borghese.

Her mother was so distressed by all she heard that she left Paris, accompanied by Cardinal Fesch who was staying with her, and travelled post-haste to Aix. The two found Pauline unwell but far from dying. Letizia sent off brief reassuring letters, such as the one to Lucien in which she said tersely: 'Paulette, with whom the climate of Turin did not agree, is somewhat more ill than usual.' Letizia and her half-brother stayed at Aix for a week and then, on 12 July, went on to Lyons. Pauline was to join them there, but she travelled by water, along Lake Bourget and then down the Rhône, as being a more comfortable means of conveyance for her. It was slower than by road, but time was not of the essence. Most of her retinue were sent on to Paris to prepare the Hôtel de Charost for her arrival in August; she had heard from Joseph, through her mother (who had become a sort of clearing-house for news of her far-flung family), that Napoleon would be returning to Paris for his birthday, 15 August.

Pauline had a short rest at her uncle's episcopal palace, then went on to Paris by road. She arrived filled with fury towards Borghese; he had cut off her funds and she had no money. The payments for the cession of her duchy of Guastalla had been held up; she had overspent her own income and there were piles of bills waiting for her attention. She had to borrow from the banker Laffitte until Napoleon reached Paris and had time to see to her affairs. But how would he receive her after she had disobeyed his commands?

Chapter 10

Napoleon to the rescue

Napoleon was at St Cloud on 14 August and Pauline saw him a few days later. It was the first time the two had met for nearly two years, which probably explains Napoleon's forgiving mood; or perhaps his mind was beset with so many problems of magnitude that Pauline's escapades assumed minor importance. Just what passed between them is not known, but Pauline came away smiling and next day wrote to a friend: 'The Emperor was charming to me. I am to stay in France, and he is going to arrange about my financial affairs and estate when he returns from Germany.'

Her financial affairs certainly needed putting in order. Her secretary, chamberlain and man of business never knew what expenditure was being concealed from them, and the accounts were often in a hopeless tangle. Forbin's firm hand and influence had kept things in control for a time, but a whole year had passed since he had left the household. Pauline's passion for jewels was insatiable. At one jeweller's on the Quai des Orfèvres she spent more than a quarter of a million francs in a single year; one acquisition alone, a necklace of thirty-four diamonds of the finest cut, cost 135,000 francs (about £30,000 today). Her ideas of making economies – Napoleon had probably pointed out the desirability – were to give strict orders that the candles were to be snuffed out as soon as the last guest had departed, and that a set of chairs had to be moved from one room to another instead of a new set being bought.

However, Pauline had to keep her creditors quiet with promises for a few more months. Napoleon left Paris in September to meet the Tsar at Erfurt, and when he returned a month later, having obtained a promise of Russian aid against any uprising in eastern Europe, he had no time to spare to deal with Pauline's finances. He merely sent her one of the three fine sables given to him by the Tsar (more was to be heard of this sable) and then he was off on his travels again, to the opposite end of his dominions, to Spain, where matters were going badly for Joseph and the army.

Napoleon had increased the year's levy of conscripts to a quarter of a million, and had transferred the pick of his veterans from Germany and Italy to the Pyrenees in less than a month by using relays of waggons. By the beginning of November there were 120,000 French troops on the Ebro. By early December the French were back in Madrid and Napoleon was planning the utter destruction of the British forces in Spain. On New Year's Day, while pursuing the British retreating towards Corunna, a courier galloped up to him with dispatches from Paris. Napoleon learnt that Austria was re-arming and that Fouché and Talleyrand were plotting together against him. That night he handed over command of the army to Soult and sped furiously back to Paris in bitter wintry weather.

At last, at the end of January 1809, Pauline heard through Grand Marshal Duroc that Napoleon had made provision for her to receive an annual income of six hundred thousand francs, as from the beginning of the year. In addition, she was given the château of Neuilly and its estate. Pauline was duly grateful for the money, though it was not nearly enough for her style of living and social responsibilities; at least, it made her independent of Borghese. And she was delighted with the château which was less than an hour's drive from her town house. It had been built in the neo-classical style in the middle of the previous century and stood in a vast park (most of which is now the modern suburb of Neuilly), but was close enough to the Seine for lawns to slope down from the rear of the château to the river bank. It had belonged to Murat and Caroline, but when Napoleon had 're-shuffled' his family and given Murat the throne of Naples left vacant by Joseph the château and estate had been ceded back to the French state, in other words to Napoleon. During their tenure, the Murats had added two wings and furnished the house in Empire style.

A month later, on 1 March, Napoleon made further financial arrangements for Pauline whereby her income for the year was increased to more than one million francs. In return she readily agreed to appear in public with Prince Borghese whenever he was in Paris on official business as governor-general; and quite likely she promised to be more discreet in her love affairs. She went to live at Neuilly in the spring, and with her new craze for making economies she gave orders for furniture and ornaments to be transferred from one house to the other. But when news reached her of Napoleon's victory at Eckmühl – he had taken the field against the Austrians in April – she celebrated by buying a dinner service and a small yacht costing twelve thousand francs which was kept moored on the Seine at Neuilly but never used by her.

The time came for Pauline to take a cure, which was becoming an annual summer event in her life, and she heard from her youngest brother, Jerome, that Aachen was an excellent watering-place. Jerome had married Princess Catherine of Württemberg two years previously and it was proving to be a happy union.[1] The Emperor had made Jerome King of Westphalia and he was taking his duties seriously. Madame Mère was going to Aachen; so was Louis, then living in Paris but apart from his wife. Pauline decided to join them, though after some hesitation. She had never been farther north than Paris in her life. But everyone seemed to be going to Aachen that year, it was obviously the fashionable spa, and it was nearer for news from the battlefields in Austria. Pauline had been greatly alarmed when reports reached her that Napoleon had been wounded at Regensburg (the hurt was in fact very slight), and after the murderous battle of Wagram he sent a special courier to tell her that he was safe.

When Pauline reached Aachen, the war against Austria was over and Napoleon was dictating terms to the other Emperor, Francis. The season at the spa was a merry one, with much dancing, card-playing for high stakes, intrigues and flirtations. Pauline found the waters very beneficial, so that with improved health and an abundance of pleasure she was in a happy mood. Neither the hypochondriac gloom of Louis (who had always been the sickly one of the family) nor the parsimonious attitude of Madame Mère (who, now sixty years of age, grumbled more than ever at rising prices as her own fortune increased) could dampen Pauline's spirits. She had plenty of admirers, of course, but either Napoleon's admonitions were still having effect or else no man succeeded in arousing her passions. One prominent visitor,

Beugnot, chief administrator of the Grand Duchy of Berg, wrote of Pauline: 'She had been followed to Aix-la-Chapelle [Aachen] and did not know whether to choose to perceive it; and there she found more than one adorer . . . She treated the matter with charming levity. At sight of her I said to myself, not without keen regret, "Happy are those still in the time of life when one is permitted to worship at such a shrine".'

Beugnot met Pauline at dinner at her mother's, where much of the conversation turned on the high cost of living. Letizia asked Beugnot how much he paid for various items, and to show how shrewd he was he gave abnormally low prices; whereupon Letizia requested him to obtain the items for her at the prices he paid. Pauline had been listening with amusement to Beugnot talking himself into her mother's trap, but she got him out of it by changing the conversation.

She and her mother stayed on at Aachen until well into October, and then left only because Napoleon returned to Paris and summoned his court and his family to Fontainebleau for three weeks of formal receptions and balls. He was in need of constant diversion, for he had returned from Austria with the firm intention of divorcing Josephine; but he had to prepare himself for the wrenching, heart-breaking announcement to the woman he had once loved passionately and for whom he still felt a deep affection. He had been driven to this momentous decision by reasons of State and his own over-riding ambitions. To ensure the hereditary succession he needed a son, for he realised that Joseph, his legal heir, would never be accepted by the French nation. And there was the annoying fact that the royal families of Europe regaded him as an upstart; but if he made a marriage alliance with one of the foremost royal houses . . .

Pauline just had time for a visit to Paris before the court gathered at Fontainebleau at the beginning of November. Everything was minutely regulated, as at the Tuileries; receptions held by Napoleon have been described as 'like military parades but with ladies present'. 'On both sides of the room there would be three rows of ladies in court dress, and behind them a line formed by the officers of the Emperor's household and those of the princesses'; then the generals in uniforms glittering with gold, the senators, the councillors of state, the ministers, all richly dressed, their breasts covered with the stars and ribbons that Europe offered us on its knees.' Napoleon would go round the room speaking only to the ladies, then depart followed by his household and leaving the guests to dance. Pauline attended court as little as possible; she found it infinitely boring. But now, at Fontainebleau, she received – like the other princesses and the high dignitaries – precise instructions regarding the etiquette to be observed and the social duties expected.

On one evening in the week the Emperor held a reception followed by music and cards. On two evenings plays were given, one being followed by a ball in Caroline's apartments, the other by one in Pauline's apartments. Certain days were fixed for hunting, guests being invited to accompany the hunt in carriages or on horseback, as they preferred. Napoleon went hunting not because he enjoyed the sport but because it was the regal thing to do. He and his entourage wore hunting-jackets in the Imperial colours, green laced with gold; but Josephine and the princesses had each adopted individual colours for their riding-habits and those of the ladies of their households – though very few, certainly not Pauline, intended to be seen on a horse. Josephine's colours were purple embroidered in gold; those of Hortense were blue and silver; of Caroline, pink and silver; and of Pauline, lilac and silver. The meet must have been a splendid sight: to the loveliness of the women, the fine physique and dashing bearing of Napoleon's marshals and aides, were added the vivid hues of the costumes, all against the background of the glorious autumnal tints of the forest.

The days were nevertheless a time of great strain for Napoleon, who could not bring himself to make the fatal announcement to Josephine. She, however, could hardly mistake the signs – Napoleon's reserve, the little time he spent with her, the closed doors between their two apartments. But he kept putting off the moment, and the person he turned to for comfort was Pauline. Nearly every evening he sought her companionship, and it must be supposed that he confided to her the step he was about to take – much to her satisfaction and probable delight. Pauline could understand his feelings and state of mind better than anyone; and who else could he turn to at this crisis in his private life? Joseph was in Madrid, with troubles enough of his own;

Lucien was at Frascati, as obdurate as ever; Louis was at hand, but far from being in hand, having put the interests of his Dutch subjects before those of Napoleon; and Jerome was fifteen years his junior. But in any case Pauline was the only one of his family with whom he could relax; she knew just the men and women and the kind of parties that gave him the most amusement and distraction. These small, intimate gatherings in Pauline's apartment started late in the evening and their lack of convention was a relief to all concerned.

Pauline had very soon understood a particular need of Napoleon's too, at a time when he was keeping apart from Josephine and yet was living at home, so to speak; and when his keen eye fell appreciatively on her plump, blonde lady-in-waiting from Turin, Christina Ghilini, she nodded with quiet satisfaction. Pauline was only too happy to be of some assistance to Napoleon after all he had done for her; normally there was so little that she could do. However, Napoleon did not have an easy conquest.

On the morning of 9 November he dashed off a note to Pauline:

> I am going hunting at twelve-thirty. Come along to the meet. Are you feeling well? The weather is lovely. It was a delightful time last evening, but was then spoilt by unexpected obstacles. What I suspected two days ago has proved true and I can see no means of getting round it. Afterwards there were many tears, and she said she wished to leave on Tuesday. Many promises exchanged, and we parted at midnight.
>
> I'm writing her a note. I don't want her to leave for a fortnight. Let me know what she said, and bring her to the meet.
>
> *Adieu, petite princesse.* I'm afraid she won't be very nice to you this morning.

Pauline, with her amoral outlook and permissive attitude to sex, could just not understand Christina's hesitations; and she dismissed the girl's scruples by telling her peremptorily that one never said 'no' to the Emperor. But he was no great lover and did not believe in wasting time on preliminaries; the breach had to be stormed at once and the whole business quickly dispatched. It was no way to woo a girl with romantic ideas.

Nevertheless Christina became Napoleon's mistress, but not until he was back in Paris. In late January 1810 she went to Turin to see her father and told him of the affair. He returned with her to Paris in the vain hope that the Emperor would marry her. By then, Napoleon had completed negotiations for his union with the Emperor Francis's daughter, Marie-Louise; he saw Christina again, but only to break off the affair.

Napoleon had been unable, while at Fontainebleau, to screw up enough courage to tell Josephine of his decision to obtain a divorce, and she had to wait until the court was back in the more familiar setting at the Tuileries to hear from his lips what she had realised was inevitable. On 15 December 1809 the Senate declared their marriage null, and next day Napoleon and Josephine read the prepared statements of dissolution in the presence of all available members of his family and a few high officials. This painful scene took place in the Emperor's study at the Tuileries. All were in full court dress: Pauline and her mother, Louis and Hortense, Jerome and his wife, Caroline, Cambacérès . . . Josephine broke down in the middle of reading her statement and Cambacérès had to finish it for her: '. . . The dissolution of my marriage will make no difference to my feelings . . . The Emperor will still find me his best friend . . . We are both proud of the sacrifice we are making for the good of the country . . .'

Pauline, despite her hatred of Josephine, could hardly help feeling sorry for her in this moment of triumph for her in-laws. But most of Pauline's emotions were for Napoleon, standing there with arms folded and his face twitching as he tried to master his feelings. She could imagine better than anyone present what he must be suffering.

During the next few months she did all she could, in her particular way, to help Napoleon. The ceremonies in connection with his marriage to Marie-Louise drew to Paris representatives of all the crowned heads and the nobility of Europe, and Napoleon was most eager that they should be entertained in impressive style. That winter of 1810 was the most glittering and festive that Paris had known for the past decade. The Comédie Française was in its heyday, with Napoleon's friend Talma as the brightest male star. The leaders of Paris society vied with one another to give the most original balls and receptions. Senator Count Marescalchi, who held the diplomatic sinecure of representing Napoleon, King of Italy, at the court of Napoleon, Emperor of the French, brought fancy-dress and masked balls back into fashion; several of those he gave at his mansion on the Champs Elysées numbered Napoleon among the masked guests. An even greater success was the 'Chessboard Ball' given during Carnival week. This was an idea of Caroline Murat's; the prettiest of the ladies-in-waiting took the part of pawns, but one of Pauline's ladies, Madame de Barral, was the red queen, while chamberlains and aides-de-camp of the Imperial households represented other chess pieces. As for Pauline, she gave ten grand balls or receptions at the Hôtel de Charost. Besides wishing to please her brother – and, after all, the large sums of money he had bestowed on her were not intended wholly for her personal establishment and enjoyment – Pauline's ambition was to excel all other hostesses in the splendour and elegance of her receptions. There can be no question that she achieved her purpose. Only the choicest and most elaborate dishes appeared at her table or buffet, served on gold or silver plates; the most fashionable orchestra of the day, Julien's, played at her dinners and dances; the chandeliers burnt more brightly than elsewhere; the conversation was more sparkling and amusing. As for herself, no other woman had such magnificent dresses or could appear equally graceful, and her jewels outshone those of visiting royalty. It was at this time that she wore one of her famous girdles, the one with false emeralds surrounded by real diamonds; it had cost her only 13,000 francs but looked to be worth a million. Everyone stared at it, fascinated, and women raved about it; Pauline laughed quietly to herself.

In private she performed several services for Napoleon, apart from facilitating his affair with Christina Ghilini. In preparation for the arrival of Marie-Louise at Compiègne, Pauline tried with the assistance of Hortense to teach Napoleon to waltz. But all their efforts were in vain. Pauline did succeed, however, in persuading him to employ a better tailor. 'Your clothes never fit properly,' she told him frankly. 'And why are you so obstinate about not wearing braces? Your breeches always look as if they are falling down.' Napoleon dutifully changed to Léger, who tailored for Joseph, Murat and other prominent figures.

Pauline was thoroughly enjoying all this social activity and the opportunities to shine as the leading hostess – until she heard that her husband was coming to stay at the Hôtel de Charost. He, like all Napoleon's relatives, had been instructed to be in Paris in good time to attend Court for the arrival of Marie-Louise and the wedding at the beginning of April. Pauline had not forgotten the indignities she had suffered – according to her version – while in Borghese's power at Turin. Now she was completely independent of him. She at once gave her household precise instructions about the arrangements during the Prince's stay. He would be given the first floor and she would move down to the ground floor; this and that furniture had to be removed from one room and put in another; the bathroom equipment had to be rearranged elsewhere. When Borghese arrived with his retinue she announced that she had no room for them and that she had rented a nearby house, at his expense, where his chamberlains, equerries and servants would have to lodge. He would have to pay, too, for all meals taken at her house; but she would graciously place a carriage and horses at his disposal.

The long-suffering prince accepted all this philosophically. Any intention he may have had of prolonging his stay in Paris after the Emperor's marriage was dismissed from his mind. But Pauline was taking no chances and she continued to plague and torment him, a process at which she was adept. She kept sending him messages to complain that he was making too much noise above her head and that it was bad for her nerves, until Borghese and his staff were creeping about on tiptoe. If he wished to see her, he had to give adequate notice. When the Emperor asked him one morning how the Princess was, he had to confess that he had not seen her since dinner the day before yesterday. She sent back one of his notes – the chief means of communicating with her – because it was addressed to 'Princess Borghese' instead of 'Her Imperial Highness the Princess Pauline'. Altogether Borghese must have felt like giving a great sigh of relief when Napoleon and Marie-Louise were married and he could return to Turin.

After the wedding Pauline became extremely busy with the

preparations for a grand fête she had decided to give at Neuilly in honour of the Emperor and his new Empress. She gathered round her artists and architects, musicians and dramatists, ballet-masters, designers, caterers and experts of all kinds. The planning went apace, money was no obstacle, and the outcome of it all was the most magnificent and elaborate open-air fête ever held since the grandiose days of the Monarchy. It was both a triumph and a disaster for Pauline.

She invited about five hundred people to Neuilly for the evening of 14 June.[2] The festivities opened with a one-act light opera specially composed by Henri Berton, *La Danse Interrompue*, which ended just as daylight was fading and the grounds were lit by hundreds of coloured lanterns hanging in the trees. At this point the Emperor and Empress made their appearance, and as they strolled through the gardens, followed at a respectful distance by the guests, orchestras concealed behind shrubs and judiciously spaced out one from the other played soft enchanting airs, statues came alive and descended gracefully from their pedestals to weave and dance before Their Majesties and scatter flowers in front of them, leading them towards a Temple of Hymen. From there they progressed to other artistically devised structures of woodwork and painted canvas, the last one being a model of the palace of Schönbrunn, Marie-Louise's summer home outside Vienna. On returning to the terrace, Napoleon gave a signal which started up a marvellous fireworks-display, the set piece being a Temple of Glory; and amidst it all, while the guests exclaimed in wonder, the celebrated lady tightrope-walker, Signorina Saqui, began her act on a high wire, a flaming torch in either hand. When everyone's senses had been thoroughly titillated, supper with five different menus was served on the lawns. While Their Majesties and some two hundred guests sat at table, two hundred and fifty less-favoured people ate standing at a buffet; and a cold meal was provided for the actors, musicians and men of the Foot Guards on duty. Dancing began at midnight and continued until dawn.

Pauline went to her bed tired out but with the warm congratulations of her guests ringing in her ears. The fête had been a triumph in the opinion of those present, was talked about for weeks and remembered for years. But for those who had not been present it was thought of as a terrible, almost a criminal, waste of money. Ugly rumours were soon circulating in Paris regarding the cost of Pauline's fête; the organiser of the fireworks-display alone was known to have been paid five thousand francs, and the total amount spent was generally put at one hundred thousand. This, people muttered, meant that in a few hours there had been expended a sum equal to the taxes paid by several provinces in a year, and all for the benefit of a privileged few; it was the way to ruin.

At this time, the summer of 1810, mounting taxation and increasing conscription were turning the nation against Napoleon. The people had had enough of war and were asking only if it would ever end, so that they could begin to benefit from the glorious conquests. Even the peasantry – the backbone of Napoleon's power – was becoming alienated; in the past six years nearly a million young farmers had been taken by conscription, many never to return. Instead of a balanced budget, there was now a deficit of fifty-seven million francs. The British blockade and Napoleon's embargo on British products were stultifying commerce and causing shortages and hardship – and also, of course, giving rise to a flourishing black market.

Napoleon was always highly sensitive to public opinion, and when he read police reports on the deplorable impression that Pauline's fête had made in Paris and beyond he quickly ordered her to repeat it for the benefit of four or five thousand representatives of the middle classes; the invitations were to be sent out by the municipal authorities.

There was still time to retrieve the situation to some extent. But Pauline, by her behaviour, completed the disastrous effect. She remained aloof from this second lot of guests, did not receive any of them in her salon, and provided no supper nor even refreshments. They could only walk about the grounds and view the bedraggled decorations. Men left in sullen anger, women in a fury, saying that they were being given the Court's leavings. For days afterwards, in shops and courtyards, tales of Pauline's reception were retailed at first- and second-hand. Her reputation was torn to shreds and old stories of her scandalous behaviour were revived. Some of this, inevitably, rubbed off on Napoleon.

Pauline was obviously at fault, but it would be unfair to

condemn her too harshly. The long preparations for the fête and the event itself must have tried her strength to the limit. She could rightly say that the second lot of guests were not there by her invitation, that they had been imposed upon her; and, her character being what it was, her natural reaction would be to demonstrate uncooperation. She may even have thought that she had spent enough money already.

The sudden accession to wealth and high position at an early age, and by no effort of her own, was beginning to ruin the goodness in her, the spontaneous gaiety and natural generosity. She was becoming too self-centred, too immersed in her own pleasures. But what else was there for this grass-widow caught up in the web of history?

Fortunately, she was about to be wrenched out of herself by another love affair even more passionate than the last.

Chapter 11

The galloping lover

In September 1810 the Court, including Pauline, was at Fontaine-bleau, and from there Napoleon directed affairs of state and pursued the war in Spain. His trusty chief-of-staff, Marshal Berthier, Prince of Wagram, was with him; and with Berthier was Captain Jules de Canouville, one of his four aides-de-camp. These young men were the military dandies of their day. Scented and corseted, they carried their toilet articles in their cartridge-boxes; in their splendid, colourful uniforms they were ready at a word from Berthier to lead a charge with gallantry, to take an enemy battery with impetuous dash, deliver a message across a bloody battlefield or ride five hundred leagues non-stop with important dispatches.

Jules de Canouville was outstanding in this small dedicated group. He came of an old Norman family, and at the age of seventeen had enlisted as a private in the Sixteenth Dragoons; six years later he had his captaincy, and now at twenty-five was on Berthier's staff with further promotion in sight – and further conquests of the fair sex. He was not the most handsome of men, having a hooked nose and a thick, sensual mouth, but his dark eyes had a burning, voluptuous look and his broad-shouldered, virile figure in a tight, gold-laced uniform could set women's hearts fluttering. He was said to have a sword and a spirit which commanded the respect of men, an eye and an energy which promised protection to women. To this kind of protection Pauline was never averse; he soon attracted her attention and before long they were madly in love.

It was indeed madness for Pauline to have an affair at Fontaine-bleau, right under Napoleon's nose and in a château where the etiquette observed and the great number of courtiers present made privacy almost impossible. Moreover, Canouville was well known for his indiscretions regarding his relations with women; he could never keep his boudoir triumphs to himself, and even this liaison with the Emperor's sister was no exception. Pauline returned his passion with ardour and sincerity, and she had no hesitation about acceding to his requests for some tangible proof of his triumph. Everyone at Court soon knew about the couple – except, apparently, Napoleon. On 22 October Canouville was made a Baron of the Empire, probably at the request of Pauline, but a fortnight later Napoleon was taking a very jaundiced view of the new Baron.

It was largely due to one of those tangible proofs that Canouville fell into disgrace. Napoleon had been presented with three magnificent sables by Tsar Alexander I after their meeting at Erfurt; he had kept one for himself, given one to Bernadotte's wife and the other to Pauline. Canouville saw her sable and gave a broad hint that it would set off his uniform very well. A short time later he was wearing it at a military review and his horse began to back towards the group of resplendent Marshals around the Emperor, in fact his mount's hindquarters barged into the flanks of Napoleon's mare. Canouville succeeded in mastering his high-spirited horse and regained his position among Berthier's staff officers; but Napoleon had recognised the sable. He was prompted to make a few enquiries and learnt what everyone else had known for some time. That same afternoon he took Pauline severely to task for her indiscreet conduct – or so it can be assumed, for she left Fontainebleau precipitately and in a huff. 'I am leaving tomorrow at eleven o'clock', says a note of hers dated 6 November. 'I shall be in Paris at four. My health obliges me to leave Fontainebleau.' And Canouville was given orders to leave instantly with dispatches for Masséna in Spain – perhaps Napoleon remembered how he himself had more than once got rid of an undesirable officer (because he desired the wife) by sending him off with urgent dispatches.

Canouville, burning to be back in Pauline's arms, rode the six hundred leagues to Salamanca at a gallop. But when he reached army base headquarters he learnt that communications with Masséna, then in Portugal, had been cut. The French were pressing Wellington back to the lines of Torres Vedras, through country stripped of food and shelter, and were being continually harassed by Spanish guerrillas. Masséna had had to detach half a brigade in order to make sure of getting a report back to

Napoleon. All this was explained to Canouville by General Thiébault at Salamanca, but the mud-splashed, begrimed captain could not bear the thought of waiting about for communications with Masséna to be re-established.

'My dispatches could go just as well with yours when you are able to send them,' Canouville proposed to Thiébault, an old social acquaintance. 'What impropriety would there be in my handing them to you?'

'I should not receive them,' replied the General.

'And if I left them on your desk?'

'Well, I should have to see that they were taken up. But you would not get any receipt for them. You would remain responsible, and I should report the matter.'

Canouville thereupon convinced himself that he would be taking important news to Paris if he returned at once to report that it was impossible to communicate with Masséna. Thiébault said that he had already reported the fact a dozen times to Berthier, and that it was ridiculous for Canouville to ride all that way only to get a severe rebuke. But Thiébault was past forty, he had lost the fire of youth and he was not in love with a beauty like Pauline. Canouville declared that for him an hour in Paris was worth a lifetime. He asked for a meal and a camp-bed, and next morning started back across northern Spain without a single escort.[1]

He had his hour in Paris, which probably extended to a night or two with Pauline – for what woman could resist such a lover, and would Pauline even want to? – but three weeks later he was back again in Salamanca, asking for his dispatches. He eventually got through to Masséna with them, but by then they were quite out-of-date – except for the instruction that Masséna was to keep Captain de Canouville with him until further orders.[2]

Meanwhile, in Paris, Pauline was complying with Napoleon's wishes that she should play a major part as a society hostess. Marie-Louise's confinement was due in the second half of March, and Napoleon wanted her to be diverted by constant entertainment; and then there were the receptions and festivities for the kings and princes who came to Paris for the birth and baptism. He particularly asked Pauline to organise, in addition to the weekly receptions she gave at her town house, a grand costume ball during Carnival week and to lead a quadrille at a ball at the Tuileries on the night of Mardi Gras. Napoleon knew that beauty and brilliance would attend her wherever she went. And she responded nobly; her loyalty to him – her only loyalty – remained unchanged despite the fact that she was pining for the lover from whom he had separated her.

Pauline was by now the only one of Napoleon's brothers and sisters still at his side and upon whom he felt he could still rely. Joseph and Jerome were serving him badly in their respective kingdoms; each seemed to think he was a real monarch instead of Napoleon's nominee and was inclined to act independently. Louis had so identified himself with his kingdom of Holland that he had abdicated rather than agree to its becoming part of the French Empire, and had gone to live in Bohemia. A month later, in August 1810, Lucien had sailed from Civita-Vecchia with his large family and household, bound for America; but a storm drove the ship into Malta, Lucien was made prisoner by the British, and was now living under household arrest in England. Elisa and Caroline were in different parts of Italy, each wrapped up in her own affairs, and in any case Napoleon had never expected much from them.

Between January and March 1811 Pauline entertained or was present at other people's entertainments on at least five nights every week. This all took a heavy toll of her limited strength, and it was not altogether love of ease that caused her to be carried from the Faubourg St Honoré to the Tuileries or elsewhere in her well-cushioned sedan-chair borne by two tall footmen in green livery. There were eight days of rehearsal for the quadrille at the Tuileries, and then Pauline scored another social triumph when she appeared in a tunic of gold-embroidered muslin with a small shield of golden scales over her bosom and a light helmet of burnished gold surmounted by ostrich feathers on her head, representing ancient Rome. She had golden bracelets set with cameos round her arms, and wore purple silk sandals with gold leg-bands which had a cameo affixed to each crossing of them; the ornament that held the shield to her bosom was the most magnificent cameo of the Borghese collection, the one representing Medusa dying. In one hand she carried a light lance embossed with gold and precious stones. This priceless figure moved slowly and languorously to her place in the quadrille, her white plumes undulating and shimmering in the polished surface of the gold helmet, while everyone looked on spellbound. When the quadrille ended a young woman representing Egeria presented Pauline with a magic mirror in which was depicted a happy and glorious destiny.

It seemed most appropriate; in these early months of 1811 everything was auguring well for Napoleon and his vast Empire, and his union with the most illustrious of European dynasties had put the keystone upon his self-confidence. The birth of a son on 20 March gave him the assurance of a dynasty of his own blood, and he exultingly exclaimed, 'Now begins the finest epoch of my reign.'

Pauline was almost as glad as Marie-Louise when the baby was born.[3] As soon as the baptism had taken place with great ceremony in Notre Dame, Pauline retired to Neuilly for a few weeks. On 25 June she set out for her annual cure, going again to Aix-la-Chapelle (Aachen). The weather was cold and wet; in fact the summer of 1811 was bad everywhere, with a consequent poor harvest that brought hard times to the rural population and increased the discontent. Pauline was more restless than usual. The house she had rented did not please her, so she had all the partitions taken down and the interior re-arranged to suit her wayward fancy. Then she moved to Spa, in the neighbouring province of Liège, and from there made a short visit to Antwerp to see Napoleon, who was inspecting the coastal fortifications of the Low Countries and introducing the new Empress to his Dutch and Flemish subjects. At last, in September, at some point in her restless journeyings, Pauline received the news she had been long waiting for and the lack of which had caused her to be irritable and peremptory to persons around her.[4] Canouville was back in Paris.

He had taken part in the battle of Fuentes de Oñoro on 5 May and been slightly wounded. A week later Masséna was relieved of his command and replaced by Marshal Marmont, Duke of Ragusa (he who had politely refused Napoleon's offer of Pauline's hand in marriage when on his staff in Italy). Canouville had seized upon the departure of Masséna to obtain permission to return to his duties as aide-de-camp to Berthier in Paris, and had galloped northwards like a courier carrying urgent dispatches.

He and Pauline were reunited at Neuilly in early October. The lovers resumed their frank and open intimacy; she was joyful at recovering her handsome and amusing Jules, and he was blind to everything save the happiness of being once more with his beautiful Paulette. Napoleon was still in the Low Countries and not expected back in Paris for some weeks. The two were immersed in their glamorous adventure for a whole month, living openly as man and wife and giving small, intimate parties at Neuilly with dancing to the music of Julien's orchestra. Many tales of their intimacy and indiscretion have been told and repeated in print, some true or partly so, most of them fabrications. As typical as any, and having no reason to be doubted, is the story of the dentist Bousquet who was called to Neuilly to extract one of Pauline's teeth.

When he was shown into the Princess's bedroom he found a young man lounging there in dressing-gown and with all the appearance of having just got up. Pauline drew back in fear as the dentist laid out his instruments, and the young man endeavoured to reassure her.

'For the past three nights you've suffered so much with that tooth that neither of us has had a wink of sleep. It can be taken out in a moment, and you'll be saved hours of agony.'

'Yes indeed, Your Highness,' Bousquet said to the young man, naturally taking him for Prince Borghese. 'And there will be no ill effects of any kind.'

'You see?' said Canouville (who the young man was, of course) to Pauline.

'It's easy for you to talk. I'd like to see you stand it.'

'All right, I'll have one out just to show you how easy it is.'

Canouville stepped across to the dentist and pointed to a tooth that was beginning to decay. Bousquet quickly extracted it, with no cry of pain from Canouville. Pauline was so touched by this proof of devotion that she overcame her fears and let the dentist operate on her.

When Bousquet was being shown out he told some members of the household that the Princess would now be free of pain and added: 'Her husband was most anxious about her. It will be a pleasure for me to recount what I have just witnessed, for they are indeed a model pair, which is rare in persons of such high degree.'

And off he went quite unaware of his mistake, while his remarks were rapidly repeated throughout the household, giving everyone a good laugh.

Pauline and Jules continued to throw discretion to the winds even after Napoleon returned to St Cloud. She must have known that Napoleon would be informed of her conduct, but by now she refused to be deprived of her lover for even a few nights. As for Canouville, he was infatuated and could no more impose a brake on his ardours with Pauline than on his impetuosity when leading a headlong charge. Inevitably, the blow fell from on high. One day at the end of November Berthier received the following instructions from Napoleon: 'Major Canouville is to report at Danzig and take up his duties with the Second Chasseur Regiment. His commission is at the War Ministry and I have already signed it. As from this date he ceases to be your aide-de-camp. Inform him that he is not to return to Paris on any pretext whatsoever, unless he has a direct order from you to do so.'

The soldier had to obey without question; the Princess took the edict with outward submission and inward despair, then began to use what influence she had to obtain Canouville a posting to another regiment or staff appointment that would bring him nearer to her. But the lovers were still hundreds of leagues apart, she in Paris and he in Danzig, when springtime came. Then Murat arrived in Paris and she seized the occasion to beg him to get Canouville appointed to his staff. Like other men, Murat could never refuse his lovely sister-in-law anything she asked, and he at once applied to Clarke, the Minister for War, for Canouville's services as aide-de-camp. The wary Minister knew the ground was hot where Canouville was concerned and so forwarded Murat's application direct to the Emperor. A cold reply came back through Berthier that 'it was not convenient to appoint Major de Canouville one of the aides-de-camp to the King of Naples'.

Pauline could do no more on her lover's behalf. By then Napoleon was at war with the Holy Alliance and in need of every soldier in his Empire able to bear arms. He led his Grand Army towards Russia and fatal consequences; and among the tens of thousands of soldiers from many countries was Jules de Canouville.

Pauline was heartsick and irritable; her amorous excesses had brought on the inevitable inflammation and she was suffering from other ills, real and imagined. Her mother became very worried about her condition. In June Pauline went to Aix-les-Bains and rented a house for the season. Women were predominant among the visitors and most of them were anxious about husbands, brothers or lovers with the armies of the Emperor in Spain or eastern Europe. Pauline received news of Napoleon through several channels, but from Jules she heard only irregularly and after long delays. At times she grew so disturbed when no word came from him that she sent a courier to the battle-front to gather news of him. She had given him a number of costly presents but all she had from him were a few locks of his hair, which she wore woven into a bracelet. In pain though she was, she dictated letters to the head of her Paris household giving details of a splendid dress-sword she wished to be made for Canouville. 'Above all, do not forget that the diamonds to ornament the hilt must be inserted in such a way that they can be easily removed or replaced as desired.'

Her thoughts were with Canouville but, true to her dominating instincts, she still craved for the visible admiration and attention of men. Sick or well, she could not exist without it. Fate was kind to her and provided two devoted slaves to dance attendance upon her during those long summer weeks of illness and anxiety spent by the shores of Lake Bourget.

Chapter 12

A double escort

Aix-les-Bains, or Aix-en-Savoie as it was then called, had never known such a brilliant summer season as that of 1812. The leaders of Empire society had decided that it was the place to frequent, and people of lesser prominence followed by the hundreds. Pauline's friend Laure wrote, 'In 1812 it was the smart thing to go and take the waters at Aix-en-Savoie . . . People crammed together, as many as twenty in one bedroom, but they were none the worse for it. . . .' Taking the waters had become a fashion, especially among the ladies; a fashion that the doctors supported and encouraged, for it meant good business for their profession. Medical knowledge of the properties and efficacy of the waters at different spas was in its infancy; in general, all the waters were good for all ills. As for society, it mattered not whether the waters of a particular spa were sulphurous or had a high magnesium content, were very warm or quite cold; the essential was to know that one would there meet everyone who mattered.

Pauline had spent a month at Aix after her escape from Turin in 1808 and was no doubt enchanted by the town's situation on a hillside overlooking Lake Bourget and backed by the 5,000-foot Mont Revard. The lovely lake sheltered by high wooded hills and mountains provided opportunities for interesting excursions by a means of transport much more comfortable for her than a jolting carriage or even a litter conveying her along a rough track. However, the local authorities were thrown into something of a panic on learning of the imminent arrival of the Emperor's sister, mother and other relatives, and the important personages who had decided to follow them. Aix was ill-prepared for sudden publicity and the influx of a great number of visitors. The Préfet wrote urgently to the mayor ordering all the rubbish and rubble to be cleared from the streets, and for the many beggars to be transported elsewhere. There was no clubhouse or suitable building for social gatherings in the vicinity of the baths, but something would have to be provided where the visitors could at least meet to gamble. Playing at dice or cards for high stakes was a major pastime of these idle people. In the event, gambling took place that season in a wooden structure in a kitchen-garden on the slope behind the baths.

Accommodation was severely limited, as evidenced by Laure Junot's description, but Pauline was handsomely lodged – through influence or by being first in the field – at the Villa Chevalley, a three-storey house with stabling, standing in its own grounds high above the town, yet only a short distance from the baths by a steep path. From its front windows there was a fine view of the lake and the range of hills rearing up from the opposite shore, while the back gave a sight of the dominating Mont Revard.[1] Later arrivals at the spa, in addition to Madame Mère and her half-brother, Cardinal Fesch (who shared lodgings as usual for economy's sake, even if they had not been obliged to do so by the scarcity), were Joseph's wife Julie, Queen of Spain, and her sister Désirée, now married to Bernadotte (who, as Crown Prince of Sweden, was about to betray Napoleon); Josephine was there too, also women of lesser rank but social prominence such as Madame de Rambuteau, the Duchess of Ragusa (Marmont's wife) and Madame de Sémonville. Men were in short supply.

Pauline followed her cure under the direction of Doctor Demaison, the Inspecteur des Thermes (Baths Superintendent), and a Doctor Buttini of Geneva who was called in for consultation. They decided that taking the baths and drinking the waters were not enough in her case, and prescribed a rigorous diet of soup without salt, and whey. They diagnosed an acute inflammation throughout the abdominal region, and recommended frequent application of leeches to the parts affected and daily bathing in whey. None of this treatment appeared to alleviate the poor patient's almost constant pain (some was probably due to it); so Jean-Nicolas Corvisart, Napoleon's favourite medical adviser, was summoned from Paris. He disagreed with the local doctors but otherwise seemed as baffled as they were. 'A series of rare complications', he wrote, 'has resulted in a condition that is a malady *sui generis*, of which I do not think the exact nature and limits are known. A thousand times unhappy is the Princess who suffers from it, and equally unfortunate are the physicians called in to attend so ambiguous a case.'

This was of little help to the Princess, who might well have done better to send all the doctors packing. Her own remedy was as good as any, which was complete rest and an admiring circle of men. She knew how to make illness become her. Visitors to the Villa Chevalley found her reclining on a chaise-longue in the garden, dressed in the most captivating of négligés. An English boudoir-cap with bows of pink ribbon rested on her dark hair. Her dressing-gown was of Indian muslin with open-work embroidery, bordered with pale-rose muslin and fastened with bows of similar material; the trimmings were of English point lace. 'In the midst of her muslins, laces and bows she looked as lovely as an angel.' Her conversation was almost exclusively concerned with her ills and the remedies prescribed for them, and in her uninhibited way she was most explicit about the kinds of medicine and the number of douches she took daily.

A favourite diversion was to have François-Joseph Talma, the greatest dramatic actor of the day, come and read or declaim parts from Shakespeare, Molière and Racine to her and a small group of friends. Pauline already knew Talma through Napoleon, who had long been an enthusiastic admirer of the great tragedian. When Napoleon had his meeting with the Tsar at Erfurt in 1808 he had taken the Comédie Française headed by Talma with him, and so kept a promise to the actor that he would one day perform before 'a parterre of kings'. Talma was acting at Chambéry during the summer of 1812 and taking advantage of the proximity of Aix to drink the waters there – and to be invited to join the circles of high society there in force. He loved grandeur and had a romantic mind; although almost fifty years of age, he aimed to play the great lover off stage as well as on, and he became deeply enamoured of Pauline. He had an unbounded hero-worship of Napoleon (that nothing ever weakened, not even Waterloo), and this extended in some degree to most of the Emperor's family.

Another man often in attendance on Pauline was of very different character and calibre. Antoine Duchand was a handsome young artillery officer who had been severely wounded at the siege of Valencia the previous year. He belonged to a Grenoble family of financiers, and after partly recovering from his wounds at home had come to Aix to convalesce. His attentions to the ailing princess were so assiduous that gossip accused him of guarding her like a sentinel. In her then state of health, even the most malignant gossip could hardly infer that his guard was more pressing. But Pauline responded to his undisguised admiration; as her strength returned and she was able to walk out a little, it was on his arm that she leaned, her dainty hand tucked under his blue dolman.

In late August Doctor Corvisart sent from Paris a report on Pauline's health which recommended that she should spend the winter in the south of France. 'Residence in a mild and warm climate throughout the winter is indispensable for the renewal of Her Imperial Highness's health', he wrote. 'She should remain there until the spring of 1813. Permission to do this should be asked for at once.' The mere prospect had a beneficial effect upon her. She at once sent off a request to the Emperor, though she was firmly resolved to go whatever the answer. 'I cannot disregard this advice of my doctors,' she said, as it suited her.

Her health improved and she began to go out more. One day in early September she organised an excursion to the abbey of Hautecombe on the other side of the lake. It was originally a Cistercian monastery, and had been the burial place of the House of Savoy until 1731. There were twenty people in the party, including Colonel Duchand in full dress uniform, Talma, the Duchesse d'Abrantès and her current lover, Maurice de Balincourt. They gathered at the little lakeside harbour of Aix to be rowed across in several boats. Pauline, as often happened, was late in arriving. But when she did join the others, being carried down in her chair, she presented a pretty picture in a daring polonaise with a richly-embroidered underskirt trimmed with fine Valenciennes lace, and wearing an Italian straw hat with three gorgeous scarlet plumes and ribbons to match.[2]

Pauline and her party had an alfresco lunch and then visited the abbey. They returned to the boats in the early evening to cross the lake again. It had been a successful day, and as the boats glided slowly through the water, the only sound being the dipping of the oars, the setting sun gave a brilliance to the white stone outcrops on the heights of Mont Revard; the lake became streaked

with milky shadows as daylight faded, and then the yellow globe
of the moon slowly rose above the mountain crest. Pauline was in
one of her romantic moods – the impulse behind her arranging
the outing. She saw Laure and Maurice holding hands, and her
own soft fingers stole out in search of a hand . . . Talma's or
Duchand's?

Talma left Aix six days after the excursion to Hautecombe as
he had engagements to keep in Geneva and Lyons. Only a
day later he wrote the first of a series of passionate letters to
Pauline:

> I have left you at last, my love, and am now separated from
> you for a long time . . . I set out at daybreak yesterday and
> looked up at your windows for the last time. Tears came and
> sobs choked me as I sent you from afar the tenderest hopes and
> wishes for your health and happiness. There were multitudes
> waiting here to see me, but these tributes of public interest
> and regard, of which I should once have been so proud, touch
> me not at all now. Their only value in my eyes is that they might
> make me more worthy of your affection . . . If you do not write
> to me, my heart will be plunged into despair and I shall believe
> you have forgotten me. I promised you that I would destroy
> all your letters, and I repeat that pledge.

Similar burning, declamatory letters reached Pauline at almost
daily intervals. Talma sent them poste restante addressed to
'Mademoiselle Sophie' and they were collected by Pauline's
majordomo, Ferrand. What did Pauline think of their ardent,
dramatised phrases?

> I have been overwhelmed with visits and invitations but
> have escaped from them as much as I could [wrote Talma],
> for they only increase my torment. I want only to be alone with
> memories of the happy hours spent with you, of all your tender-
> ness and goodness. . . .
> I am conscious of but one event in my existence – the moment
> you thought me worthy of your affection, the moment when
> I knew my destiny was to live for you alone. . . .

And much more in the same strain. Then he at last received a letter from Pauline and went into raptures:

> Oh my dear one, what horrible anxiety you have dispelled! All yesterday I was beside myself, and then – your letter arrived at 8 p.m. My dear one, your charming, tender letter touched me to the heart. Words cannot depict the emotion, the joy I felt when I read that you had wept while reading my letter. Yes, my dear one, I shall obey you; yes, I respect the weakness and the suffering that you are still experiencing. It is a horrible sacrifice that I make for you, but it is enough for me that such is your will ... My Pauline – for I need to call you by so sweet a name – I prostrate myself at your feet . . . On my knees, I beg you to let me come to you for a single hour.

A week or so later he began to get a little desperate:

> Pauline, you do not know the depths of my love for you nor what wounds you have inflicted on my heart . . . I know you are going to leave on the 6th, but I had to learn of it from others. Pauline, you are leaving and I shall never see you again! Was there ever a fate like mine? Will you not write to me at Lyons? My God, how unhappy I am!

Nevertheless he kept up the exhortations and started asking her for souvenirs, first for a length of Madras that she had worn, 'to put round my neck in the mornings', then for a bust of her ('I shall give you no peace until it is sent me'), and later for a boat, one of the light skiffs that Pauline kept on the lake at Neuilly: 'Give me authority to take one of your boats. As I am going to shut myself up in my country house it would give me great pleasure to have this boat as a present from you.'

He was still writing to Pauline at the end of the year, when he was back in Paris and she was in the south of France. By then, his letters had taken a still different turn. In one dated 23 December 1812, when he was considering retiring from the stage after a quarrel with a dramatic critic, he wrote:

> . . . It would be assuming too much to believe that my annual salary will be continued. But one of my friends has

offered me a share in one of those licences which the government grants for the exportation of goods to England. He has
just lodged an application for one with the Minister of Commerce and Manufactures, but although well backed it needs
to be even more so, in order to make success certain . . . You
would not refuse to assist me . . . The thing to do, then, is for
you to be so extremely kind as to write to the Minister strongly
recommending Monsieur Marguerite, merchant of Le Havre,
and saying that you take a special interest in the success of his
application . . . But, my dear one, there is no time to be lost,
for the matter is already in hand . . . Perhaps it is indiscreet
to ask this of you at a time when you are not equal to taking
thought for the troubles of others; but, dear and loving friend,
to whom shall I turn if not to her who has shown such kindness
to me, to whom it would be so sweet to owe all?

However, Talma did not leave the Comédie Française, so this
matter of an export licence was not pursued. Instead he wrote
offering his service as agent, having learnt that Pauline was
thinking of buying the château of Petit Bourg. 'From the
information I have obtained, I think it would suit you to perfection. Would you like me to go and see it and report on it?'

Pauline sent her man of business, Michelot, to look at the
château, but Talma went too and then sent her a detailed report
which ended, 'For myself, I desire it from the bottom of my
heart, as I might hope to spend a good part of my life not far
from you.'

Pauline never bought the château, and even if she had no one
who knew her well would have imagined her living there, or
anywhere else, for very long.

In another letter Talma offered to carry out commissions for
her. 'I have seen some very good watches set with fine pearls for
seven louis – really very cheap.'

Pauline must have been highly amused by these letters, to
which she never replied; nor, apparently, did she show them or
mention them to any of her friends such as Laure. Memoir-
writers of the time, never hesitant to add to the number of
Pauline's lovers, did not include Talma among them. His letters
remained unknown for one hundred years, until Talma's copies

of them were discovered in the Bibliothèque Mazarin to which they had been bequeathed by Talma's friend, the dramatist Pierre Lebrun, and were published. Modern French biographers of Pauline have seized upon them as evidence of yet another lover in her life, and even Carlton, the one biographer of her in English, made a rare error of judgment in believing that Talma's passion was reciprocated.[3] For surely these are not the letters of one of a pair of lovers. They are not even the work of a man truly in love. And work they were, for Talma drafted each letter several times; four rough drafts exist of one letter dated 25 October 1812 from Lyons. He polished his phrases, dramatised the situation, studied the niceties of words to strike the imagination and 'make the tears flow from his dear one's eyes'. If tears flowed from Pauline's eyes they were due to helpless laughter.

During the time that Talma was at Aix Pauline was in no state of health to take a lover. Moreover, she was becoming increasingly worried at not hearing from Canouville. This did not mean that Pauline placed great importance on being faithful in love, far from it; but the anxiety added to her ills. Poor Talma's role was to restore her spirits, to remind her of more interesting attachments than the adoration of an elderly actor. And, with feminine wile, she played off the ageing tragedian against the youthful colonel. It was Duchand's hand that she held in the dusk on the return journey from Hautecombe – Duchand, an army officer like Canouville and who was only thirty-two, the same age as herself. And it was Duchand who followed her south when she finally left Aix-les-Bains. But by then she was in a deplorable state. News of Canouville had at last reached her. He was dead.

Canouville had been killed at the battle of the Moskova. A miniature of Pauline was found on his breast, under his uniform, by a brother officer who tactfully gave it to Murat. He eventually returned it to Pauline.

At first no one dared tell Pauline that her lover had fallen in battle. Word of his death had reached Paris on 27 September, at the same time as the news of the taking of Moscow. One of Napoleon's equerries sent a message to the head of Pauline's Paris household, but it was not passed on. Pauline read of Jules's death some time in October, in a newspaper which a kind soul sent her.

'The frightful news is known now,' her majordomo Ferrand wrote from Aix on 25 October, '. . . and it will be a long time before anyone can speak to her of her grievous loss. She weeps continuously, eats scarcely a thing, and is obviously endangering her health. My only hope is that the approaching journey may do something to ease her grief.'

Pauline eventually left Aix at the end of October, crossed a rough and stormy Lake Bourget and journeyed down the Rhône to Lyons, as she had done before, and there stayed for a few days with Cardinal Fesch; then she continued on her way to the Mediterranean.

Nine days before she left Aix, Napoleon had begun his retreat from Moscow. Four days before, an attempt to overthrow the government and seize power in Paris had almost succeeded.

Pauline arrived at Hyères on 3 December and was soon joined by Duchand. He was obviously devoted to her, for she was still in a poor state physically and morally.

'This journey has been insupportable', wrote one of the ladies of her household. 'Her health is unchanged. She has been here four days and is no better. She tried her milk diet again but it did not agree with her, so she is now taking only soup. The pains are severe, and blisters have again been applied. It is most distressing. May God help us!'

On 18 December Napoleon arrived back in Paris, having handed over command of the remnants of the Grand Army to Murat, and published a communiqué giving full details of the terrible losses. It is doubtful whether Pauline learnt how badly things were going for Napoleon until she received a letter from her mother (who wrote fairly regularly to Pauline but complained of never receiving a letter in return). Madame Mère was writing round to all the family, urging everyone to demonstrate solidarity with Napoleon in this time of misfortune, to revive the clan spirit. 'I should have thought you would have written to the Emperor as soon as you were able,' she scolded Pauline. 'If you have not yet done so, I urge you not to put off this duty any longer.'

Pauline did write, but seems to have been more concerned about her own health than her brother's troubles, for in a letter to her at the end of January Napoleon said: 'I have your letter of 20 January, and am distressed to learn how bad your health is. You would have done better to come to Paris than to have allowed yourself to be sent from place to place by doctors who hope to do you good. You would have done better to go to Nice than to Hyères. I see no objection to your going to that town.'

Duchand had just said farewell to Pauline; he was fit again and the army had need of him. Whether he received his recompense before departure, one does not know; but Pauline had been faithful to Canouville's memory for long enough. In any case, she and Duchand were not parting for ever, so far as they knew; and when he had left, Pauline became increasingly restless and discontented. She decided to go to Nice, where she had recovered her spirits and her health five years before, and her chamberlain, Clermont-Tonnerre, was suddenly kept very busy making arrangements. He had arrived from Paris almost at the same time as a new physician for Pauline – Doctor Espiaud, who had been recommended by Madame Mère and approved of by Corvisart. By now Pauline had most of her official household around her, and proceeded to put them all to great trouble by preferring to travel to Nice by sea. It was, however, the simplest way – when one was the Emperor's sister and could obtain the use of a naval frigate. She and her retinue embarked at Toulon and two days later, on 8 February, reached Nice.

A large villa had been rented for Pauline, a different one from the previous stay, and once installed she began to make the lives of her attendants a positive misery, as she usually did when in ill-health and bored. But this time her efforts extended to pestering her retainers elsewhere, at Montgobert and Neuilly, with niggling instructions: flowering shrubs were to be brought from Montgobert for the gardens of the Hôtel de Charost; the birds at Neuilly must be protected, no shooting was allowed and cats had to be driven from the grounds. Letters poured forth, to her stewards and gardeners, to suppliers and jewellers too.[4] But it was her ladies-in-waiting who had to write them. At the same time as she ordered two strings of pearls at fifty thousand francs each she was making economies – in her manner. Madame de Cavour, still patiently in attendance, complained in a letter to the head steward at the Hôtel de Charost: 'It is bad enough to be employed all day as a secretary; I ought not to have to provide the stationery. The amount of writing I have to do for the Princess is simply enormous. Please send me a large box of writing paper, quill pens, Spanish wax, wafers, envelopes, etc.' Pauline reduced the size of her household – the secretary was obviously one of the first to go – and lowered the salaries of those remaining. 'Anyone who complains can leave too,' she said sharply. But she was only scraping at the problem: she still had enormous expenses, and her chief source of revenue – Napoleon and his civil list – had almost dried up.

Chapter 13

Into exile

Pauline spent the summer of 1813 – a disastrous year for Napoleon – among the high craggy hills of Upper Provence. She left Nice early in May, going by sea to Fréjus and then being carried in a litter inland, past Draguignan to Gréoux, where she had benefited so much from the relaxing climate six years before and which held such happy memories for her. This slow overland journey of about sixty miles, up hill and down dale, took her through a countryside she was very fond of; the winding tracks found a way from one hilltop village to the next, past vineyards and olive-groves, with a few fields in the bowls formed by encircling hills. The villagers must have stared hard at the lumbering procession as it passed through the narrow streets or perhaps halted for a while in the little tree-lined square with its running fountain: the Princess in her litter, with some local officials and notables walking in attendance on either side; the baggage carts, a few carriages, and some horses being led by grooms. It was not often that such diverting sights broke the monotony of the days in these remote villages.[1]

At Gréoux Pauline stayed at the same hotel as before. She had very few staff with her, and engaged maids and other servants from the local population. It is doubtful whether she visited her pavilion in the woods; Pauline was not inclined to sentimentalise over the past. The rest and the quiet did her a lot of good; probably the waters of Gréoux did too – at least she believed they did, which was the next best thing. The news she received, chiefly from her mother, about distant events was not reassuring. Joseph was back from Spain, having lost his kingdom and much else. In Germany, while Napoleon was winning one battle his generals were losing four. But even if Pauline had been fully aware of the dangers threatening Napoleon's power, of the checks in policy and defeats in battle that he suffered in 1813, their significance would probably have escaped her. Although she was always greatly concerned about Napoleon's safety when he was in the field, she never doubted that his political and military genius would triumph. Why should she?

Despite the peace and beauty of the countryside around Gréoux, Pauline was bored. And this bored idleness caused her to dwell far too much upon her ailments; she was in danger of becoming a hypochondriac. Ignoring Napoleon's other preoccupations, she wrote to him in late August about her health and her desire to spend another winter by the Mediterranean. Her doctor, Espiaud, was baffled by her illness but had acquired an influence over her and was insisting on a return to Nice for the winter. He was probably thinking of himself too – if the Princess went to Paris, as her mother and Napoleon were urging her to do, he would become subordinate to Corvisart or other eminent physicians. Napoleon replied from Dresden after his victory there: 'I have received your letter and see with regret that your bad health continues, and can only agree with the advice given by your physicians. I approve of your staying in whatever place promises you a quick recovery and an early return to Paris.' Pauline clinched the matter by declaring that anyone who tried to prevent her going to Nice simply desired her early death.

Beneath her maddening, capricious character there were those qualities of generosity and kindness which frequently suddenly emerged when least expected. Impelled by no known reason, but sensing that Napoleon was in financial difficulties, she sent some of her finest jewels to Paris with instructions to sell, and then offered the sum raised – some three hundred thousand francs – to Napoleon. It was the only way in which she could help him. Her letter bearing the offer reached Napoleon just after the holocaust of Leipzig, which left him hopelessly outnumbered and almost surrounded by the forces of the Coalition. On 26 October, while withdrawing his shattered army towards the Rhine, hotly pursued by Blücher, he found time to compose an optimistic reply to Pauline:

My dear sister, I have received your letter of 13 October. My expenses have been considerable this year and will be even greater during the coming one. I accept the gift you wish to make me, though such is the goodwill and the resources of my people that I think the means are assured for meeting the enormous expenditure that the campaigns of 1814 and 1815 will require, whatever the outcome of events. If this European coalition against France continues further and I have not obtained the successes I have every right to expect from the bravery and patriotism of the French, then I will make use of your gift and of all those that my subjects care to make me.

This letter reached Pauline after she had left Gréoux for Nice. Before leaving she had distributed presents to the local people who had looked after her and been of service to her, as she usually did after a prolonged stay in a place. These were mostly valuable and tasteful presents, like the one given to her chamber-maid who was also called Pauline – a needle-case of Sèvres porcelain, gold mounted, with the bust of a woman wearing a sprig of flowers on the lid, and the words *'Pour l'Honneur et l'Amour'*.[2]

When at Nice, Pauline received several letters from her mother urging her to leave that area, as the rapid deterioration in Napoleon's military situation made it 'likely to be overrun by the enemy'. But Pauline took no notice; either the war seemed too remote or she was so low in spirit that it was impossible for her to make up her mind – which she never found easy to do at the best of times.

Napoleon had rejected a peace offer by the Allies: the condition that France return to her boundaries of 1791 was shameful and dishonourable in his eyes. Enemy forces closed in from the north, the east and the south-west. For two months, February and March, with only fifty thousand men, Napoleon repeatedly defeated much larger forces marching on Paris. But the French had had enough. The marshals and the politicians deserted the Emperor and made terms with his enemies. Marmont opened the gates of Paris; Talleyrand formed a provisional government which declared that Napoleon had ceased to reign. On 6 April 1814 he abdicated.

In mid-March, as Lyons was occupied by Austrian troops, Nice had been cut off from communications with Paris. Letters, newspapers and visitors ceased to arrive. A British warship, the *Curaçao*, sailed into the harbour. However, Pauline was now set in her ways, and, seemingly indifferent to all else, prepared to

go and take the waters at Gréoux again. She left Nice at the end
of March and went by sea to Fréjus, as before; two or three days
after landing, she was at Le Cannet, a village two miles east of
Le Luc, and there news reached her of the Emperor's downfall.

At once, she snapped out of the indolent mood and general
lethargy which had been weighing her down for so long. Perhaps
it was the suddenness of this crisis in her life, perhaps it was that
hard core in her complex character which she only revealed in
moments of real stress; there was certainly her loyalty to
Napoleon. In any case, at a time when Napoleon was at a low ebb
she rose to the occasion with unexpected courage and dignity.
All thoughts of self vanished. Instead of proceeding to Gréoux,
she decided to stay where she was on learning that Napoleon
would pass through Le Luc on his way to Fréjus to take ship for
Elba.

She was in a house called Bouillidou, a large farmhouse amid
cypress and olive-groves which was rented by Monsieur Charles,
the postmaster at Le Luc and an old acquaintance of the Bonaparte
family. When he heard of her intention to stay on and await
Napoleon's coming, he vacated the house for her.[3] News reached
her from her mother and Fesch that they were on their way to
Rome by way of Lyons and the Mont Cenis. A letter arrived from
Bacciochi, Elisa's husband, then in Marseilles, proposing that
Pauline should accompany him to Rome. Pauline could easily
have gone to Rome to live; despite her differences with Borghese,
she was still an Italian princess.

'The Emperor will shortly pass through here, and I wish to see
him and offer my sympathy,' she replied to Bacciochi. 'If he will
permit me to follow him, I will never leave him. If he refuses,
I will then go to Naples. I have not loved him because he was a
Sovereign, but because he is my brother.'

Napoleon arrived at Bouillidou on the afternoon of 26 April,
accompanied by a few senior officers who had remained loyal
to him and were going to share his exile and by four commissioners of the Allies whose task was to watch over him. During
the journey through the Royalist south, Napoleon had been
threatened by hostile crowds, and after a particularly nasty
incident at Orgon he had put on an Austrian uniform and a
Russian cloak – borrowed from the commissioners – to avoid

being recognised. It was in this garb that he greeted Pauline. She refused to embrace him until he had changed into his French Guards uniform. Then she threw herself into his arms, weeping.

After all the betrayals and desertions of the past few months, this evidence of Pauline's love and her devotion to him must have been balm to his tortured mind.[4] They spent four hours together in private – talking of what? No one knows; any reconstruction of the gist of their conversation is pure supposition. But they would have talked about money, as anyone would in such a sudden change of circumstances – much more sudden for Pauline than for Napoleon. He had left huge debts behind as Emperor, but still possessed a very large fortune in his own name.[5] She was in debt and had little income, but her jewels were of great value (these extravagant purchases were now proving to be wise investments) and she owned property worth several millions. Napoleon would have advised her to sell Neuilly and her town mansion before they were sequestrated by the Bourbon government. The two would have talked about the future – they did in fact, for next morning Napoleon dashed off a note to the British commissioner, Colonel Sir Neil Campbell: 'Princess Pauline, sister of the Emperor, wishes to go to Elba, but owing to ill-health cannot leave for five or six days. His Majesty requests that an English frigate be ordered to take her to the island.'

Napoleon stayed the night at Bouillidou and continued his journey next day. On 28 April, he went aboard the frigate *Undaunted,* captained by Thomas Ussher, and was received with military honours and a salute of twenty-one guns. Five days later Napoleon landed on Elba.

Pauline remained at Bouillidou for three weeks, and recovered much of her energy and old spirits. She may even have welcomed the sudden turn of events. Previously she had been sinking into a useless, vain existence; now there was a purpose in life again – and Duchand had returned to her. He had fought bravely at Bautzen and had been created a Baron of the Empire after Leipzig, where he had rushed up his guns and repulsed an attack by superior forces. Now, the fighting over, he turned up at Bouillidou a day or two after Napoleon had left, and became Pauline's confidant as well as her lover. He proved to be a true friend as well, and offered to go to Paris on her behalf. His financial background enabled him to give her good advice, and when he left on 15 May he had her power of attorney to sell her properties and other effects, also a letter to her representatives in Paris telling them to 'listen to him as though he were myself . . . he is my only friend'.

A few days later, Pauline left France – but bound for Naples, not Elba. However, she had first to decide which ship she would take. It would surely have happened to no one but Pauline: three ships were waiting for her to go aboard. The commander of the *Curaçao*, Captain Tower, had offered the services of his ship; he was an admirer of Napoleon and, now, of Pauline too, having paid his respects to her before she had left Nice; Colonel Campbell had probably passed on to him the contents of Napoleon's note. The *Undaunted* had returned from Elba for her, at the request of Napoleon. And Murat had sent the frigate *Laetitia* from Naples.

Pauline chose to sail in the *Laetitia*, which put to sea from St Raphaël on 19 May. She thought she was seeing the last of France, of Provence, for a long time, perhaps for ever, but one of those sudden Mediterranean storms sprang up, she became very seasick, and the *Laetitia* put in at Villefranche to wait for calmer weather. She sailed again on 30 May. On the afternoon of the third day out, the Neapolitan frigate rounded a long headland, tacked across a bay and dropped anchor in the almost land-locked harbour of Portoferraio, the little capital of the island of Elba.

There has always been some mystery about Pauline's journey. Why, having expressed her determination to join Napoleon on Elba and received his agreement, did she take ship for Naples – to join Murat, one of Napoleon's betrayers? Why, having apparently changed her mind and abandoned Napoleon, did she allow the *Laetitia* to put in to Portoferraio? Some writers have explained the latter by saying that the frigate was forced to take shelter from a storm. But it would be most unusual for another storm to blow up in those waters at that time of year; and even if one had, there were other harbours much less difficult for a sailing-ship to make in rough weather.

When Napoleon and Pauline had discussed the future, that evening alone together at Bouillidou, the name of Murat would have come into their conversation. He had abandoned Napoleon, but if he had taken the field in support of him it would have made little or no difference to the final outcome. As it was, Murat still held a large bridgehead and an army in Europe for the Napoleonic cause – if that had a future. Napoleon was a realist; if he could not forgive Murat, he could make use of him. Moreover, Napoleon feared being forcibly taken from Elba, where he would be defenceless (at the time, 26 April, the few hundred soldiers to form his guard, as allowed in the Treaty of Fontainebleau, were still marching across France under command of General Cambronne and had hardly reached Lyons); but warships and troops from Naples could arrive at Elba in a couple of days. For one reason and another, it would be good policy to be assured of Murat's support in the future – and Pauline was the best person to act as Napoleon's emissary, for she and Murat had remained friends and it was to her that Murat had written in March to explain the reasons for his conduct and hinting that he could be called on if needed. He had thought that Napoleon might make peace with the Allies, but had never expected him to abdicate.[6] However, no plans could be made at the time, and Napoleon had left Bouillidou for Elba fully expecting Pauline to join him there. But in the meantime the *Laetitia* arrived at St Raphaël – in other words, there were communications between Murat and Pauline. And, knowing what was in Napoleon's mind, she decided to go to Naples there and then; though she would first want to see Napoleon, to get instructions from him and to inform him of the latest communication from Murat.

Admittedly, this is chiefly supposition. Pauline could have changed her mind – never very difficult for her – but it is scarcely conceivable that she would have gone to Elba just to tell Napoleon so, after her expressions of loyalty and affection, knowing that he had been neglected by every other member of his family. Equally discreditable is the explanation that the *Laetitia*'s arrival off Portoferraio was fortuitous. The frigate did not just shelter behind the headland; she sailed boldly round into the harbour flying the Neapolitan flag and was greeted with a salute of twenty-one guns which she returned round for round. And Pauline went ashore to stay the night and all the following day at Portoferraio.

Jerome Bonaparte presents his bride, Princess Frederica Catherine of Württemberg, to the Bonaparte family

by J. B. Regnault

The Comte de Forbin

from a sketch by Ingres (1812)

Napoleon was away visiting another part of the island when he heard the rumble of a gun-salute. An hour or so later he rode his horse down to the shore of the bay, found a boat to take him across to Portoferraio, and went aboard the *Laetitia*. A few moments later, brother and sister were greeting each other affectionately. When they stepped ashore, at about seven in the evening, a large crowd was gathered along the quayside to cheer them. Some Elbans mistakenly raised the cry, 'Long live the Empress!' – taking Pauline for Marie-Louise, whom Napoleon was expecting to come to Elba and whose forthcoming arrival he had announced to his new subjects.

The two were driven in an open barouche up to the heights above the town where Napoleon's residence, the Casa dei Mulini, stood on a cliff a hundred feet above the sea. The house was still being repaired and extended, and had scaffolding all round it, but Napoleon had taken up his quarters there with his small staff (moving from cramped accommodation at the town hall), though the habitable rooms were as yet sparsely furnished. Napoleon gave up his bedroom to Pauline and slept on his camp-bed in an adjoining room. It was a far cry from St Cloud and the Hôtel de Charost.

Next day, a hot, sultry wind, the sirocco, was blowing; and the sun beat down on the Mulini in its exposed position.

'You can't stay here,' Pauline declared to her brother. 'There must be some place in the mountains or in the woods where it would be cooler for you to live in the summer.'

Napoleon looked at her. She was wearing nothing but a diaphanous dress over her naked body, and stood fanning herself quite indifferent to the sidelong glances of some of Napoleon's household.

'Yes, I known of a place about four miles from here, in the woods of San Martino,' he replied. 'There's a barn and land that the owner's prepared to sell. I've already had an architect make an estimate for converting the barn into a summer villa. Including purchase, the cost would amount to nearly two hundred thousand francs. But the whole of the island's revenues for a year come to little more than that. And I have my troops and my household to pay, apart from anything else.'

Later in the day Pauline was alone with General Count

Bertrand, who had been grand marshal of the palace at the Tuileries and was now Napoleon's 'Minister of the Interior'. His loyalty to Napoleon went back seventeen years, and was to last until the end.

Pauline was carrying one of her jewel-caskets. She took out a cluster of diamonds and gave it to Bertrand. 'There, that should buy the San Martino property, and pay the architect and the builder.'

That evening Pauline went aboard the *Laetitia* again. Napoleon accompanied her to the jetty, where she said farewell, kissing his hand and embracing him. Whether she was the bearer of secret messages from Napoleon to Murat, pardoning him for his past betrayal and warning him to be ready for an attempt by Napoleon to regain his throne, is a matter for conjecture; but several writers have argued in support of such a thesis, Louis XVIII's head of police was inclined towards it, and later events tend to give it credence. In any case, Pauline promised to return to share her brother's exile on Elba.

Murat and Caroline gave Pauline a friendly welcome and put at her disposal the Villa Favorita, by the sea at Portici, near Herculaneum. She was soon comfortably settled in, but with a very reduced number of personal attendants. Only one of her previous household had followed her into exile – Madame Ducluzel, who had been with her for at least seven years and was her housekeeper at Gréoux; she was now promoted lady-in-waiting, which meant lady of all work. Pauline's circumstances were very reduced too, and she was seized by fear of poverty. Of course she was not poor, but wealth is a relative term; for seventeen years she had been able to indulge her every whim without thought for the cost, and had known that Napoleon was in the background to extricate her from any real difficulty. However, Pauline faced up to the situation with new-found energy. She sold some diamonds to obtain ready money. She wrote to her agents and to Duchand in Paris, pressing for a quick sale of her properties. And she remembered that she had a rich husband with legal obligations towards her.

But first she wrote to her mother in Rome (Madame Mère and Cardinal Fesch had arrived there at the end of May and, the

Pope having given them permission to stay, had taken up residence again in the Palazzo Falconieri):

I have suffered so much that I need to recover near you, dear Mama. Tell me when you intend to join the Emperor on Elba. He seems to desire that very much, and bade me tell you so. I hear with sorrow that Elisa has been to Vienna. Yet she wrote the Emperor that she wished to go to Elba . . . I hope Joseph will go as he promised. It would be very bad of him otherwise. We must not leave the Emperor alone. It is now that misfortune has overtaken him that we must show our attachment to him.

Duchand wrote from Paris that money was scarce and prospective buyers were slow in coming forward for either of her residences. Pauline had set a price of 900,000 francs on each. The Hôtel de Charost had been occupied for a time by Austrian officers who had drunk all the wine in the cellars. Pauline sent a stream of letters giving detailed but frequently contradictory instructions as to the furniture and effects she wished to be crated up and sent to her at Portoferraio. Included among them were various clocks and carpets, a billiard table and a folding step-ladder, servants' liveries (if still in good condition), the stock of West Indian rum (a taste Pauline had acquired when at San Domingo), six beds with all their curtains and hangings, and a walnut night-commode. The first consignment filled sixty packing-cases, which were sent to Marseilles to be shipped to Elba. Then she heard better news from Paris – Michelot was negotiating the sale of the Hôtel de Charost to the Duke of Wellington. The Duke had been appointed ambassador to France and had taken a great liking to the mansion. Duchand brought the price down to 800,000 francs (which was still twice what Pauline had paid for it) and agreed to accept payment by instalments. Wellington moved into the *nid de Pauline* and signed the inventory of contents on 26 August.[7]

Pauline had heard nothing of her husband, so she wrote to Lucien in Rome asking for news, saying 'It is my desire to be on good terms with him if he is willing to reciprocate.' But Borghese, understandably, was not willing. Since Napoleon's abdication he had been trying to dissociate himself from the Bonapartes. From Florence, where he had gone after leaving Turin, he wrote through Lucien that if the château of Neuilly were sold the proceeds had to be deposited with a notary until his rights had been determined; and he instructed his agent in Paris to demand the return of all his personal property, especially a collection of 175 pictures. When Pauline heard of this, she wrote to her steward to prevent the removal of any of the Prince's belongings. A long-drawn-out battle ensued between their respective representatives.

Meanwhile, Madame Mère had joined Napoleon early in August, crossing to Elba from Leghorn in a British sloop, the *Grasshopper*, one of the ships employed on patrolling the waters round Elba. Colonel Campbell sailed with the sloop to collect Madame Mère and her much-reduced household, and accompanied them to Portoferraio. Napoleon became impatient for Pauline to join them, and eventually received word from her that she would be able to leave the last week in September. He sent his 16-gun brig, the *Inconstant*, the one ship he was allowed to protect the island and himself against raids by Barbary pirates. But when the vessel arrived, Pauline was not ready. For a whole month the *Inconstant* swung at anchor in the Bay of Naples, awaiting the good pleasure of the dilatory princess. She thought of going to Rome to see Lucien – the *Inconstant* could then take her aboard at Civita-Vecchia; she thought of going to the hot springs on the island of Ischia . . . then there seemed a prospect of selling Neuilly (which came to nothing, and before the end of the year all properties in France belonging to the Bonaparte family were confiscated by the State). Pauline at last went on board the *Inconstant* on 29 October. Two days later, Campbell noted in his diary: 'Napoleon's sister Pauline arrived here today on board of his brig, escorted as far as the Piombino channel by a Neapolitan frigate, which then returned to Naples without any communication with Elba.'

Chapter 14

Pauline on Elba

Napoleon gave the upper floor of the Mulini to Pauline; he no longer had any illusions that Marie-Louise would come to occupy it. The alterations and extensions to the house had been completed and the rooms furnished – perhaps this was what Pauline had been waiting for; she liked her comforts more now. The Mulini was no palace but a pleasant enough residence for two people and their personal attendants. Napoleon had five rooms and a bathroom on the ground floor, also an ante-room, a wardrobe-room, a guardroom and two rooms for the servants and officers on duty. But only one room, the Grand Salon, was of good proportions and had windows overlooking both the narrow street and the garden. It had the only painted ceiling too, done in the illusionist style of *trompe l'œil* which was so popular with Napoleon, and depicted a vast military tent with spears, shields and flags between the folds. The kitchen had been built out from the garden side of the ground floor and, at an angle from it, a Salle des Fêtes for receptions and dancing.

Pauline's accommodation was better than her brother's. She had nine rooms and a large bathroom that extended out over the kitchen. There was one apartment of four rooms, originally intended for the King of Rome – Pauline gave one of these to Madame Ducluzel for her bedroom – and a second four-roomed apartment which was to have been Marie-Louise's; the room between was the best in the whole house, extending over four of Napoleon's rooms and having eight windows, four on either side, which flooded it with light. Its ceiling was painted in *trompe l'œil* to evoke Napoleon's victorious campaigns; spears and pikes supported an awning, and brightly-clad Victories seemed to be juggling with laurel-wreaths. This room became Pauline's drawing-room. A private staircase near the bathroom enabled her to slip down to the garden without using the main stairs. There was a flower garden and a kitchen garden, dominated at the far end by the Medici fort on the headland but open on the seaward side, where a low wall ran along the top of the slope which ended in a steep cliff. Here against the wall Napoleon had built himself a stone seat; in one direction was a wide view of the Tyrrhenian sea with the Italian mainland in the distance, in the other direction the lighthouse and the entrance to the bay. No ship could reach Portoferraio without being seen from this point.

The Mulini, with its plain white front and green shutters, the garden of freshly-planted flowers and splendid views over the sea and the town, was a most agreeable place for retirement from the world. It was also a very safe place.

The island capital had been built in the shape of an amphitheatre, the back turned from the sea, with tiers of houses coming down to the harbour which, because of the curving entrance from the bay, had – has – the strange appearance of being in the heart of the countryside. Ramparts all along the quay cut off the town from the harbour, except for the one entrance, the Porta a Mare. And there was only one way into the town from the countryside, by the Porta a Terra, a tunnel about one hundred yards long burrowing through the rock on which one of the forts stood. Carriages and horses had to take a circuitous way round the town by the one road, which led to the forts on the heights. But people on foot could use a number of steep paths and flights of steps between the houses.

Pauline had noted these handicaps to easy movement on her first visit, and this time had brought a pony-cart with her. None of her own furniture had arrived, but she found that the rooms at the Mulini were already well furnished with pieces that had been, as Napoleon put it, 'in the family'. Finding little to his taste at Portoferraio, Napoleon had sent his brig across to Piombino to strip the villa belonging to his sister Elisa.[1] His men had made a thorough job of it, even taking up the parquet floor and taking down the shutters; but they had scrupulously left a receipt for everything. This loot was not enough to furnish the whole of the Mulini, but providence had sent a ship to take shelter in the cove at Porto Longone, on the south-east side of the island. Napoleon heard that the cargo included furniture belonging to Prince Borghese which he had sent from Turin to

Genoa for shipment to Rome. So while the Prince was being carried across Italy in his berlin, his furniture was being unshipped and carried across Elba in carts. 'Like that, it hasn't gone out of the family,' Napoleon chuckled as he told Pauline the story, which undoubtedly amused her too.

She was pleased to find that many improvements had taken place since June in Napoleon's little capital. Chamberpots were no longer emptied out of windows nor was kitchen-refuse thrown into the gutters to be washed down by rain, when rain fell. Napoleon had imposed fines on people who continued these traditional practices and had organised a refuse-collecting service. The flights of steps and the slopes with a gutter down the middle prevented carts from being used, so men with large wicker baskets on their back went up and down, blowing trumpets to call the attention of housewives. Paving-stones had been put down and trees planted in the two small squares, lamps erected at strategic points and benches placed along the quay; and roads were being made between the chief villages – there were only two carriage-roads on the whole island when Napoleon took possession.

There was much more animation in Portoferraio than there had been in early June. Napoleon's guard had arrived, over seven hundred officers and men – including a contingent of Polish lancers – instead of the four hundred allowed (which meant additional expense for the Emperor of Elba), and they were billeted in the three forts on the heights above the town. Together with the French garrison of about two hundred which had been on the island when peace came, commanded by the governor, General Dalesme, and with recruits from among the islanders, Napoleon had more than a thousand men under his command. Every morning a military parade was held in the main square, the Piazza d'Armi, by General Cambronne.[2] There was much coming and going of resplendent officers between the Mulini and the town hall in the Piazza d'Armi, where General Bertrand lived and had his offices; between these two places and the fort on the headland, where General Drouot, the Minister for Defence, had his offices. There were three other Ministers in Napoleon's government: Balbiani, who had been the Sous-Préfet, was now Minister of Justice; Peyrusse had received promotion to Minister of Finance; and a prominent Elban, Doctor Lapi, was a kind of Minister of Health and in command of the National Guard. Napoleon had also appointed a civil and a military household. The former consisted of two secretaries and four chamberlains, among them the mayor, Traditi, who all wore purple uniforms when on duty. The latter, headed by General Bertrand, consisted of seven orderly officers, all Elbans, whose uniform was sky-blue with silver piping. And Napoleon had given his island kingdom a flag of his own design: a white field having a red diagonal with three golden bees on it.[3]

Every Sunday morning the little court attended Napoleon's levée, with Bertrand regulating the ceremonial as though still grand marshal at the Tuileries. Then, accompanied by his ministers and chamberlains, Napoleon walked down to pay his respects to his mother, who was living at the Casa Vantini, a modest house rented from one of Napoleon's chamberlains. From there they all continued down to the Piazza d'Armi and went to Mass at the 'cathedral', at the opposite end of the square to the town hall, where the vicar, Monsignor Arrighi, officiated – he was a Corsican who claimed to be a 'cousin' of the Emperor, and had been appointed his chaplain.

These comic-opera trappings of a kingdom had certainly enlivened the compact little town, but by the time Pauline arrived the novelty had begun to pall and the enthusiasm had waned; boredom had descended again, especially among the military. Pauline soon swept it away. She gathered round her a bevy of young women and organised balls, theatrical performances and receptions. She was in her element, and she had the field to herself. As sister of the lonely Emperor she was in any case the first lady in the land; but the three Generals, Drouot, Dalesme and Cambronne, and Colonel Campbell, were all bachelors. Bertrand was married and his wife Fanny – a tall, graceful woman and a distant relative of Josephine – had joined him with their three children when she was eight months pregnant; the baby had lived for only three months and Countess Bertrand had taken a dislike to Elba and hardly ever went out. Pauline often called on her at the town hall, and was warmly welcomed, but Fanny never returned the visits.

The first of Pauline's entertainments was a buffet-dance with one-act comedies during the intervals between dancing. She chose the cast from among the young officers and the daughters of the leading families of Portoferraio, and directed the rehearsals, which were gay affairs. It was held in the newly-decorated Salle des Fêtes at the Mulini. Napoleon, at Pauline's bidding, sent instructions to Bertrand:

> Invitations are to be issued throughout the Island, although there must not be more than two hundred guests at one time. Presuming there are more than two hundred people on the Island to be invited, two sessions must be arranged. The invitations are to be for nine o'clock. The refreshments will be served without ice, because of the difficulties of obtaining it. There will be a buffet, served at midnight. The cost must not exceed one thousand francs.

If only two hundred guests turned up, the expenditure allowed would provide refreshments and a buffet of adequate, but hardly royal, standards. However, without doubt it was a great occasion for the gentry of Elba. Dressed in their best, they drove up to the Mulini in a simple trap or a high-wheeled cart, and entered the 'palace' between a double row of Polish lancers in full dress uniform and with sabres at the present, and by the light of spluttering torches held by servants. Pauline took an active part; she danced several times with Cambronne, seeing that the old soldier was bored with the sedentary, peaceful life on Elba, and although his awkwardness as a dancer raised a few smiles among the guests, she complimented him sweetly. She changed out of her magnificent ball-gown (Napoleon noticed the jealous looks it occasioned and afterwards told her to dress more simply in future) to take a leading role in the two short plays, *Les Fausses Infidélités* and *Les Folies Amoureuses*. The party ended in the small hours with a tumultuous fandango danced by the wife of the major commanding the Polish lancers, Baroness Skupieski, who was Spanish by birth; Pauline had appointed her a lady-in-waiting.

The entertainment was such a success that Pauline urged Napoleon to build a theatre. He would not go to that extent – he probably thought by now that he might not be present to see its completion – but he gave orders for an existing building to be converted. And in view of the shortage of public funds he evolved a scheme for the boxes and stalls to be sold outright before the work began. The purchasers formed a society to which they gave the florid name of Accademia dei Fortunati, and they had the words *A noi la sorte* – we are the lucky ones – inscribed on the front of the building. This was a deconsecrated church which had been used as an army store for several years and stood halfway up the carriage-road from the harbour. The work went ahead rapidly, giving useful employment to the troops, and early in January 1815 the Teatro di Vigilanti, as it was called, was ready for its opening night.

There were twenty army bandsmen in the orchestra pit, and the boxes and stalls were filled with the social life of Portoferraio, everyone beaming with pleasure. *A noi la sorte!* – it was painted above the stage too. The drop-curtain had been painted by an artist from Piedmont, and it showed 'Apollo, banished from the heavens, watching over the flocks and happily teaching shepherds' – an Apollo with a distinct facial resemblance to the Emperor. The ladies had been greeted by ushers who addressed a complimentary remark to each – a refinement thought of by Pauline, who had recruited some young officers for the purpose. Napoleon had given her the official title of 'Organiser of Entertainments on the Island of Elba'. Suddenly orders rang out from the porch – the Emperor was arriving with his mother and sister. The conductor raised his baton and for the first time the Elban anthem (another bright idea of Napoleon's) was heard – not a martial tune but a popular air from one of Grétry's light operas: 'Where can you better be than among your family?'

Napoleon stood in the Imperial box acknowledging the ovation from 'his family'. To emphasise still further that he was done with the past he had discarded his green Guards uniform for the blue of the Elban National Guard. He sat down between his mother and Pauline, the one stiff and upright, the other languorous in tulle over her flowing curves. Behind them were Traditi, the mayor and chamberlain, and Colonel Campbell in his tight-fitting, red-and-gold uniform, more than ever convinced that Napoleon was definitely settled on Elba. In the next box Generals Bertrand, Cambronne and Drouot were presenting a stern front to the proceedings.

A fife-band came on to the stage to perform, was suitably applauded, and then the curtain rose on a vaudeville given in Italian by a company of players brought specially from Leghorn. They followed it with a comedy given in French with a strong Tuscan accent. The Elbans were highly delighted with both, more so than the privileged few who had seen much better in Paris.

The Emperor and his mother left after the comedy, having no intention of taking part in the fancy-dress ball which was to follow. For a while the theatre became a hive of activity as people withdrew to the back of their boxes and changed into the costumes they had brought with them, presently emerging dressed as Punch or as pierrots, clowns or harlequins.

Pauline appeared as 'a girl from Procida' (an island in the Bay of Naples), wearing a red skirt, green bodice and a white, wide-sleeved blouse – the colours of the Italian flag of independence; was this her idea or Napoleon's? She opened the ball with Cambronne, who was a Sicilian bandit; but she soon gladly abandoned him for some of the young officers, who competed for the honour of dancing with the celebrated sister of the Emperor. Sedate waltzing gave way to the tarantella. This lively, whirling Italian dance, in which the men leapt after their tantalising partners like satyrs after nymphs, allowed liberties that Pauline's partners were not slow to take nor she to permit. The young women of Portoferraio took their cue from her, and their elders began to frown. Still – *A noi la sorte!* It was an evening to remember. The next entertainment organised by Pauline would be remembered much longer and by many more people. . . .

Napoleon, his mother and Pauline usually spent their evenings much more quietly, playing cards – *écarté* or *reversi* (an Italian game in which the winner is the player who makes the least tricks) – after dinner at the Mulini with one or two of the generals. Madame Mère was happy and contented; she had sent for some of her furniture and she seemed quite prepared to spend the rest of her days living at the rented house with just two ladies-in-waiting and a chamberlain, Colonna, a Neapolitan. She occupied much of her time doing embroidery, sitting by the window with her balls of wool on a side-table that held portraits of all her children. She had no need to worry about them any more, they were all safe and well off, and Lucien (whom the Pope had recently made Prince of Canino) had become reconciled with Napoleon. She opened her door to Elba's notables and her purse to its poor. She suddenly became generous, almost lavish. She sent one of her ladies, Madame Blachier (born a Ramolino and so a 'cousin' of hers), to Rome to fetch all her jewels, which she then offered to Napoleon. He was greatly touched by her gesture but refused them, accepting only a diamond clasp for his sword-belt. She no longer said 'Let's hope it lasts!' for she was convinced that it would.[4]

Pauline was not so sure; but, like her mother, she was happy at Portoferraio, breathing the same air as in her native Corsica and living among people who spoke Italian. Like her mother, she would have been content to stay on Elba. Her mind could grasp the scope of this tight little kingdom, whereas the Empire had been a concept utterly beyond her. The leading position she had was unchallengeable and satisfied her vanity. She was no longer bored; she was leading a calm and regular life, and not for many years had her health been so good. She had the admiration of men, but no lover as yet. There was a certain Captain Cornuel whom Napoleon had appointed as her equerry and to watch over her safety; whenever she went about the town, in a sedan-chair or in her pony-cart, he was seen striding along at her side. People said . . . But a love affair was difficult while sharing the Mulini with Napoleon; he was again domineering, even forbidding her to dress in all her finery. However, he sometimes went away for a day or two, to Porto Longone or the villa at San Martino; perhaps a time would come . . .

By February Pauline could hardly help being aware that greater events might well come first. Living in close proximity to her brother, she realised that if she and her mother were content on Elba, he was not. Napoleon was forty-five and had a pronounced middle-age spread and a flabby face, and suffered from a bladder complaint and other ailments; he was past his peak physically, and mentally too, but his brain was still superior and intensely active. He had exercised his mental powers on organising Elba;

now he was restless for a wider field, for the pace and challenge of power and all that went with it. Pauline could understand that Elba must seem a pathetic little stage to him; instead of commanding a quarter of a million men he had no more than a thousand. There was so much else he missed – even the family rows. Some of the news from abroad was not reassuring. The Allies were said to be planning to remove him to the Azores or the West Indies or even to St Helena. There were warnings of plots against his person. On the other hand, there were reports from France of discontent with the Bourbon government; while the Allied representatives at the Congress of Vienna were divided over the settlement of Europe, and two power blocs were forming round the treaty table.

Napoleon was biding his time, waiting for a propitious moment. In the meantime he continued playing a part. There was no lack of reports to the Allies of his peaceful intentions and even his decrepitude: a monarch who planted trees, built a theatre and a summer villa, who played 'blind-man's buff' with his sister and her ladies, and slipped sardines surreptitiously into the pocket of his grand marshal, could not be considered a threat to the world. Colonel Campbell was so convinced that Napoleon had settled down for good that he applied to London to be withdrawn. Napoleon asked him to remain, and Bertrand gave him a sort of testimonial which said in part, 'I cannot stress enough how agreeable Colonel Campbell's company and presence are to the Emperor.'

The island was full of spies or agents, most of them French, who sent their reports, in which gossip, second-hand information and fact were impartially mingled, to the French Consul at Leghorn or to the Governor of Corsica. There were also spies in Corsican and Italian ports and along the coast of southern France whose assignment was to report on persons travelling to or returning from Elba. Every ship to Elba had among its passengers a number of agents – some going to report to Napoleon, not to spy on him – pretending to be friars or fishermen, traders or tourists. Visitors to the island came from all over Europe – including Englishmen on the Grand Tour, which was now not complete without a sight of Napoleon – and on some days there was quite a crowd outside Cambronne's quarters, where permits to stay on the island were issued. Armed with a permit, the holder then went down to Bertrand's office at the town hall and joined the queue of applicants for an audience up at the Mulini. These visitors brought money to the hotel and lodging-house proprietors, the shopkeepers and traders, and the Treasury not the least.

Most of the spies were inexperienced, but one was astute and persevering enough to gather valid items of information which, if extracted from the wealth of dubious material, could have aroused alarm when passed on to Vienna or Paris. He was Alessandro Forli, so his papers said, but was known at Portoferraio as the 'Oil Merchant', for he did in fact sell olive-oil as a cover for his spying activities. He reported to Mariotti, the French Consul at Leghorn. In December his report included a scrap of conversation between Napoleon and Drouot: 'Well, General, what do you think? Would be it too soon to leave the island during Carnival week?' In January, the 'Oil Merchant' gave as his opinion that the King of Naples was in league with Napoleon, supporting this with the story that whenever a military man asked Drouot for employment, 'the General tells him . . . to go to Naples, as those who serve the sovereign there are serving the Emperor'.

It was time for Napoleon to act, and the right opportunity seemed to come in mid-February. The 14th was Shrove Tuesday, and Pauline was arranging for a masked ball at the Mulini that evening. The Carnival spirit was everywhere; there were parties up at the forts and at the houses of leading citizens; there were stallholders and cheapjacks crying their wares under the plane-trees in the main square, and practical-jokers were mingling with the crowd. At the Mulini, Napoleon was receiving a secret agent, Fleury de Chaboulon, who was reporting on the political situation in France. Fleury had arrived at Portoferraio the previous evening, disguised as a sailor, on a felucca from Lerici. He had been Préfet at Rheims in 1814, but had resigned when the Bourbon government was formed. Now he was an envoy of Maret, Duke of Bassano, who had been Napoleon's Minister of the Interior, and brought word of plots to overthrow the Bourbon government.

On Ash Wednesday was held the traditional procession round the town – the 'Burial of the Carnival'. It brought an end to the festivities and, this year, the beginning of Napoleon's preparations for escape. The procession was led by Colonel Mallet, the stern-faced commander of the Guard, dressed as a pasha – swathed in some of Pauline's cashmere shawls – and riding Napoleon's white parade-horse, Intendant. Behind him came Don Quixote and Sancho Panza, a tall, thin Polish officer on the most skinny horse in all Portoferraio and a plump catering officer on a small mule. They were followed by army bandsmen dressed as pierrots and a score of floats carrying the pasha's harem – though moustaches were visible under the veils, and the hands tossing flowers to the spectators were noticeably hairy. One float, however, unmistakably contained young women dressed as gypsies, with festoons of muslin and dangling beads, who were throwing carnations and branches of flowering mimosa to the joyful people lining the route. It was whispered that the flowing draperies of one of the gypsies concealed Princess Pauline herself. The High Command of the island brought up the rear, the mournful faces of the Generals giving the impression that they were following a real burial procession. It made its way round by the carriage-road and arrived laughing and shouting and with band playing in the Piazza d'Armi.

What buffoonery, thought the observers in Allied pay, quite persuaded that Napoleon was content to lord it over an island of clowns. Pauline was organising festivities to cover his preparations for escape as she had four years earlier to entertain the court waiting for the birth of his child.

That evening, while the carnival procession was keeping all Portoferraio amused, Fleury had a second interview with Napoleon and then slipped away on a felucca bound for Naples. Next day, 16 February, Colonel Campbell called at the Mulini to inform Napoleon that he was leaving for Leghorn, and added that he intended making a brief visit to Florence for some medical attention. It seemed to Campbell to be a good time to have a break from Elba.

'I hope you will be back by the twenty-eighth,' said Napoleon.

'Why the twenty-eighth, Sire?'

'Because Princess Pauline is giving a ball that evening and we should be happy to have you among our guests.'

Campbell gladly accepted the invitation and took his leave; later in the day he sailed for Leghorn in HMS *Partridge*. Hardly had the British ship cleared the bay than Napoleon was giving the first of his orders: the *Inconstant* was to be refitted and made ready to sail by the twenty-fifth; the two small cargo vessels at Rio Marina, the port for the island's iron-mines, were to be brought round to Portoferraio – but fully loaded to prevent suspicious surmise, one with timber and the other with ammunition from the citadel at Porto Longone.

On 17 February Napoleon sent Madame Mère's chamberlain, Colonna, to Naples with letters for Murat that authorised the bearer to 'sign any agreement that you may desire concerning our affairs . . .' and added '. . . Colonna will tell you many great and important things. I count on you and above all on the utmost speed. Time presses. . . .'[5]

Time did indeed press, and all Napoleon's mental energy revived. Each preparatory move for embarking his troops was offset by an order designed to show that he had no intention of changing his circumstances. On the day he had two pairs of boots issued to each of his soldiers he went down to the quayside and bought a portable hut that had been recently unloaded. 'It will come in useful for my journeys about the island,' he said loudly. The spies did not know what to make of these indications.

There was a scare on the 23rd when the *Partridge* was sighted making for Portoferraio. Napoleon ordered the suspension of all suspicious movement of men and supplies. However, the ship was not bringing Campbell back early but cruising around while waiting to return to Leghorn for him on the 26th. Her commander, Captain Adye, put in at Portoferraio, was rowed ashore, and spent a few hours in the town. Noticing nothing abnormal, he sailed again in the afternoon. Napoleon learnt through Bertrand, who had had some conversation with Adye, that the *Partridge* would be at Leghorn on the 26th. That was the day, then, when Napoleon and his transports would set sail for France.

On the 24th Napoleon put an embargo on the island. No fishing vessel was allowed to leave (the 'Oil Merchant' paid a skipper handsomely to take him across to Piombino, but the boat was fired on from the *Inconstant* while crossing the harbour and forced to put back); all troops were confined to barracks.

In the midst of all these preparations and upheavals Pauline had continued with her arrangements for the ball at the Mulini, but at her brother's request had brought it forward three days, to the evening of the 25th. Right to the last, the date of Napoleon's departure had to be kept as secret as possible. While Pauline was dancing with the guests, Napoleon was drafting his proclamation to the people of France. The 26th was a Sunday; Napoleon held his levée as usual, but appeared in his green uniform of a colonel of the Guard with a grey riding-coat over it and his cocked hat held under his arm. Then he announced his departure. 'Gentlemen, I shall be leaving you this evening. France wants me back. Signor Lapi, I appoint you governor of the island. My friends, never shall I forget you! I leave in your care those who are most precious to me – my mother and my sister.'

He had told his mother the previous evening that he was going to land in France, to march on Paris. 'Go and fulfil your destiny,' the brave old lady had told him. 'You were not made to perish on this island.'

Pauline would have liked to dissuade him, but she knew it was useless. She had a vague foreboding that she would never see him again. She had done all he had asked of her during the past fortnight, but it seemed inconceivable to her that with a thousand men he could regain dominion over France. Better a sure hold on Elba than this mad venture across the sea. Nevertheless, later in the day she offered him her finest diamond necklace, worth half-a-million francs. Napoleon, much touched, asked her to give it to his trusted valet, Marchand, who was packing in the next room.

Her face was wet with tears as she handed the necklace to Marchand. 'The Emperor has asked me to put this in your charge,' she said. 'If things go wrong he will surely have need of it. And oh! Marchand, if they do, never abandon him. Take good care of him. Adieu.'

She gave him her hand to kiss. Marchand tried to console her. 'Everything makes me hope it is only "au revoir", Your Highness.'[6]

'I do not think so,' she murmured miserably.

At five that afternoon the drums beat to arms; by seven all the troops and their officers were embarked. Napoleon and Bertrand drove down to the quayside in Pauline's pony-cart, took leave of the assembled Elban authorities and were rowed out to the *Inconstant*. Night was falling; the lights from hundreds of lanterns were twinkling along the top of the ramparts, which were dense with people. From the decks of the *Inconstant* and the four small transports came the vibrant strains of the *Marseillaise* as the sails filled and the little fleet began moving across the bay. The last great gamble was under way. For Elba, the *epoca napoleonica* had ended.[7]

Chapter 15

Arrest and escape

On Monday, 27 February, the *Partridge* sailed from Leghorn with Campbell on board, but Captain Adye found only light airs along the coast and by daylight on Tuesday was still some miles off Portoferraio, becalmed. Campbell eventually had himself rowed ashore in one of the ship's boats. There was a calm in the town too, an unnatural calm. And the *Inconstant* was missing. Campbell hurried to the town hall and learnt the awful truth. Madame Bertrand declared her ignorance of any plans of Napoleon's and Campbell went up to the Mulini, only to find that Princess Pauline was with her mother at the Vantini house. Down he went, was received by Pauline and met with a similar blank attitude.

'She . . . protested her ignorance of Napoleon's intended departure,' Campbell wrote later, 'and of his present destination; laid hold of my hand and pressed it to her heart, that I might feel how much she was agitated. However, she did not appear to be so, and there was rather a smile upon her countenance. She inquired whether the Emperor had been taken? I told her I could not exactly say he was, but that there was every probability of it. During this conversation she dropped a hint of her belief in his destination being France, upon which I smiled and said, "Oh no, not that far, it's Naples." For I fancied she mentioned France purposely to deceive me.'

Campbell returned to the *Partridge* and sailed away to scour the sea. Pauline had at least learnt that Napoleon and his ships had got clear away; now she was most uneasy in her mind for her own safety. Campbell might return and make her prisoner, hold her as a hostage. Elba, emptied of French troops, suddenly seemed a most insecure place; and the hush that hung about the Mulini served to accentuate her fears. She knew that Murat was supposed to send a ship to collect her, her mother, Madame Bertrand and her children, when he learnt of Napoleon's escape.

But how long would that be, and would the ship evade patrolling enemy vessels?[1]

The problem was where to go from Elba. Pauline remembered that Elisa had a property at Compignano, about a league from Viareggio; this was a refuge relatively easy to reach and, depending on events, she could go and join Napoleon or Caroline from there. She called upon the aid of a Lieutenant Monier, a French engineer officer who had been inadvertently left behind while on duty in a remote part of the island. He obtained a fishing-boat and fitted it up comfortably for the crossing. Pauline said farewell to her mother; the stern old lady was determined to stay until Napoleon or Murat – she hoped the former – sent a ship for her. During the night of 3 March Pauline secretively sailed away from Elba accompanied by Monier, two of her ladies and four servants. She seemed fated never to stay in one place for more than four or five months; either her restless disposition drove her to move on or circumstances beyond her control forced her to seek another residence.

This time she found that she had gone, as it were, from the frying-pan into the fire. The little group spent the night of 4 March at sea and landed at Viareggio late next morning. When the authorities asked Pauline to state her destination, she told them frankly and was allowed to proceed. She was carried the three miles to Elisa's villa in her sedan-chair, which she had thoughtfully sent on board before leaving Elba; the others walked. The place was all shut up, but the bailiff was found and he opened it; by evening Pauline and her ladies were installed on the first floor, while Monier kept guard on the ground floor. At midnight they were all roused by the clatter and jingle of a troop of cavalry. The Austrian officer in command insisted on seeing Pauline, and informed her that she was under house arrest.

The Austrian governor of Lucca, Colonel Wercklein, was a man who took his duties seriously; on being informed of the arrival of Napoleon's sister by the Viareggio authorities, he had at once sent troops to place her under guard. She was in fact a prisoner of state, if not of war, and soon discovered that she was being kept incommunicado. No one was allowed to enter or leave the grounds without permission; if a visitor was permitted to see her, it could only be in the presence of an Austrian officer;

she was not allowed to send out letters, and any arriving for her were opened and read before being passed on to her. The only consolation was that she was not quite so badly treated as Elisa, who had been arrested and imprisoned in a fortress at Brünn by order of Metternich when he heard of Napoleon's landing in France.

The news of Elisa's imprisonment and of Napoleon's triumphal arrival in Paris trickled through to Pauline, the first making her more despondent and fearful, the second cheering her and bringing hope, but also making her wonder anxiously what Napoleon would say on learning that she had not gone to Naples as arranged. For the moment, that was the least of her worries. As she was unable to correspond, she decided to send Lieutenant Monier to Paris to report on her situation, and a passport for him was obtained on 22 March.[2] At the same time, unknown to her, Murat was protesting at the treatment of Pauline and had sent one of his generals to Marshal Bellegarde, the Austrian governor-general in Milan, to demand her release.[3] But this had no effect. Pauline was left in a deplorable situation, surrounded by enemies and without a single man to call upon. Napoleon's Hundred Days were for her the most horrible period in her life since the time in San Domingo. However, she again showed her powers of resourcefulness when really pressed and in dire trouble, and reacted in her own particular way.

She fell back on her precarious state of health, never better; taking to her bed, she demanded the attentions of a doctor. The Austrians allowed a Doctor Martelli to see her; with the aid of a darkened room, hot-water bottles and make-up, she convinced him that she was suffering from some obscure ailment. She asked him for news, denounced the treatment she was being subjected to and claimed that her state of health required her transfer to the baths at Lucca. But he was too timid and cautious a man for her purpose; he merely prescribed poultices and advised that another physician be called in. His successor was much more useful. He was Doctor Vacca, who had been court physician to Elisa. By now Pauline had convinced herself that she was really ill – never very difficult for her – and concentrated on charming her new doctor. It was Turin and Doctor Vastapani all over again, but in more serious circumstances. She found Vacca amenable and took him into her confidence, and he rendered her some useful services other than medical; for instance, he helped her to by-pass the Austrian authorities with the receiving and sending of letters. He arranged for other doctors to be consulted, and with the aid of false blood and urine samples and some generous fees the medical men were led to submit to the Austrians that a cure at Bagni di Lucca was essential for the Princess. The baffled Austrians gave up, and on 5 June Wercklein sent permission for her to leave Compignano.

Having achieved her aim, the Princess was able to rise immediately from her bed of pain. Escorted by twenty Austrian soldiers and accompanied by several doctors, she arrived at Bagni di Lucca the following day.

Surveillance of her was relaxed; she soon had a little group of admirers, Russian, Polish and English, from among the international set taking the waters. She rented a villa in nearby San Pancrazio, and there in the lovely Serchio valley she quickly recovered her spirits; after those three gloomy months of incarceration, life seemed full of sunshine again. It reminded her of her stay here eleven years before, after escaping from Borghese and the restrictions in the magnificent but cavernous palace. She was able to communicate with France again, and from the faithful Michelot came the good news that he had placed 215,000 francs to her credit with bankers in Leghorn and Rome. She thought of going to join Napoleon in Paris, as most of the family had already done. Then the blow fell.

One day in late June, Wercklein gave himself the pleasure of calling on Pauline to tell her in person of Napoleon's defeat at Waterloo and his second abdication. Her world fell about her. For days she lay prostrate, unable to imagine any sort of future. A letter from Lucien in Paris, dated 26 June, gave her a little hope: 'You will have heard of the Emperor's latest misfortune and that he has abdicated in favour of his son. He is about to leave for America, where we shall all join him . . . I am going to Rome to collect my family and take them to America. If your state of health allows, we might see each other there. Goodbye, dear sister. Mother, Joseph and Jerome and I send you fond kisses.'

But this was soon followed by the awful news that Napoleon

was being sent prisoner to St Helena. This was the end of everything. Pauline cared nothing for the disappearance of the Empire; it was Napoleon and her devotion to him that mattered. She did not know what to do. She tried to get in touch with the scattered members of her family, but they were all on the move, seeking a haven themselves, except for Elisa who was still held prisoner at Brünn. A ray of light came with a letter from Duchand. He had fought like a lion at Waterloo and after Napoleon's abdication had resigned from his regiment. Pauline was in sore need of his love for her. She wrote back that 'his affection had withstood the test of calamity', but it is doubtful whether he ever received her reply, for it was seized at Lyons. Early in August Pauline heard that her mother and Cardinal Fesch were at Siena, waiting for the Pope's permission to settle in Rome. They were given assurance of a welcome by the kindly Pius VII, despite opposition by the French ambassador, and left for Rome on 13 August. Pauline decided to join them, but the Austrian authorities took two months to conclude that she was not a potential disturber of the peace of Europe. The restrictions on her movements were raised in October and she was allowed to proceed to Rome – provided she went by sea. She embarked at Viareggio on 12 October and arrived in Rome at about the same time as Napoleon landed on St Helena and a day or two after Murat was executed by a firing-squad in Calabria.

Pauline went to stay with her mother and Fesch at the Palazzo Falconieri, which the far-sighted Cardinal had bought the previous year. It was not a very satisfactory arrangement. The palace, though vast, was not large enough to hold Cardinal Fesch, his collection of pictures (which took up the whole of one floor) and his ecclesiastical attendants; Madame Mère and her household, though reduced; and a Pauline used to living her own life. Nor was the rather gloomy and priestly atmosphere to her taste. There was enough gloom in her heart; a little gaiety in her surroundings would not come amiss. She thought of moving into the Borghese palace, as she was entitled to do. But Camillo refused her access; and from Florence, where he was living contentedly with the charming Duchess Lante della Rovere, he instituted a suit for divorce, through the Rota.

I am most grateful to you for your kindness in having baths and other conveniences installed at the palace. The month of October is awful, the rain never stops. But the promenade last Sunday was very fine. My villa is just opposite the vicolo del Macao and the grounds go down to the Porta Pia, which is really delightful . . . To get to the palace I sometimes have myself driven through the park of the Villa Borghese. Whatever people may say, your villa is the most beautiful in Rome, and every foreigner thinks the same.

All this time she was of course very worried about Napoleon. Both she and her mother had written for news, and each had offered to join him on St Helena as they had on Elba. But no reply had come, and as their letters were perforce sent through the British Colonial Office they could not be sure that Napoleon had even received them. It was not until the summer of 1817 that the Bonaparte family had authentic news of Napoleon's circumstances. One of his companions, the Comte de Las Cases, was expelled from St Helena by the governor; when he reached Europe he wrote round to the family, telling of Napoleon's straitened circumstances and the unhealthy climate of St Helena. Madame Mère asked the Pope to intervene with the British government for an alleviation of Napoleon's condition, and she and Pauline sent funds to Las Cases for transfer to Napoleon. But the rest of his family were far more concerned with their own affairs and had little pity to spare for their brother's situation.

Lucien and Louis were living in Rome; Jerome and his wife were in Austria; Caroline and Elisa in Trieste, Italy being forbidden to them. Joseph was the only one to have reached America, leaving his wife temporarily in Switzerland and taking with him a fortune in bankers' orders. They had all been banished from France and were not allowed to live in countries which had a common frontier with France. Early in 1816 a law had been passed which deprived the Bonapartes of the protection of French embassies and consulates everywhere. Pauline at least escaped the police surveillance to which the others were subjected, except Lucien, a Papal prince.

Pauline was better off than most of her brothers and sisters,

all of whom had families to provide for. Her way of life had
not greatly changed; she went to Bagni di Lucca for the summer
months, and there bought a villa which she called, like the one
in Rome, the Villa Paolina. At the latter she held receptions and
reigned over a salon which became the rendezvous of a brilliant
cosmopolitan circle. She had furnished the villa in mahogany
in the latest English style and decorated the ground-floor rooms
with frescoes of Egyptian scenes recalling her brother's campaigns
in the East. The twenty acres of grounds combined the elegant
sweep of an English park with the regular patterns of a French
garden, and at a central point Pauline had built a *casino* or small
pavilion, reminiscent of the one at Gréoux, surrounded by orange
and lemon trees. One of her many British visitors, Lady Morgan,
the novelist, wrote that at the Villa Paolina, 'English neatness,
French elegance and Italian taste are most happily united . . . it is
the most hospitable house in Rome. . . .' Pauline made a point of
inviting English visitors to Rome who were admirers of Napoleon
and opposed to the British government's treatment of him. Her
one purpose in life now was to give Napoleon all the aid and
support she could; and the only way she knew, while prevented
from going to join him, was to try and induce influential
Englishmen to persuade their government to adopt a more
lenient attitude to the prisoner on St Helena.

Chief among her English visitors were Lord Holland, leader
of the Liberal party, the Earl of Jersey, Lord Brougham and the
Marquess of Douglas (soon to succeed as tenth Duke of
Hamilton). In December 1816 Metternich warned the British
government of 'the eagerness with which leading members of
the Opposition party were profiting by their sojourn in Rome to
make close acquaintance with some of the Bonaparte family'.
Elizabeth, Duchess of Devonshire, the second wife of the
fifth Duke, was in Rome during the winter of 1816–17, and one
of her letters gives a glimpse of Pauline and her guests at an
evening party:

> . . . the set now here, almost all alike flock to the Princess
> Borghese; and the grave Lord Landsdowne, the silent Lord
> Jersey, the politician Mr Brougham, all go and play *aux petits
> jeux* with Pauline. Forfeits condemned Lord Jersey to recite;

he got off by promising to waltz. Lord Cowper was to *soupirer pour une dame*, and so on. She shows her fine plate with the eagle, etc., and gets dozens of fine dresses from Paris. I admire the Pope's firmness in letting them all of that family remain at Rome, but I think that the English should put a little reason in their eagerness to go to her.

In any case, such an assemblage in Pauline's drawing-room was a social triumph. The Marquess of Douglas was a great admirer of Napoleon and had visited him on Elba. His views carried weight in England, even though he belonged to the party in Opposition. When he accompanied Pauline to Lucca in the summer of 1818 there was a revival of stories of plots aimed at the release or escape of Napoleon from St Helena. The Marquess was fifty years old, full of rheumatism, and married to an acknowledged English beauty, and Pauline seemed to have abandoned love affairs; so observers were forced to conclude that it was politics and not love that drew together the Whig nobleman and the sister of Bonaparte. But the only concession that the Opposition obtained for Pauline was that she should be directly informed by the Colonial Office of personal news of Napoleon whenever official reports arrived from St Helena.

On her return to Rome in October, Pauline fell desperately ill from a gastric fever and for several weeks she hovered between life and death. She gradually recovered, but the attack had greatly undermined her constitution, never very strong. And her convalescence was not helped by the gloomy news from St Helena and a prolonged, despairing quarrel with her mother and Cardinal Fesch.

In May 1818 Fesch had received a letter from Bertrand, writing on behalf of Napoleon, which told of several deaths among the household staff due to the unhealthy climate and asked for a doctor to be sent out, also a priest, a maître d'hôtel and a cook; the last two were to be chosen if possible from persons already in the service of the Bonaparte family. Fesch approached the Pope for help in obtaining the necessary permission from the French and British governments. Pauline offered to send her own cook, Chandelier, if he agreed to go to St Helena; and her mother contributed the maître d'hôtel from her household. Correspondence was begun respecting a suitable priest; and Doctor Foureau de Beauregard, who had studied under Corvisart and been with Napoleon on Elba, expressed willingness to join him on St Helena. But then Fesch's whole manner changed; he stopped answering letters and caused unnecessary delays, and finally selected an aged Corsican priest, the *abbé* Buonavita, who had recently suffered an apoplectic stroke, and a young doctor from Florence, Antommarchi, who knew more about carrying out autopsies than curing patients of their illness. It was not until February 1819 that the four left Rome for England and St Helena.[4] Fesch had ignored all protests from Pauline and others over his deplorable choice of men to look after Napoleon's spiritual and physical welfare. Madame Mère alone had supported all Fesch's decisions. The whole episode was inexplicable; and Pauline, ailing and weak, was distracted with anxiety. When she was able to go out, and sought an explanation from her mother, the reasons given her were beyond belief.

Madame Mère calmly announced that she, Fesch, and her chamberlain, Colonna, knew for certain that Napoleon was no longer on St Helena and that sending the four men to him was therefore a waste of time and expense! Pauline finally got to the bottom of it all, as is apparent from letters she wrote later:

My uncle, mother and Colonna have let themselves be taken in by a scheming woman, a German who is a spy for the Austrian court, who said the Virgin Mary had appeared to her and told her that the Emperor was no longer there, and a thousand other incredible things. The Cardinal is out of his mind, he says openly that the Emperor is no longer on St Helena and that he has had revelations as to where he is . . .

Mama is devoutly religious and has given lots of money to this woman who is in league with her confessor . . . The whole affair is a horrible conspiracy, and Colonna is behind it all. He is in church from morning till night . . . Mama and the Cardinal say they know positively that the Emperor has been taken up by angels and carried to a country where his health is much better . . . They tried to draw my brother Louis and myself into their absurd beliefs, but we did all we could to frequent changes of scene. Prevented from going to Genoa, she had a small villa built at Viareggio, which then had an unspoilt miles-long stretch of sandy beach and pine-groves; for two or three years she divided her time between there, Bagni di Lucca, Frascati and Rome. At the Villa Paolina in the capital she gave musical entertainments and receptions, pursuing her reputation as a society hostess. She saw little of her family, though she went regularly to see her mother, now always dressed in black and sitting amid a Napoleonic shrine. Madame Mère was still trying to obtain her son's body, but the British government seemed as scared of the effect the corpse might have if returned to Europe as of the living presence.

Pauline resumed her yearly round but now made little effort to combat her ailments. A severe attack of pneumonia caused her doctors to recommend a change of climate, and she spent the winter of 1822 in the milder air of Pisa, at the Palazzo Lanfranchi. Byron had lived there and described it as 'large enough for a garrison . . . and full of ghosts'. However, Pauline was apparently unaffected by its gloom, for when Lord Holland's son, Henry Fox, visited her there he found her in good spirits.

'The expression of her countenance is very *vif* and full of talent,' he wrote pompously in his diary. 'Her voice oppressed as she was afflicted by a cold, but very harmonious, and I was far from disappointed. Her manner is very royal . . . she was amazingly civil to me and talked a good deal. Now and then her conversation bordered on what was *leste*.'

She was past forty – forty! – and there were lines on that perfect face which no amount of cream and massage could eradicate. Her beauty was fading, but she was still vain. 'If you would like to see my feet,' she said in Rome to Princess Ruspoli, 'come and visit me tomorrow morning.' The showing of her feet was quite a ceremony, as another lady visitor, Baronne du Montet, told in her *Mémoires*:

> The Princess was reclining at her ease in an invalid's chair, her little feet well in view. A page entered with a silver-gilt basin, a napkin of fine cambric, perfumes and other cosmetics. He drew a velvet hassock up to the chair, the Princess graciously put forth a leg, the little page took off her stocking, the garter

Chapter 16

The last years

The death of Napoleon was known in London on 4 July, in Paris
on the 6th and Rome the 16th. But not until the 22nd was his
mother informed, as gently as possible. Pauline had left for
Frascati; she came hurrying back to comfort her mother, all
recrimination forgotten. Her mother was in a state of collapse;
the news had been a much greater shock to her than to Pauline,
who wrote letters to the family like the one to Hortense:

> . . . I have been very ill since this terrible news. Please let
> me know all that you hear from St Helena, and I will do the
> same for you. I am hoping to spend the winter at Genoa, if
> allowed. The sea air will do me good. I feel so distressed and
> need a change of scene . . . Mama has just applied to the
> British minister, on behalf of us all, for the Emperor's remains.
> If this meets with refusal, she will appeal to Parliament . . .
> The news of the death of our well-beloved Emperor caused
> much sorrow here. The Pope was very upset. He at once said
> Mass, himself, and for three days received no one. I can't get
> used to the idea that I shall never see him [Napoleon] again,
> and am in despair. Adieu. For me, life has lost all attraction.
> It is the end of everything. I have sworn never to receive any
> English again, without exception. They have been brutes.

Pauline eventually changed her mind about not receiving any
English, as she did about life having no attraction. Time helped
to ease her sorrows. But there is no doubt that after 1821 life
lost much of its meaning for her. Napoleon had been a dominant
force and had to some extent arranged her life for her. They had
had tussles and clashes of wills, but they were united by bonds of
affection and a subtle affinity; without him, without that father
figure, she was left adrift.

She tried to pick up the threads of her life again, but with

days wrote to everyone she thought could be of help to Napoleon
or to her in obtaining permission to go to him. Her chief appeal
was to Lord Liverpool, the Prime Minister. She enclosed a copy
of Montholon's letter and requested, on behalf of all the Bonaparte
family, a change of climate for Napoleon.

> If this request is refused [she went on], it will be tantamount
> to his death sentence, and in this case I ask permission to leave
> for St Helena . . . As my state of health does not allow me to
> travel by land, I would embark at Civita-Vecchia for England,
> and there take the first ship leaving for St Helena . . . I know
> that the Emperor's days are numbered, and I should never
> forgive myself if I had not done all in my power to soften his
> last hours and prove my devotion to his august person. Should
> there be any English vessels at Leghorn at the time of my
> departure I would request as a further favour that one call at
> Civita-Vecchia to take me to England. . . .

The last letter she wrote was to Montholon, recounting all
she had done, and adding, 'In taking these steps I have consulted
only my heart . . . I trust my strength will sustain me so that I
can prove to the Emperor that no one loves him so much as I do.'

This letter was dated 15 July 1821. Napoleon had been dead
since 5 May.

open their eyes and ended by mocking at their credulity . . .
I pass over the scenes and the quarrels and the coldness between
us which has resulted from it all.[5]

This unhappy affair made Pauline ill again, aggravated by her
inability to join Napoleon and the lack of news from him. In
June 1821 she heard that the *abbé* Buonavita was back in England,
having fallen gravely ill on St Helena, and she wrote to Lady
Holland asking her to find out, if possible, what news the *abbé*
had of Napoleon. However, early in July the *abbé* reached Rome
and went first to see Madame Mère. Fesch was there, and asked
him sceptically whether it was really true that he had seen
Napoleon. The old *abbé* was somewhat taken aback. Meanwhile
Pauline had called to bid her mother goodbye before leaving for
a visit to Louis at Frascati (he had bought Lucien's villa there).
When Pauline learnt from the porter that her mother was
engaged and the visitor was the *abbé* Buonavita she swept into
the room and demanded to speak with him. Her mother and
Fesch were still refusing to believe that the *abbé* had ever seen
Napoleon. Pauline implored her mother to come to her senses,
explained that she was the victim of an intrigue, and at last began
to shake her conviction. 'It was a terrible scene,' she wrote later,
'and I have broken with the Cardinal for good. Fortunately the
abbé had a letter to give me personally, otherwise everything
would have been kept from me. The *abbé* Buonavita has been
very badly treated, and the good old soul is deeply hurt. I am
taking him with me to Frascati, for they would not give him a
sou.'

The letter the *abbé* gave her was from Montholon, Napoleon's
closest companion during his last years, and was dated 17 March,
the day that Buonavita had left St Helena. It indicated plainly
that Napoleon was dying. 'He can scarcely bear the fatigue of a
half-hour's drive in his carriage,' Pauline read through her tears,
'and can walk about in his room only when supported. The
digestive organs have ceased to function . . . he exists only on
soups and jellies . . .' At the end came a despairing appeal. 'The
Emperor counts on Your Highness to bring to the notice of
influential people in England the true state of his disease.'

Pauline put off her departure for Frascati and in the next few

Pauline's salon at the Palazzina dei Mulini, Portoferraio, Elba
photograph by Gartano Barone

Palazzina dei Mulini, entrance

Palazzina dei Mulini, panorama

too, and began to massage, to rub, to wipe, to perfume this beautiful foot, which really was incomparable . . . The operation was a lengthy one, and the astonishment of the onlookers so great that they lost the faculty of enthusiastic praise which was doubtless expected of them. While the little page drew her stockings off and on, perfumed her beautiful feet, filed and refined the nails, she was chatting and, to all appearances, quite devoid of self-consciousness as regards her toilet.

In some ways she had not changed. Her capacity for loving needed an outlet, and she turned to the younger generation of her family. She would have preferred Napoleon's son, but he was confined to Vienna. When Jerome's first wife, the American Elizabeth Patterson, came on a visit to Rome with her son by him, Pauline received them both and took an interest in the lad – which infuriated Jerome. When, in 1823, Caroline's daughter Laetitia became engaged and Caroline had difficulty in providing the dowry, Pauline stood surety by promising to leave Laetitia 50,000 francs in her will.

Pauline also turned to a young musician she had first met a few months before Napoleon's death. He was Giovanni Pacini, a Sicilian and a prolific composer; for a time he was a possible rival to Rossini, but his energy proved to be greater than his talent. Pauline took him up and created a musical salon around him; perhaps she was thinking of Blangini and trying to recapture her lost youth. She had one of Pacini's operas performed at her villa in Rome and another at Lucca. She called him 'Nino', and in 1822 took him with her to Pisa, where he gave concerts at the Palazzo Lanfranchi. He was fifteen years younger than Pauline, and although attracted by her and flattered by her reputation, he saw her as an older woman whose demands must be held in check. He was really more interested in his career than anything else; and, unlike Talma, more apt to drop her than to be dropped by her. And in fact, after the success of his opera performed at Lucca, the Bourbon princess who reigned in Elisa's place appointed Pacini her precentor; and that was the last Pauline saw of him.

It was brave of her, it was pathetic even more. It did not make her bitter but left her desperate. It was the end of loving, the end in fact of living. For a time, her salon in Rome and her periodic moves to her villas at Bagni di Lucca and Viareggio, her new acquaintances, helped to make life just bearable. But the hand of death was upon her, and she knew it. Her complexion had become yellow and she suffered from her liver – 'as Napoleon did', she said. This was true, but he had died primarily from a peptic ulcer, probably cancerous. It was believed at the time, however, that his death, like his father's, was due to cancer. And that was her unspoken thought, her dread of the family disease. It was time to make her peace with everyone, even Camillo.

In the late summer of 1824 an approach was made through Cardinal Rivarola, a frequent visitor at the Villa Paolina, to the new pope, Leo XII. He wrote a firm but persuasive letter to Prince Borghese, pointing out that it was his duty as a Roman prince and a good Catholic to help his wife end her days in harmony. Borghese responded nobly to the appeal; on obtaining confirmation that Pauline had not long to live, he put aside his duchess and offered his wife a home. She went to join him in his Florentine palace; he received her with kindness, surrounded her with comfort and gave her all the care she needed.

Pauline then discovered that life was worth living after all. She made an astonishing recovery – certainly astonishing to Borghese, and possibly suspicious too – and began to take part in the social round of Florence. Prince and Princess Borghese were seen driving together in the Cascine park and arm in arm at the Opera. Pauline even found strength enough during the winter to give several receptions, with Borghese at her side. Her capricious nature must have appreciated the irony of the situation. But it was only a respite, a final effort of her constitution before complete breakdown. By the spring she was confined to her bed and in continual pain.

Louis came to see her, and she sent him a letter shortly afterwards on 13 May: 'I am still very ill, worse in fact than when you left. I do nothing but vomit and suffer; I am reduced to a shadow . . . They are putting down paving-stones in the street outside, and the noise is unbearable. . . .' In her own hand she scribbled a postscript. 'I am ill, ill, but I embrace you.' They were the last words she wrote, except to sign her will.

Borghese, still considerate and thoughtful for her, rented the

Villa Strozzi outside Florence, to get away from the noise in the narrow streets. There, with stoical calm, she dictated her will to her lawyer in the presence of five witnesses, including her brother Jerome. It was a long and detailed document, like Napoleon's; and, like his, was made with an eye to posterity. Altogether she had about two million francs (half a million sterling in present money) in funds and possessions to leave.

The chief beneficiaries were Caroline and her children. 'My brothers ought not to complain, for they are better provided for,' was Pauline's comment. (Elisa had died in 1820, from a malarial fever.) She left her villa and its furniture at Viareggio and 300,000 francs to Caroline, in memory of Murat. The Villa Paolina in Rome went to Louis's son Napoleon-Louis, who had married Joseph's daughter Charlotte. And the villa at Bagni di Lucca was left to Camillo, 'as a slight recognition of the sincere and faithful attachment he has shown me during my long illness'; and Pauline handsomely added for the record: 'I gratefully acknowledge that although circumstances and events have temporarily divided us, Prince Borghese has always shown the greatest attachment and loyalty towards the Emperor, my brother.'

Legacies and bequests were made to more than a hundred persons and institutions: relatives by blood and marriage, old friends and recent ones, attendants and servants, bankers, cardinals, physicians and tradesmen, churches and the poor of Ajaccio, Rome and Viareggio. The English who had sat at her table were not forgotten, despite their failure to do anything for Napoleon. To the Duke of Hamilton (the Marquess of Douglas) Pauline left her silver-gilt dressing-case, 'as a mark of my friendship', and to his Duchess two Sèvres vases; Lord Holland was given the books in her library at Rome, and Lord Gower a Sèvres tea-service adorned with portraits of famous women.

There was no mention of the lovers in her life. Fréron and Canouville were of course dead; but of the living, Forbin had accepted an appointment under the Bourbon government, and Blangini and Duchand were both married. Whether Pauline omitted them as a matter of diplomacy or through being grieved with them will never be known.

Like Napoleon, she made her peace with the Church: 'I am dying amid cruel and horrible sufferings of a long illness that I have borne with resignation and as a true Christian. I am dying without hatred or animosity towards anyone, and in the faith and doctrine of the Roman Apostolic Church. . . .'

Finally she came to the disposal of herself. She strictly enjoined that no autopsy be performed upon her and that she should not be exposed after death, 'as is the custom; I desire to be embalmed and taken to Rome, which is my domicile, and buried in the Borghese chapel of Santa Maria Maggiore'.

'Madame the testatrix', concluded the document, 'pronounced in a clear and audible voice before me, the notary, and five witnesses, the names of the beneficiaries, the legacies, and other dispositions, contained in this testament. . . .'

This last important act in Pauline's life, the dictating of her will, was a noble effort; and it revealed glimpses of her personality and the peculiar workings of her mind.

She named Prince Borghese as executor of her possessions in Tuscany and Lucca, and Cardinal Rivarola of everything she owned in the Papal States – the greater part of her estate. Then Princess Pauline Bonaparte-Borghese signed her name for the last time.

When she knew that death was near she asked to be dressed in her best court gown; a last touch of vanity. Camillo was at her bedside to the end, and he closed her eyes at one o'clock in the afternoon of Thursday, 9 June 1825. She would have been forty-five in October.

Prince Borghese carried out her last wishes, and she was buried in the family chapel of Santa Maria Maggiore – between two popes, Clement VIII and the Borghese pope, Paul V.

Some contemporary events

August 1768   Corsica ceded to France by the Republic of Genoa.

April 1770   Corsican nobility allowed to apply for assimilation with French nobility.

May 1789   States General meet at Versailles.

14 July 1789   Fall of the Bastille.

July 1790   Paoli is given amnesty, returns to Corsica and prepares elections.

September 1791   French Constitution drawn up by National Assembly and accepted by Louis XVI.

20 April 1792   Louis XVI declares war on Austria.

August 1792   Louis XVI and family made prisoner by the Paris Commune, dominated by Robespierre.

20 September 1792   Battle of Valmy; French victory over Prussians.

22 September 1792   National Convention abolishes monarchy, declares France a Republic.

21 January 1793   Louis XVI guillotined. England, Holland and Spain join Prussia and Austria against France.

February 1793   Royalist rebellion breaks out in the Vendée.

March 1793   Revolutionary Tribunals set up.

13 July 1793   Charlotte Corday kills Marat in his bath.

February 1794   Nelson sails into Bastia harbour.

5 April 1794   Danton sent to the guillotine.

1 June 1794   Admiral Howe intercepts French grain convoy west of Brest and captures six warships.

July 1794   Reign of Terror reaches its peak; culminates in execution of Maximilien Robespierre.

March 1795   Failure of French expedition to re-occupy Corsica.

April 1795   French forces occupy Belgium and Holland. Treaty of Basel; Prussia abandons everything west of the Rhine to France.

September 1795   New French Constitution: Directory of five, legislative power invested in two Chambers.

9 March 1796	Napoleon marries Josephine; and Barras appoints him GOC Army of Italy.
12 April 1796	Napoleon opens his Italian campaign.
May 1796	French victories in Piedmont.
October 1796	British evacuate Corsica.
November 1796	Battle of Arcoli; Napoleon defeats Austrians once again.
February 1797	Battle of Cape St Vincent; British crush the Spanish fleet.
April 1797	Navy mutiny at Spithead. Britain threatened with invasion; Pitt introduces income-tax.
October 1797	Treaty of Campo Formio, victorious end of Napoleon's campaign against Austrians in N. Italy.
July 1798	Napoleon reaches Cairo. Battle of the Pyramids makes him master of Egypt.
1 August 1798	Battle of the Nile. Nelson destroys the French fleet.
August 1798	War of Second Coalition against France.
9 November 1799	Directory overthrown. Napoleon becomes one of three Consuls.
June 1800	Battle of Marengo; Napoleon defeats Austrians.
February 1801	Treaty of Luneville; more French gains.
April 1801	Battle of Copenhagen.
July 1801	Concordat signed between Napoleon and the Pope, re-establishes Catholic church in France.
Autumn 1801	Bread at famine prices in England; price of loaf up fifty per cent in France.
January 1802	Elba taken over by France.
March 1802	Treaty of Amiens; uneasy peace in Europe. British tourists flock to Paris. France regains her West Indian islands which had been captured by the British.
August 1802	Napoleon elected First Consul for life.
May 1803	War breaks out again. Napoleon interns British visitors. French forces occupy Naples.
June 1803	Napoleon invades Hanover, prepares to invade England.
1803–4	British naval forces bottle up French squadrons at Brest, Rochefort, Toulon.
March 1804	Napoleon's Civil Code becomes effective.
May 1804	Napoleon becomes Emperor of the French.
2 December 1804	Coronation of Napoleon and Josephine.

4 December 1804	Spain declares war on England.
April 1805	Third Coalition between Britain, Austria and Russia.
20 October 1805	Battle of Ulm; French defeat the Austrians.
21 October 1805	Battle of Trafalgar; death of Nelson.
2 December 1805	Battle of Austerlitz; Emperor Francis asks for an armistice.
26 December 1805	Treaty of Presburg. France gains most of the German provinces and much of Italy from Austria.
January 1806	British recapture Cape of Good Hope.
October 1806	French defeat Prussians at Jena, enter Berlin. Height of Napoleon's success.
November 1806	Napoleon, in Berlin, orders continental blockade of England. He controls every port in Europe, outside the Spanish peninsula.
March 1807	British government abolishes the slave trade.
14 June 1807	Battle of Friedland; Napoleon victorious over the Russians.
June/July 1807	Napoleon meets Tsar Alexander near Tilsit, concludes treaty of alliance.
September 1807	British ships bombard Copenhagen, seize the Danish fleet.
March 1808	Murat occupies Madrid.
April 1808	French troops enter Rome. Napoleon holds the Pope prisoner.
April/May 1808	King of Spain abdicates in favour of his son Ferdinand. Napoleon holds them both prisoner.
August 1808	Wellesley lands British troops in Portugal, defeats Junot at Vimiera.
September 1808	Napoleon and the Tsar meet at Erfurt.
December 1808	Napoleon arrives in Spain, enters Madrid after defeating Spanish insurgents.
January 1809	Sir John Moore retreats to Corunna. France at war again with Austria.
May 1809	Napoleon enters Vienna. Wellington drives the French out of Portugal.
10 June 1809	Napoleon annexes Rome and the Papal States.
6 July 1809	Battle of Wagram; French defeat Austrians.
14 October 1809	Treaty of Vienna; Austria cedes territory to France and Russia.
16 December 1809	Annulment of Napoleon's marriage to Josephine.

March 1810	French troops besiege Cadiz.
2 April 1810	Napoleon marries Marie-Louise of Austria.
October 1810	Wellington withdraws behind the lines of Torres Vedras.
20 March 1811	Birth of the King of Rome.
April 1811	Wellington's forces re-enter Spain.
June 1812	Napoleon invades Russia at head of the Grand Army.
17 August 1812	Napoleon captures Smolensk.
14 September 1812	Napoleon enters Moscow.
18 December 1812	Napoleon arrives back in Paris.
February 1813	Russia and Prussia sign a treaty of alliance.
June 1813	Wellington defeats French army in Spain.
August 1813	Austria re-enters the war against France.
January 1814	Allied forces cross the Rhine.
March 1814	Wellington captures Bordeaux.
6 April 1814	Napoleon abdicates.
1 March 1815	Napoleon lands in France.
20 March 1815	Napoleon enters Paris, Louis XVIII flees.
May 1815	Murat, defeated by Austrians in Italy, flees from Naples to France.
18 June 1815	Battle of Waterloo.
15 July 1815	Napoleon surrenders to the English.
17 October 1815	Napoleon arrives at St Helena.

Notes

Full details of the books listed in these Notes can be found in the Bibliography, pp. 217–18.

Chapter 1

1. Carlo and Letizia had fought with Pasquale Paoli, the leader of the movement for Corsican independence, until French troops gained control of the island in 1769. The French authorities had pursued a liberal policy and Carlo had seen which side his bread was buttered. He had become friendly with the governor of Corsica, the Comte de Marbeuf, who obtained various grants and privileges for him. It was hardly his fault that the concessions – for plantations of mulberry trees and the draining and exploitation of a salt-marsh – brought more debts than income. He was an advocate by profession, though he rarely had any clients. He made three journeys to Paris to plead his own affairs, but had little better success; he was astute enough, however, to travel at the expense of the state and to include one or two of his children on each journey – and Letizia too, on one occasion, taking her for a cure at Bourbonne-les-Bains after a stay in Paris. When he died at Montpellier during his third journey to France he was saved from a pauper's grave only by the generosity of some Corsican friends living in the town. Although extravagant and heedless, he had a hard core of tenacity. It was her father, much more than her mother, whom Paoletta took after.

2. The archdeacon's will was discovered during the Second World War by Maître Mirtil of Ajaccio. It bears the endorsement, among others, of Napoleon – a signature still decipherable at that early age but spelt 'Napolione'.

3. The object of this expedition – four men-of-war, six frigates and several troop transports – was to create a kind of 'second front' while a French army invaded the King of Savoy's other possession, Piedmont. Overall command of the troops had been given to Colonna Cesari, a nephew of Paoli. Napoleone, full of enthusiasm for his first taste of active service, was aghast at the indiscipline of the raw French recruits – overlooking the fact that they had not been paid for three months – and he fretted at the lack of preparation and general incompetence of the leaders. Believing that his presence at Ajaccio was indispensable, he took upon himself to abandon his troops. He merely sent a letter to Colonel Cesari, written at Bonifacio

on 14 March 1793, saying, 'I'm leaving for Ajaccio this evening as there's nothing useful I can do here, and I shall be in a better position to get news from the French commissioners and to advise my comrades as to their future action . . .'

4. In order to consolidate his position, Paoli called a 'Consulta' at Corte. The thousand delegates unanimously approved his policy of independence and passed a florid resolution condemning the Buonapartes as outcasts, 'leaving them to their own remorse and public opinion which already views them with perpetual abhorrence'. (Decaux, *Napoleon's Mother*; Roux, *Monsieur de Buonaparte*; Stirling, *A Pride of Lions*.)

Chapter 2

1. Junot later married Laure Permon, daughter of the family which had befriended Carlo Buonaparte during his fatal illness at Montpellier. Junot was happy with her for a time, became a general, governor of Illyria and Duc d'Abrantès – thanks to Napoleon – then went mad and killed himself in 1813.

2. Roux, *Monsieur de Buonaparte*, pp. 270–1.

3. One of the letters of introduction given to Fréron by Napoleon was addressed to Madame Clary, Giuseppe's mother-in-law:

> Fereron [*sic*], who is going on a mission to Marseilles, will hand you this letter. I beg you, Madame, to show him all the kindness that you would show to myself. You will find him a man very ready to oblige, loyal, and a good sort. I have told him of the friendly feelings I have for your family, so he will look out for opportunities to make himself useful to you. See that it is due to you that his stay in Marseilles is a pleasant one. (First published in *Amateur d'Autographes*, Paris, 1901.)

Napoleon probably gave Fréron a similar letter for his mother. But it made no difference to her opposition to the marriage. (Fleischmann, *Pauline Bonaparte and her Lovers*.)

Chapter 3

1. It has been called *un mariage de garnison* – a shotgun wedding – by Fouché in his *Memoirs* and by some later French biographers, but there is nothing to substantiate this. Fouché's *Memoirs*, like those of Barras, were not written by the man under whose name they pass and are prejudiced and notoriously inaccurate.

2. Madame Campan later reported to Joseph, as head of the family: 'Citizeness Leclerc has been attending here for six months. She has made astonishing progress in all respects, and she did not know how to read and write French.'

3. 'We saw more of Madame Leclerc', wrote Laure (the Duchesse d'Abrantès) in her *Memoirs*, 'than of any other member of her family. She came every day to my mother, who was very fond of her and petted her by being more indulgent than her own mother to the thousand and one whims which she expressed in a day.'

4. Van Scheelten, *Mémoires sur la Reine Hortense*.

5. 'If I succeed, no glory will come to me,' Leclerc is reputed to have said at the time. 'Every favourable action of mine will be viewed as having been dictated by my brother-in-law . . . If I fail, the responsibility will be mine alone . . . I shall of course do my duty, but I have no illusions regarding the fate that awaits me. I have, moreover, neither the right nor the power to attempt to escape it. All of us now have merely to obey. We have found a master where we had hoped only for a protector.' If these remarks are authentic, then Leclerc was one of the first to note the change in Napoleon. (Carlton, *Pauline, Favourite Sister of Napoleon*.)

Chapter 4

1. A military escort accompanied Leclerc's coffin to its final resting-place at the family château of Montgobert. Napoleon gave orders for a portrait of Leclerc to be painted and hung in the Hall of Marshals at Fontainebleau, and in several other ways demonstrated his deep regret at the death of his old comrade-in-arms. The municipality of Pontoise, where Leclerc was born, voted the erection of his statue.

2. Among the lovers attributed to Pauline were the Marquis de Sémonville (who had met her at Ajaccio when she was twelve) and Admiral Decrès, the Minister of Marine. Both certainly greatly admired her and came within her orbit at this time. Both were plump and middle-aged, which did not correspond to Pauline's taste in men.

3. The official report on the autopsy and embalmment of Leclerc's body contained the sentence: 'The body has been enveloped . . . each finger, each limb separately, right to the top of the head where the bandaging ends in a little cap, underneath which is some of Madame Leclerc's hair placed there at her request as a pledge of her affection, in exchange for some of her husband's, for which she asked.' (*Moniteur Universel*, 7 January 1803.)

Chapter 5

1. When Pauline acquired the Hôtel de Charost, the decorations and furnishings were of the eighteenth century. She transformed them into the latest style of the Empire, replacing the elegant Louis Quinze chairs and settees by austere furniture which evoked Napoleon's conquests in the Orient. Like all eighteenth-century town houses, there were no corridors; one room led into the next. It was the same in the royal palaces, and this inconvenient arrangement had led to a ceremonial procedure designed to protect to some extent the privacy of the occupiers. Pauline's visitors passed from one ante-room to the next, and so into the reception-room and eventually the drawing-room, being weeded out *en route* by her staff, if necessary.

2. Fesch had written to Napoleon from Rome: 'His Holiness is delighted; the Roman nobility is pleased too; and the Dowager Princess Borghese is extremely gratified and looking forward to the moment when she can embrace your sister. She is sending to Paris her second son, Prince Aldobrandini, as a mark of her approval. She is a good woman who will make life happy for Paulette . . .' During the fighting in Italy in 1798, Camillo Borghese had joined the French forces and his brother had been with the Papal forces – so that a Borghese was bound to be on the side of the victor. (Carlton, *Pauline, Favourite Sister of Napoleon*; Dixon, *Pauline, Napoleon's Favourite Sister*.)

3. It was at Mortefontaine that Joseph had received the American envoys in October 1800, to sign a treaty regulating maritime commerce and the rights of neutrals.

Chapter 6

1. Lucien had become very short-sighted and wore a primitive form of spectacles. He had a squeaky voice, a charming smile and a generous but obstinate disposition, and was attractive to women. After he married his mistress, Alexandrine Jouberthon (who already had a child by her first husband), she was received by his mother, by Joseph, Louis, Caroline and Hortense during Napoleon's absence from Paris, which infuriated him when he heard of this on his return. 'I am trying to restore moral values, and a woman like that is brought into my family!' he exclaimed. It was Napoleon's attitude towards Lucien that had chiefly decided their mother to leave Paris for Rome. 'The child of mine I love most,' she said more than once, 'is the one who is suffering the most.' (Decaux, *Napoleon's Mother*.)

2. On 18 May 1804 a senatus-consulte proclaimed that 'the government of the Republic is vested in an Emperor who takes the title of Emperor of the French'. The new Constitution was later approved by more than three million votes to three thousand.

3. This statue of Pauline is now on show at the Villa Borghese in Rome.

Chapter 7

1. Madame Mère paid Lucien 600,000 francs for his town house, the Hôtel de Brienne, one of the best in Paris and situated in the heart of the aristocratic Faubourg Saint Germain. The grounds were extensive; at the end of one wing was a private chapel where Madame Mère attended Mass every morning. The building is now the French War Ministry.

2. Napoleon had ordered his sisters to give a ball once a week. Pauline had the Wednesdays, Caroline the Fridays; Hortense, who escaped from Holland and her husband as much as she could, had the Mondays. Pauline agreed with Caroline to share their evening receptions on alternate Mondays – they were near neighbours, the Murats having recently bought the Hôtel de l'Elysée.

3. One of the last entertainments that Pauline attended was at Malmaison on 19 March, St Joseph's day. Josephine having returned, Pauline and Caroline arranged for some amateur theatricals to celebrate her fête day – not because they loved her, but because it gave them an opportunity to play leading parts. Among the other people involved were Laure Junot and her husband, Madame Ney and Monsieur de Montbreton. Pauline was carried to the rehearsals and read from an armchair her part of a young fiancée. When the time came, however, she acted her part very creditably, although her singing was out of tune. Her costume of a peasant bride was most becoming. The other sketch had been specially written by Caroline's secretary for her and Junot – with whom she was then having an affair – and gave only a small part to Laure. Pauline was much amused. (Carlton, *Pauline, Favourite Sister of Napoleon*: Cole, *The Betrayers*; Decaux, *Napoleon's Mother*.)

Chapter 8

1. For many years after Pauline left Gréoux, the villagers adopted her grotto and clearing in the woods as a place to picnic themselves. The tree became known as 'the Princess's oak'. It is still there, as are the stone slab, the flight of steps and the circular pavilion. The

last has survived the years well; much of the frieze clearly remains, but the wall has been covered with graffiti by people staying at the Château de Laval, which is now a holiday home for employees of a Marseilles firm.

When I was there in late September the château (just a large country house and much altered since Pauline's time) was shuttered up and only the caretaker was in residence, in one of the outbuildings. He kindly led me through the woods to Pauline's pavilion; without his guidance the place is impossible to find, and besides it is all private property and his permission is necessary. The sight of that elegant pinkish-brown pavilion on top of a short, steep slope, partly screened by bushes and trees, arouses thoughts of *La Belle au Bois Dormant*.

To reach the Château de Laval you follow the road out from Gréoux to Valensole for about one mile, and the entrance drive is on the right, over a small stone bridge.

2. Gréoux-les-Bains, a charming little spa, very quiet and still somewhat out of the way, claims to be the oldest spa in Europe. Proof that its waters were known to the Romans is provided by a votive stone inscribed to 'The Nymphs of Gréoulx' by Eilia Faustina, wife of Consul Vitrasius Pollion and a cousin of Marcus Aurelius, which now stands in the park behind the Thermal Establishment.

The sulphurous, radioactive waters are reputed to give relief to rheumatism, arthritis, bronchitis, sinusitis, asthma and nasal disorders in general. Pauline suffered from none of these, but she must have benefited from the wonderful climate, which is most relaxing.

The Templars in their wisdom had a commandery at Gréoux and built a hospital by the waters. Their old castle was being lived in by its owner in Pauline's day, but is now just an imposing ruin.

3. The Château de La Verdière is still owned by the Forbin family. It is open to the public every afternoon from two-thirty to six, and is well worth a visit. The small boudoir, which still contains the *causeuse,* is shown, but Pauline's bedroom is not.

However, at La Barben the bedroom she occupied and the adjoining boudoir are shown to the public and are said to be furnished as during her stay. The pretty boudoir is circular, with ceiling and walls decorated by F. M. Granet, a Provençal painter and contemporary of Pauline. The bed is a single one, quite narrow. Both here and at La Verdière the rooms given to Pauline are quite small and very feminine, and are tucked away in a remote part of the vast building. Forbin knew Pauline's tastes, and by arranging for her to have these rooms and not a large, ornate bedchamber he presumably felt he would be pleasing her. The deduction is that she preferred the small and the intimate to the grandiose and the ceremonial. One can understand better why she attended Court only when she could not avoid doing so, and why she could leave her magnificent residences for long periods to live in comparative simplicity at health resorts, to stay in a furnished villa or at an inn.

Chapter 9

1. The *Almanach Impérial* for 1808 gave the household of Princess Pauline, Duchess of Guastalla, as:

Cardinal Spina, Archbishop of Genoa	High Almoner
L'Abbé Saint-Geyrat ⎱ L'Abbé Maussac ⎰	Chaplains
Madame de Champagny	Lady of honour
Madame de Barral ⎫ Madame de Chambaudouin ⎬ Madame de Bréhan ⎭	Ladies-in-waiting
Monsieur de Clermont-Tonnerre ⎱ Monsieur de Forbin ⎰	Chamberlains
Monsieur de Montbreton	Equerry
Monsieur du Pré Saint-Maur	Secretary
Doctor Peyre	Physician
Mademoiselle Millo	Reader

Madame de Champagny's husband was then Napoleon's Minister for Foreign Affairs. Cardinal Spina had a sinecure; he had paid a courtesy call on Pauline while she was at Nice but had not been received, for he arrived at a moment when she was deeply engaged with Blangini. One of the chaplains celebrated Mass every Sunday morning in the drawing-room; this was the minimum of lip-service demanded by Napoleon, so Pauline dutifully attended.

She did not remain long enough in Turin for all of her Piedmontese household to assemble, but among those who attached themselves to her were Madame de Cavour, Madame de la Turbie (who later married Monsieur de Clermont-Tonnerre) and Mademoiselle Ghilini (later Madame de Mathis.)

2. Pauline had a point over the question of precedence, though it was a cruel thing for her to say. When Jerome married Catherine of Württemberg in August 1807, Murat, Grand Duke of Berg, Caroline's husband, had protested at being placed after Prince Borghese in the order of precedence at the ceremony. Ségur, the Grand Master of Ceremonies, replied that he had referred the

matter to the Emperor, 'who has told me that . . . within the family
Prince Borghese takes the rank of the Princess his wife, and that
I should place him before Your Highness.' Napoleon emphasised
the point by writing to Murat that, 'Your rank in my palace is
determined by the rank you have in my family, and your rank in
my family is determined by my sister's rank . . .' What was true for
Murat was true for Borghese. (Cole, *The Betrayers.*)

Chapter 10
1. The present head of the Bonaparte family, Prince Napoleon, is
   descended from Jerome.
2. Caroline was among her sister's guests at Neuilly, and in a dis-
   approving way she noticed many changes. Pauline believed her
   looks were best displayed against a plain background, and she had
   re-upholstered the rooms in monochromes; her bedroom was all
   blue, her boudoir all orange, and so on. There were changes in
   the gardens too; new walks had been laid out and summer-houses
   built.

Chapter 11
1. General Thiébault tells in his *Memoirs* of being interrupted during
   a game of chess with Laure Junot (this at army base headquarters!)
   by the arrival of Canouville: 'Everyone rose and went towards
   him with exclamations appropriate to the doleful appearance of
   this dandy of the Court . . . After telling us he was the bearer of
   dispatches for the Prince of Essling [Marshal Masséna], he came
   to the real motive of his journey and repeated to all of us what he
   declared he could not tell anyone, what everybody already knew,
   what he was all on fire to tell us – that he had recently become the
   lover of Pauline Bonaparte, Princess Borghese. While he related
   the details of his adventure he mingled them with sighs fit, as the
   Duchess said, to blow the candles out.'
2. When Canouville returned to Salamanca and eventually got
   through with his two-months-old dispatches, Masséna was at
   Guarda, a mountain village on the Portuguese frontier, trying to
   hold up Wellington's advance. Masséna spent several days reading
   and replying to Berthier's dispatches (for he knew the Emperor
   was behind them) instead of proceeding with his troop dispositions.
   This delay gave Wellington time to bring up more forces; the two
   corps of Junot and Ney were driven back with the loss of several
   hundred prisoners, and Wellington's forces re-entered Spain. Thus

was added another instance of the far-reaching effects of Pauline's charms. (Bryant, *Years of Victory, 1802–12*.)

3. Marie-Louise had a difficult confinement, and Doctor Dubois asked Napoleon which he should save, the mother or the child, if matters reached that point. Napoleon promptly told him to save the mother, much to the relief of Marie-Louise, who had feared she would be the one sacrificed if necessary.

The Parisians knew that the birth of a daughter to the Emperor would be announced by a salute of twenty-one guns, the birth of a son by one hundred guns. At a quarter-past-nine in the morning the first gun sounded. Everyone fell silent while twenty-one guns were fired, but when the twenty-second was heard a great cry of joy rose from the streets – the King of Rome was born. All the dignitaries and courtiers who had been waiting at the Tuileries until late at night, and had then gone home on being informed that the birth was delayed, now hurried back to offer their congratulations. (Cronin, *Napoleon*; Decaux, *Napoleon's Mother*; La Tour du Pin, *Journal d'une femme de cinquante ans*; Stacton, *The Bonapartes*.)

4. During Pauline's stay at Aix-la-Chapelle and at Spa a Monsieur de Montrond found his way into her circle, and some biographers have taken gossip for fact and added this middle-aged rogue and libertine to the roster of Pauline's lovers. He had been implicated in the intrigues of Talleyrand and was suspected by Napoleon's police of carrying on a treasonable correspondence with Royalist agents. He was exiled from France and went to live in Antwerp. The probability is that he hoped Pauline would ask Napoleon to pardon him and allow him to return to France. He paid court not to Pauline but to her reader and confidante, the Comtesse de Saluces (Mademoiselle Millo, who had married one of Napoleon's equerries). He failed in all his endeavours and went to England the following year, 1812. For some years he lived in London and frequented the gaming clubs, where he entertained the 'bucks' with highly-coloured tales of social life under the Empire and with exaggerated or fanciful accounts of his relationship with Princess Borghese. Even the clubmen of the Regency, who were not particularly squeamish or moral, regarded Montrond as a scoundrel. (Blyth, *Hell and Hazard*; Chanlaine, *Pauline Bonaparte*; Fleischmann, *Pauline Bonaparte et ses Amants*; Maxwell, H., *The Creevey Papers*.)

Chapter 12

1. The Chevalley family, after whom the villa was named, returned to live in it for many years after Pauline's departure. A brother

and sister, contemporaries of Pauline, lived to be centenarians and were prominent in working for the union of Savoy to France in 1860. The house can still be seen, at the junction of the Boulevard des Côtes and the Rue Bain Henri IV. It has a little of its grounds remaining, but is otherwise hemmed in by later buildings. It is now municipal property and is rented privately, and cannot be visited without permission. But although the house itself is unchanged from Pauline's time, nothing remains that can be connected with her four months' residence except a few pieces of Empire furniture in the drawing-room.

2. The date of the excursion to Hautecombe was 7 September and, all unbeknown to Pauline's party, Napoleon's army was fighting on the Borodino one of the bloodiest battles of the period. Junot, Duc d'Abrantès, said later: 'That night was one of the most horrible I ever passed . . . incessant rain, no wood for fires, and groans and cries of agony on every side.'

3. The reason for contemporaries of Pauline not suspecting that Talma was her lover was, according to Carlton, that the actor had often been invited to private gatherings made up almost exclusively of members of the Imperial family at which plays were performed, and so his frequent appearances in Pauline's company aroused no special comment.

   Talma continued writing to Pauline until March 1813. In July of that year he was sending equally passionate letters from Dresden to a former mistress, Madame Bazire: 'I am mad about you, angel and treasure. I cover you with kisses, your little nose and all the the rest . . .'

   Talma was one of the faithful few who, after Waterloo, went to Malmaison to say farewell to Napoleon before he left France for ever, and was a witness of his dramatic parting from his mother.

4. Borghese wrote from Turin to enquire after Pauline's health and added that he was planning to go to Paris and expected to stay at the Hôtel de Charost. Pauline at once sent detailed instructions to her steward there, saying what the Prince was to be allowed to do and what he was not – chiefly not. Certain rooms were to be closed off; the liveries must not be used; no expense was to be charged to the Princess; her horses were not to be taken beyond the Bois de Boulogne. Borghese decided not to go to Paris after all. (Carlton, *Pauline, Favourite Sister of Napoleon*; Abrantès, Laure Permon, Duchesse d', *Mémoires*.)

Chapter 13

1. There is a passage about this journey in Barras's *Memoirs* which is obviously second-hand yet has the ring of truth about it. Unreliable though these *Memoirs* are, neither Barras nor his ghost-writer could possibly have invented the incident; nor is there any reason for doing so.

    'The Princess was going to take the waters at Gréoux. Passing by Aulps, Her Highness became really ill. Being in the state of health she was, she had to be carried in a litter. She halted on some rising ground, in a meadow near an estate belonging to Monsieur César Roubaud, at whose house she was to spend the night. Some gentlemen respectfully took off some clothes and laid them on the grass, so that the Princess might sit down without risking anything from the damp. Monsieur Desbains, sub-prefect of Grasse, with hair *à l'oiseau royal,* offered his back to support the Princess's, while General Guyot lay down at right-angles and placed the Princess's feet on his stomach...'

2. This needle-case is still in the possession of descendants of Pauline's chamber-maid, though it has now left Gréoux. It was recently given by M. and Mme J. Negre, owners of the Hotel des Alpes at Gréoux, to their married daughter. But Madame Negre still possesses a full-length mirror that belonged to Pauline. This is in the Villa Pauline, a house that belonged to Monsieur Negre's great-grandfather, who was bailiff at the Domaine de Laval and probably had much to do with the construction of Pauline's pavilion. The mirror has a carved gilt frame and the glass is still untarnished. It is probably Venetian, and one that Pauline took with her on her travels. The hotel where Pauline stayed was recently demolished and a new one built on the site, but local people can remember being shown 'Pauline's bedroom'.

3. Bouillidou stands in its own grounds below the hilltop village of Vieux Cannet, and has magnificent views southwards to the Massif des Maures. It still belongs to the Colbert family, as it did in Pauline's time, and except for the addition of a tower is little changed.

4. Pauline was the only one of Napoleon's family who troubled to see him after his downfall. All the others passed by on the other side. Joseph and Louis went to Switzerland, Jerome to Württemberg; Marie-Louise returned to Vienna; Lucien sailed for Rome; Caroline and Murat remained in Naples; and Elisa went to Vienna to complain about the Austrian seizure of her Italian property.

5. Soon after Napoleon reached Elba, he and his treasurer, Peyrusse, went through the accounts and reckoned that he had with him

nearly four million francs in gold and silver (about one million pounds today). Napoleon told Peyrusse that it was all to be kept as his war-chest and only touched if absolutely necessary. He would try to balance his budget from the island's taxes and revenues. He had little expectation of the two million francs due annually from Louis XVIII under the terms of the Treaty of Fontainebleau. Pauline, like the rest of the Bonapartes, was entitled to 300,000 francs annually under the Treaty; but she never reckoned on it either. So neither was disappointed. The Treaty allowed Napoleon to retain his title of Emperor and gave him the sovereignty of Elba. (Bartel, *Napoléon à l'Ile d'Elbe*; Christophe, *Napoleon on Elba*.)

6. '. . . How can I describe the horror of my situation?' Murat wrote to Pauline. 'The Emperor is at grips with the Allies, France is in a bad way, and everything makes it my duty not to go and die in their defence. Everything binds me to my new country. The fate of my children and my subjects has prevailed. I have taken up arms for them and, apparently, against the man I revere . . .

'However, I am not yet an enemy, and I hope peace will come before the King of Naples has to decide on action . . . I have had to save my children, whereas I should have lost everything without any good to them or to France.

'Ah, my dear sister, pity me! I am the most miserable of men . . . Remember that you always have in me a devoted friend.'

There was obviously some hypocrisy in this letter; Murat's chief concern was to keep his crown at all costs. But having kept it – for a time at least – he was prepared to change sides again, if events were propitious. Murat was a braggart and an opportunist, but no one has ever doubted his courage.

In his recent biography of the Murats, Hubert Cole produces strong circumstantial evidence of correspondence between Murat and Napoleon while the latter was on Elba, showing that the two became reconciled. The Murat family archives contain several hand-written notes indicating that Napoleon was counting on Murat's support for any future action. (Chanlaine, *Pauline Bonaparte*; Cole, *The Betrayers*.)

7. Pauline's town house is still the British Embassy, and it was the first to be owned by the British government. The contract of sale was signed on 24 October 1814 and the first instalment was paid immediately. This good news reached Pauline soon after her return to Elba. The remaining instalments were paid as they fell due and were completed in 1816. Pauline's elaborately-carved bed with a golden eagle atop the baldachin was never removed, and with other of her furniture is still in the Embassy; moreover, all are actually

used. A recent British ambassador to Paris has written that the interior has been gradually restored to its Empire appearance, after the transformations in Victorian times, and that the house is now very much as when Pauline was living there. (Dixon, *Pauline, Napoleon's Favourite Sister*.)

Chapter 14

1. Napoleon had made Elisa Grand Duchess of Tuscany and Princess of Piombino. She too, like Murat, had made a pact with the Austrians; but it had availed her nothing, for her territory had been occupied, and she had fled.
2. Cambronne is chiefly remembered in France today because of a single rude word attributed to him: when surrounded at Waterloo and called upon to surrender, he replied '*Merde*'.
3. Napoleon knew that the arms of the Medici, who had ruled Elba for three centuries, had a red bar on a silver field. So he artfully tried to please the Elbans with a reminder of their Florentine past, and the French veterans with the addition of the Imperial bees.
4. Although Napoleon refused to take his mother's jewels, he did not refuse to take her money. She had a considerable fortune deposited with various bankers, chiefly in Italy, and she placed some of these funds at Napoleon's disposal; the taxes and revenues of Elba were proving not nearly enough for his needs. Her contemporary biographer, Baron Larrey, estimated that she contributed over two million francs to the budget of the tiny realm. In addition she assisted all the Corsicans who came to Elba in search of a job or some function, until the Customs and the port officials and the police were nearly all compatriots of hers.
5. These letters are among the Murat papers in the French National Archives. While there is no proof that they were ever received or sent, Colonna certainly left Elba for Naples at that time; and Murat sent a ship to Elba to collect Pauline and her mother.
6. Marchand remained faithful to Napoleon; he accompanied him to St Helena and was present at his death-bed. Napoleon had made him a Count.

    Pauline's necklace was lost after Waterloo, left behind in Napoleon's carriage when he escaped on horseback.
7. Napoleon, when back in Paris, gave the Mulini to the town of Portoferraio. Today the house is still much as when he and Pauline were living in it, but there is little of the original furniture; it was all seized by Ferdinand III when he regained possession of Tuscany, including Elba, after Waterloo. In the garden is a statue of the

Galatea, a nude woman on one knee, for which Pauline served as the model. It is a replica of one made by Canova which is in the Napoleonic museum at San Martino.

Portoferraio has not changed very much. The Sea Gate is still the only way into the town from the quayside; but a new road has been built out to the country, and the Land Gate is closed. The town hall and the church still confront each other across the main square, now called the Piazza della Republica.

Chapter 15

1. Napoleon landed at Gulf Juan near Antibes on 1 March. News of his escape to France reached Naples on 4 March. Murat sent a 74-gun man-of-war to Elba, and Madame Mère, her two ladies and the Bertrand family arrived in Naples at the end of March. Madame Mère was joined by Fesch and Jerome; on 13 May, after Murat's defeat at Tolentino, the three sailed for France in a French frigate, the *Dryade*. They arrived in Paris on 1 June.

2. Monier was a long time on the road. When he at last reached Paris and reported, Napoleon gave orders for a strong protest to be sent to the Grand Duke of Tuscany, demanding Pauline's release, and for the frigate *Dryade* – then at Toulon – to sail to Leghorn for her to go aboard. But these orders were never executed; they were probably set aside temporarily while the ministerial offices dealt with the hectic preparations for the campaign that ended at Waterloo.

3. Murat had ordered his troops to advance on the Austrians. He was in Bologna early in April, and his troops reached the line of the Po. He was everywhere greeted by cheering Italians, whom he called on to fight for a united Italy; but they were cheering the departure of the hated Austrians more than the arrival of the Neapolitans, and were happy for the latter to do the fighting for them. When the Austrians concentrated their forces, Murat was quickly driven back, his army disintegrated, and he had to flee from his kingdom. (Bear, *Caroline Murat*; Carlton, *Pauline, Favourite Sister of Napoleon*; Cole, *The Betrayers*.)

4. The four arrived at St Helena on 20 September 1819. 'It is just such a selection as I should expect from my uncle Fesch,' commented Napoleon bitterly. The French historian Frédéric Masson calls the episode the most tragic in all Napoleon's captivity.

5. The woman whom Pauline calls a spy was more probably a clairvoyant or a professional trickster preying upon Madame Mère's anxiety, inducing her to believe what she wanted to believe.

Madame Mère was seventy years of age and going blind; Fesch was thirteen years younger, and the only possible explanation of his conduct is that the priest-ridden atmosphere of Rome had brought on a religious mysticism.

He and his half-sister had separate households by then, but they were as inseparable as ever and spent every evening together at her home. Fesch had full authority to act for her; he and Bertrand were the intermediaries, as Napoleon had soon given up writing to his family when he found that all his letters were opened by the governor, Hudson Lowe.

Madame Mère had bought the Palazzo Rinuccini, a dignified seventeenth-century building at the corner of the Corso and the Piazza Venezia. During her lifetime it was called the Palazzo Bonaparte. The Misciattelli family bought it in 1915, and it was restored by the late Marchese, who there found more than a hundred of Madame Mère's letters. (Decaux, *Napoleon's Mother.*)

Bibliography

English

BEAR, JOAN, *Caroline Murat*, Collins, 1972.

BONAPARTE-WYSE, OLGA, *The Spurious Brood*, Gollancz, 1969.

BRYANT, SIR ARTHUR, *Years of Victory, 1802–12*, Collins, 1944.

CAMPBELL, SIR NEIL, *Napoleon at Fontainebleau and Elba*, London, 1869.

CARLTON, W. N. C., *Pauline, Favourite Sister of Napoleon*, Butterworth, 1931.

CHRISTOPHE, ROBERT, *Napoleon on Elba*, tr. Len Ortzen, Macdonald, 1964.

COLE, HUBERT, *Christophe, King of Haiti*, Eyre & Spottiswoode, 1967.

COLE, HUBERT, *The Betrayers*, Eyre Methuen, 1972.

CRONIN, VINCENT, *Napoleon*, Collins, 1971.

DECAUX, ALAIN, *Napoleon's Mother*, tr. Len Ortzen, Cresset, 1962.

DIXON, SIR PIERSON, *Pauline, Napoleon's Favourite Sister*, Collins, 1964.

FLEISCHMANN, H., *Pauline Bonaparte and her lovers* (tr.), John Lane, 1914.

KEMBLE, JAMES, *Napoleon Immortal*, John Murray, 1959.

LEWIS, GWYNNE, *Life in Revolutionary France*, Batsford, 1972.

MAXWELL, H. (ed.), *The Creevey Papers*, John Murray, 1903.

STACTON, DAVID, *The Bonapartes*, Hodder & Stoughton, 1967.

STIRLING, MONICA, *A Pride of Lions*, Collins, 1961.

WEINER, MARGERY, *The Parvenu Princesses*, John Murray, 1964.

French

ABRANTÈS, LAURE PERMON, DUCHESSE D', *Mémoires*, Paris, 1905–13.

BARTEL, PAUL, *Napoléon à l'Ile d'Elbe*, Paris, 1947.

BEUGNOT, COMTE, *Mémoires*, Comte Albert Beugnot (ed.), Hachette, 1959.

BLANGINI, F., *Souvenirs*, Paris, 1834.

CHANLAINE, PIERRE, *Pauline Bonaparte*, Buchet-Castel, 1959.

CHATEAUBRIAND, F. R. DE, *Mémoires d'Outre-tombe*, Nelson, Paris, 1937.

FLEISCHMANN, H., and BART, P., *Lettres inédites de Talma à la Princesse Pauline Bonaparte*, Fasquelle, 1911.

FLEURIOT DE LANGLE, P., *La Paolina*, Paris, 1944.

FOUCHÉ, JOSEPH, *Mémoires*, Flammarion, 1945.

GOBINEAU, MARCEL, *Pauline Borghese, Sœur Fidèle*, P. Amiot, 1958.

KÜHN, J., *Pauline Bonaparte*, tr. G. Daubié, Plon, 1937.

LECLERC, GENERAL VICTOR, *Lettres*, Leroux, Paris, 1937.

LEVY, ARTHUR, *Napoléon Intime*, Paris, 1893, and Nelson, 1937.

MADELIN, LOUIS, *Fouché*, Plon, 1955.

MARCHAND, L. J., *Mémoires*, Plon, 1952.

MARTINEAU, GILBERT, *La Vie Quotidienne à Ste Hélène au temps de Napoléon*, Hachette, 1966.

NABONNE, BERNARD, *Pauline Bonaparte*, Paris, 1963.

PELLET, M., *Napoléon à l'Ile d'Elbe*, Paris, 1888.

PONS DE L'HÉRAULT, *Souvenirs et Anecdotes de l'Ile d'Elbe*, Paris, 1897.

ROBIQUET, JEAN, *La Vie Quotidienne au temps de Napoléon*, Hachette, 1946.

ROUX, GEORGES, *Monsieur de Buonaparte*, Fayard, 1964.

THIÉBAULT, PAUL, *Mémoires du Général Baron Thiébault*, Plon, 1895.

THIERRY, A., *Notre Dame des Colifichets,* Paris, 1937.

TOUR DU PIN, MARQUISE DE LA, *Journal d'une femme de cinquante ans,* Paris, 1924.

TURQUAN, J., *Les Sœurs de Napoléon*, vol. 1, Paris, 1927.

VAN SCHEELTEN, W. F., *Mémoires sur la Reine Hortense*, Paris, 1833.

Local publications

FRANÇON, FRANÇOIS, *D'Aix-en-Savoye à Aixilia*, Editions de Trévoux, 1972.

PEROUSE, GABRIEL, *La Vie d'Autrefois à Aix-les-Bains*, Editions Dardel, Chambéry, 1967.

POITEVIN, EMILE, *Gréoux-les-Bains*, Michel, Grande Rue, Gréoux, 1971

Questa è l'Elba, Ente per la Valorizzazione dell'Isola d'Elba, Portoferraio, 1960.

Index